THE PRESENT AGE
IN BRITISH LITERATURE

THE PRESENT AGE

IN BRITISH LITERATURE

BY

DAVID DAICHES

INDIANA UNIVERSITY PRESS

BLOOMINGTON & LONDON

CONTENTS

CONTENTS

PREFACE

THIS book deals with the British literary scene, and the American reader will find some things familiar and some unfamiliar. The account of the general background, presented in Chapter I, concentrates on the effects on British culture of the Second World War and its aftermath, and such matters as the economic position of the young writer, the state of the literary magazine, and the influence of the British Broadcasting Corporation, belong to the purely British phenomena discussed. On the other hand, the revolution in poetic taste and technique discussed in Chapter II was an Anglo-American phenomenon which cannot be adequately discussed in terms of only the British or only the American situation. The Imagist movement was begun in London by a group of British and American writers and developed simultaneously in America. The symbol of Anglo-American co-operation here is contained in the fact that the movement was first adequately reported by two poets, one American and one English, both writing from London in a Chicago magazine. The activities of Eliot and Pound in London were followed with equal excitement by the *avant garde* on both sides of the Atlantic. And if the English critics I. A. Richards and F. R. Leavis pioneered in the development of attitudes and techniques appropriate to the literature which the poetic revolution produced, their work was extended, refined, systematized, and elaborated by generations of devoted American critics who have explored the implications of that revolution to a greater degree than any British writer has done. New movements in fiction, too, were watched and commented on with eager interest in America, where the little magazines of the 1920s kept a close eye on Eliot, Joyce, and others. *Ulysses* was serialized in Margaret

Anderson's *Little Review* in New York. Indeed, Joyce has had more influence, and has been discussed and explicated to a much greater extent, in America than in Britain. D. H. Lawrence, too, was early recognized in America and his work was eagerly followed and, after his death, copiously commented on. The most popular and influential single book on the modern movement in literature was Edmund Wilson's *Axel's Castle*, which discussed Joyce and Yeats for an American audience from a European perspective.

The American reader, in reading of the 'red thirties' in Britain, will be able to make his own parallels and contrasts with the age of the Depression and the New Deal in America. The Depression was another Anglo-American phenomenon, though not so spectacular in Britain as in America. The social consciousness which it encouraged was a phenomenon of the 1930s on both sides of the Atlantic, and the American reader interested in the kinds of fiction this produced might compare, say, Ralph Bates's *Lean Men* with Steinbeck's *Grapes of Wrath*. By contrast, he might compare the Southern Agrarian movement in American letters and the combination of social conservatism with literary experimentalism in certain American writers with a similar combination in the work of Eliot and (a different but not altogether unrelated phenomenon) Wyndham Lewis.

As American literature has become more independent and fully developed, its relations with English have become more mutually profitable and stimulating. As is noted on page 17, the American novelists who are most American in idiom and subject matter arouse most excitement and admiration in Britain. Similarly, Joyce and the later Yeats, both fiercely idiosyncratic writers, have commanded sustained and widespread attention in America. (Both Joyce and Yeats, incidentally, were Anglo-Irish, not English: the reader may draw from this what conclusions he wishes.) In short, what Anglo-American literary relations have shown over the past forty years is that a national literature is most vigorous when it is playing its part in an international movement and that, paradoxically, cultural independence encourages and thrives on cultural inter-dependence. Eliot and Auden crossing the Atlantic in different directions are significant symbols here. The situation is very different from that of the Jamesian American in Europe.

The problem of 'mass media' and of popular semi-literacy, touched on in Chapter I, has reached graver proportions and has been the subject of more, and more troubled, investigation in America than in Britain. This is not because of any greater degree of literary purity in Britain, but simply because the cultural problems of an industrial democracy are bound to be spelt out larger in America than in Britain. Almost every one of the phenomena that offend the British visitor in America, from certain kinds of advertising to soap operas and comic books, are to be found in Britain too, though not always so blatantly or on such a large scale. The cultural problems of America are the cultural problems of all western democratic societies, and often the observer of the British scene has only to turn his eyes to America to see more clearly what is happening in his own country. Nevertheless, differences of tradition, of social organization, of educational methods and standards, remain, and can be seen reflected in the literature and in the reading public in each country.

As I have noted on page 173, American critics have made much more determined efforts to grapple with recent English literature than British critics have done. And recent literature is discussed in American universities to an extent and with an intensity that are not found in British universities. Physical distance gives certain advantages: the British literary scene viewed from America can be seen more coherently than in Britain. On the other hand, one inevitably misses some things by not belonging to the society whose culture one is discussing. If I may strike a more personal note, I should like to express the hope that my own position, as an Englishman who has lived in America and taught at American universities, has something at least of the advantages of both perspectives. It was in America that I was first asked to lecture on modern British literature, and it was in classes and graduate seminars at the University of Chicago and at Cornell University that I first systematically explored the subject of this book. Indeed, the first five chapters really represent a distillation of my American teaching of modern British literature. (To 'teach modern British literature' is a phrase that could only be uttered in America or with respect to America.) It is appropriate, therefore, that I should take this opportunity of expressing my gratitude to American universities for enabling me to look more closely and with a new perspective at the literature of my own country.

Jesus College,   D.D.
Cambridge, England
October 1957

PUBLISHER'S NOTE. This book is appearing in England as volume V of a series of Introductions to English literature.

CHAPTER I

GENERAL BACKGROUND

I

THE period of British cultural history which saw the brittle gaiety of the 1920s, the social consciousness of the 1930s, the world war followed by the welfare state of the 1940s and the chastened readjustments (if that is not a premature diagnosis) of the 1950s, is not easy to describe in general terms. The Second World War does not appear in retrospect to have been the cultural watershed that in some respects the First was. The increasing tempo of the reaction against Victorianism (or what that generation conceived Victorianism to be) in the 1920s did not precipitate the revolution in values which was at one time predicted, nor did the pattern of Left-wing thought which emerged in the next decade as a result of the depression turn out to be an accurate prediction of the mood and method of the great social changes that took place during and immediately after the second war. Who in the 1920s could have foreseen the vogue of Trollope, or the rehabilitation of Victorian architecture sponsored by John Betjeman, or Aldous Huxley's turning from witty disillusion to mystical contemplation? Who in the 1930s foresaw that an *avant garde* that was agnostic and Left-wing would soon give way to one that was Right-wing and religious, or that the credulous idealism of 'popular front' intellectuals would soon be regarded, not only by such satirists as Angus Wilson but almost by a whole young generation, as considerably more out of date than the moral fervours of Carlyle and Ruskin? One may talk of the cynical and experimental 1920s, the troubled and earnest 1930s, the embattled and hard working

I

1940s, and the concern with security (both social and intellectual) of the 1950s; but where, in all this, does the true line of English culture run? We are perhaps too close to it all to be able to see any coherent pattern. We can see some of the details, however, and they call for some discussion.

In the matter of literary techniques, the 1920s proved to be one of the most fruitful periods in the whole history of English literature. In fiction, the so-called 'stream of consciousness' method was born, matured and moved to its decline within this single decade. In poetry, the revolution wrought by Pound and Eliot and the later Yeats, by the new influence of the seventeenth century metaphysicals and of Hopkins, changed the poetic map of the country. As far as technique goes, the period since has been one of consolidation. Nothing so radically new in technique as Eliot's *Waste Land* has appeared since, nor have later novelists ventured as far in technical innovation as Joyce did in *Ulysses* and *Finnegans Wake* (the latter, though published in 1939, was largely written in and belongs in spirit to the 1920s). The sense of excitement which all this experimentation produced, the battles, the mutual abuse, the innovating exaltation of the little magazines, seem very far away now in the 1950s, and were already lost by the end of the 1930s. A period of consolidation is not exciting, nor is it easy to describe with the literary historian's eye.

It might perhaps be said that in the 1920s the most important writers were more serious as artists than as men, while in more recent years they have been more serious as men than as artists. The Second World War forced a new kind of reflectiveness about human affairs on many British people. This was nothing spectacular, nothing like the dramatic shift from the patriotic idealism of Rupert Brooke to the bitterly disillusioned satire of Siegfried Sassoon or Richard Aldington that took place during the earlier war. It was marked by such things as a sign in a London bookshop in 1942 reading 'Sorry, no Shakespeare or "War and Peace".' There was a surprising amount of re-reading of the classics—partly attributable, it is true, to the paper shortage which resulted in a reduction of the number of new books published—and a great demand for historical works and discussions of general human problems in what might be called semi-popular form; such phenomena as the 'Pelican' books in the Penguin library are indicative of this demand. Even the most sophisticated tended to look for books with something to say rather than for new methods of expression. The problem of the artist in modern society— his 'alienation', his inevitable bohemianism—which had so agitated writers in the preceding two decades, suddenly lost much of its interest, and when some interest revived again after the war it was more often than not concerned with the sober question of how the writer was to make a living.

The shift in emphasis from technique to content, if one can describe it thus crudely, did not represent a clear-cut movement. Indeed, at times it looked as though the first response of writers and critics to the Second World War was to emphasize their status and integrity as men of letters rather than as citizens concerned with the immediate problems posed by the war. The tone of *Horizon*, the literary periodical founded early in the war by Cyril Connolly as an assertion of the claims of current literature in the midst of international conflict, was from the beginning more aesthetic, more removed from the immediate pressure of events, even than T. S. Eliot's *Criterion* which it can be said to have succeeded. And if we compare the tone of *Horizon* with that of John Lehmann's *New Writing* (which first appeared in 1936 and continued in various forms during and for a while after the war) the difference between the deliberate aloofness of the writer in the 1940s and his strenuous commitment to the issues of the day in the 1930s is even more striking. *New Writing* really represented the mid-1930s, even in its war-time forms. Though it proclaimed its devotion to imaginative literature it continued

3

the documentary reporting and social interests of the 1930s into the 1940s (e.g. in the series 'The Way We Live Now' in *Penguin New Writing*). And documentary writing of all kinds flourished during the war. But *Horizon* represented more fully the tone of literary London in the war days. It did not last, however; *Horizon* itself closed down a few years after the war ended, and Cyril Connolly's elegant prose and uncommitted sophistication was suddenly seen to be old-fashioned. A general air of tired seriousness seemed to spread over the face of English letters; writers were no longer mandarins, but people trying to earn a living by their pen. When the *London Magazine* was founded in 1954, edited by John Lehmann, it was with no clear-cut programme or new artistic creed. From the first its general air was one of mild competence; it was as though the magazine were standing by to transmit any new creative impulse when it came.

Though 'little magazines' continued to spring up sporadically after the Second World War, they no longer played the important part they had done between roughly 1914 and 1935, the great experimental period of modern English literature. These magazines reflected the fragmentation of the audience for literature, so characteristic of our period, in that they were produced by coteries and appealed to particular sectional interests. Perhaps Rossetti's *Germ* was really the first of the little magazines in England; but it was an exception in the Victorian period in its deliberately limited appeal. *The Yellow Book*, which ran from April 1894 until April 1897, was in a sense the second English little magazine; but it was much more popular than either the *Germ* or its own twentieth century successors. Arthur Symons' *Savoy*, founded in January 1896 to continue and surpass *The Yellow Book*, was less popular, and barely survived a year. When we come to the *Egoist*, founded at the beginning of 1914, we are in the true modern tradition of the little magazine. *The Egoist* was started as a feminist magazine (with Richard Aldington on its editorial staff), but under the influence of Ezra Pound and others it became for a time the unofficial organ of the Imagist movement, printing poetry by Pound, Aldington, 'H.D.', F. S. Flint, John Gould Fletcher, Amy Lowell and D. H. Lawrence. T. S. Eliot also contributed, and in 1917 he became editor, continuing until the demise of the magazine in December 1919. Parts of Joyce's *Ulysses* first appeared in *The Egoist*. The political and literary weekly *The New Age*, under the editorship of A. R. Orage, printed T. E. Hulme's series of articles on Bergson in October and November 1911 and, in the course of the next few years, most of Hulme's important critical pronouncements. The political and literary influence of *The New Age* on some important critical and creative minds is seen clearly in Edwin Muir's autobiography. *The Little Review*, published in New York by Margaret Anderson, was well known in that small group of English *avant garde* writers and critics who followed its serialization of Joyce's *Ulysses* in twenty-three parts from March 1918 to December 1920, when the serialization abruptly stopped as a result of a charge of obscenity brought against the magazine by the U.S. Post Office. T. S. Eliot's *Criterion* ran from 1922 to 1939, acting in general as the organ of the new classical revolution. *Wheels*, an annual anthology edited by Edith Sitwell from 1916 until 1921, published the Sitwells and some prose-poems by Aldous Huxley, and engaged in a species of brilliant verbal clowning which combined virtuosity with weariness. Wyndham Lewis's *Blast, Review of the Great English Vortex*, appeared first in 1914 and once more in 1915; it preached Lewis's views on art and letters and printed also Eliot and Pound. Far less of a 'little' magazine was J. C. Squire's *London Mercury* (he edited it from 1919-1934) which represented the uncommitted traditionalists, reflecting a point of view which its holders would have considered central and its opponents middlebrow. Middleton Murry edited *The Athenaeum* from 1919 to 1921 and *The Adelphi* from 1923 to 1930.

5

In the 1930s there were little magazines which responded to the tastes and ideals of the post-Eliot generation. *New Verse*, edited by Geoffrey Grigson, ran from 1933 to 1939: it was one of the most Catholic of the *avant garde* anthologies printing new poetry that was original and interesting whether it was by Auden or by Dylan Thomas. More limited in scope and interest were *Twentieth-Century Verse*, edited by Julian Symons from 1937 to 1939, and *Poetry (London)*, started just before the Second World War by Tambimuttu to reflect what for a short time appeared to be a 'new romanticism'. Looking back on all this from the middle 1950s one is aware of a loss of excitement and experiment. There is today in England no literary *avant garde*.

The quiet social revolution brought about by such innovations as the national health service, the Education Act of 1944, high taxation of the middle classes and full employment, produced an inevitable though not always a clearly discernible change in the patterns of English culture. The aristocratic implications, or at least the overtones of expansive middle-class leisure, that could be seen in different ways in the work of Eliot, the later Yeats and Virginia Woolf, had no meaning in the welfare state. Some recent novels show the post-war intellectual as a precarious provincial moving with a combination of bewilderment and sardonic observation in a world which lacks any sort of tradition, a world where the older patterns of behaviour—aristocratic or genteel— are parodied by vulgar and opportunistic pragmatists who get what they can out of each situation in which they find themselves. Social class, the theme which had been the background pattern of the English novel since its beginnings, now for the first time ceases to have meaning in a world where education and income bear no necessary relation to each other. Virginia Woolf had been accused by some critics of developing a kind of sensibility dependent on a certain degree of wealth and leisure (which of course is no proof that the sensibility thus developed was a bad thing); now it seemed that a society of working class prosperity, business 'fiddles' to minimize income tax, and a sharp drop in the relative (and often in the absolute) standard of living of the professional classes and 'intellectuals', left no room for sensibility. Was this a crisis of middle-class culture?

We are too close to it all to be able to say. But we can point to some interesting facts. For example, the *London Magazine* was originally subsidized by the *Daily Mirror*, a popular tabloid newspaper, which thus employed some of the profits made out of vulgarity and sensationalism to support 'culture'. And then there is the influence of radio and television. The BBC recognized the distinction between lowbrow, middlebrow and highbrow in their three programmes, the Light, the Home and the Third. One of the aims was apparently to introduce a few good serious works, in music and drama, on the Light programme, in the hope that some listeners to it might be attracted to the Home, and to introduce on occasion a really highbrow feature on the Home Service in the hope of making a few converts to the Third Programme. The BBC has thus thought of its function as educational and cultural, not merely as the provision of light entertainment. This artificial separation of the different 'brows', however, reflects something not altogether healthy in the state of a culture. The Elizabethan groundlings saw *Hamlet* as a blood-and-thunder murder mystery, while the better educated saw it as a profound tragedy—but each saw the same work. In our present culture, the murder mystery and the serious tragedy are represented by different works, the former trivial and merely entertaining, the latter self-consciously highbrow and probably appealing to only a tiny minority of sophisticates. This is one aspect of the problem of the fragmentation of the audience for works of literature which has long been a feature of our civilization. It is significant, for example, that the BBC programme which introduces new poetry is a regular

Third Programme feature: interest in new poetry is the mark of the extreme highbrow.

The BBC is a force, however, and is probably responsible for the remarkable increase of musical knowledge and musical taste in the country. It is in the more popular forms of art that radio and television most seriously threaten standards, by the very fact that they are catering to the same audience every night. The old music-hall entertainer perfected his act in months of playing it over and over at the same theatre, with a different audience each night, and then took it on tour in the provinces. He had time to develop an art-form of his own, however popular or crude it might be. But with a show going on the air every week, and the same audience listening each time, the situation is radically changed. The standard is bound to fall when there is the necessity of a weekly change of programme, no matter how talented the authors and performers—and the same is true of television and of the cinema. All this has its effect in due course on literature and on the public for literature.

Commercial television, which purveys merely entertainment and aims at the largest possible audience, can obviously take no chances and is bound to appeal to the lowest common denominator. It cannot afford to risk losing part of its audience by trying out something difficult. It must entertain first and foremost, and entertainment must be directed at a wholly relaxed and passive audience. Is entertainment as such an important part of the life of a civilization? Few would deny that in some sense it is. But the relation between art and entertainment has always been a shifting and a complex one, whereas the selling of guaranteed mass audiences to advertisers means immediate superficial entertainment at the most popular level at all costs. Is popular art bad art? The answer to that depends on the kind of society that fosters it. Today the answer is often but not always 'yes'. In the past art has had its own complex relationship with entertainment on the

8

one hand and with religion or at least with ritual on the other. Modern commercial entertainment has re-established contacts with ritual—a strange and frenzied ritual of hero-stars and 'personalities'.

It is not surprising, therefore, if the writer who is concerned with the problem of maintaining a discriminating audience for serious literature (or serious entertainment, for that matter) does not welcome commercial television even if he sees in it opportunity for improving his economic status. Non-commercial television has its own problems, but there can be no doubt that, like sound radio, it has played a part in the diffusion of culture. Nobody who has seen farm labourers watching television at a rustic public house and observed the thrill with which they have responded to *Swan Lake* and the half comprehending fascination with which they have watched *King Lear* (these are two real instances) can deny that television can act, and in some respects in this country has acted, as a remarkable educational and cultural force. There seem to be two quite contradictory forces at work in our culture. When we consider the exploitation of literacy (of mere literacy, that is to say) by the 'yellow' Press and all the stereotyped vulgarities of, say, the stories in some of the more popular women's magazines, to go no lower; when we think of mass production ousting individual craftsmanship, the prevalence of bad films, the complete unawareness of even the existence of any such thing as artistic integrity or literary value among so many people; when we think of the loss of that simple but genuine folk lore which the total illiterate possessed, for the sake of a minimal literacy which merely exposes its possessor to exploitation and corruption—when we think of all this, we are in despair about modern civilization. On the other hand, when we see the enormous numbers of relatively cheap paper-bound editions of the classics, as well as of serious works of history and biography, selling daily, or observe the unprecedented numbers of people who

9

appreciate good music and ballet, or reflect that an industrial worker or farm labourer whose grandfather may well have led an almost animal existence has now the opportunity of reading and hearing and viewing works of art of various kinds to a degree hitherto impossible, then one takes a much more rosy view. Which is the true picture? Both are true, and, paradoxically enough, both are sometimes true for the same people. The diffusion of culture is a sociological fact, and, further, diffusion does not always imply adulteration. The real problem seems to be an utter lack of discrimination, a lack of awareness of the *absolute* difference between the genuine and the 'phoney'. Where so much in the form of art and of pseudo-art is thrown at people, where the cultural centre of the nation is itself non-existent or at least problematical, discrimination on the part of the individual is most necessary, and lack of it most dangerous. The ordinary reader in Pope's day, though he belonged to a tiny minority when compared with his modern equivalent, was probably no better able to discriminate between, say, real poetry and imitative sentimental rubbish which followed the conventional forms of the day; but the coherence and stability of his culture and the critical tradition of his time made individual discrimination less necessary. The paradox of our time is that individual discrimination is most necessary when it is least possible.

2

The 1930s were the political decade. The rise of Hitler forced into political awareness a whole generation that had hitherto thought of politics as a dirty game or as an exalted activity for the chosen few. It was the red decade, too, for bewilderment and concern in the face of Hitlerism (whether aroused by Hitler's grandiose nihilism or by his organized cruelty) very frequently took the form of a rapid turn to the

Left, which alone seemed to have an explanation of what was happening all over Europe. We look back now in some wonder at the naïveté with which the official Communist explanation of Fascism as the dying throes of the last stage of monopoly capitalism was accepted by so many ardent and well-meaning young men, and at the move towards 'socialist realism' and other forms of socially conscious literature which resulted. But the Communist explanation was the only one of any plausibility at all that was put forward—Original Sin had not yet become fashionable, although T. E. Hulme and T. S. Eliot had made much of it. In the universities, a generation's idealistic goodwill was swept into the anti-fascist Left, and in the process Communism and fellow-travelling with Communism became the obvious marks of the young man (and not only the young) who looked with horror and compassion at what was happening to the Europe of his time. The Left Book Club was the great sign of the times; it was a tremendous educational campaign led by Victor Gollancz and John Strachey in the interests of a more-or-less Marxist interpretation of recent economic history, a vaguely conceived popular front Socialism, and a humane liberal attitude in general. These three elements were not always compatible, but it must be remembered that the basis of the movement was emotional although it pretended that it was logical.

First the Nazi-Soviet pact and then the coming of war changed all that. 'Socialist realism' faded out rapidly, leaving in its wake only a tendency towards the documentary; in a fight for survival Left and Right lose much of their meaning; the facts of life were seen to be in some respects simpler and in others much more complex than the Left Book Club authors had allowed. Nevertheless, when the war was over, the British people, wanting a fuller and richer democracy than had been possible under the old régime, turned out the hero Churchill and his Conservative government and elected a Labour government with an overwhelming majority and a clear mandate to put into effect the welfare state. The Labour Government did what it was elected to do; the accumulated influence of decades of reforming thought was spent; and by the end of the 1940s Left-wing thought had become old-fashioned among the same kind of bright young men who would have gone Communist or near-Communist in the mid-1930s. The Left Book Club, so quaintly old-fashioned when looked back on in the 'fifties, was partly responsible for Labour's victory in 1945; it may have over-simplified and even falsified in its desire to impose a clear and progressive pattern on events, but it had also reiterated certain basic truths about British society and about the facts of British economic life and the need for changing them. The writer who had been a young man in the 'thirties looked now at the changed scene and decided that politics was not for him. The welfare state, and the degree of equalitarianism which accompanied it, were good and useful things, but they did not nourish the imagination. To be non-political is, consciously or not, to be conservative; to turn from social and political problems to individual and moral ones is to become, in some sense of the word, religious. And so the literary fledgling at Oxford and Cambridge (these universities were particularly sensitive to these shifts) was a Left-wing agnostic in 1935 and was more likely than not to be Right-wing and religious fifteen years later.

Other factors were involved in the shift—disillusion about Soviet Russia, for example, and a realization among many intellectuals that the kind of life they lived was better in most essential respects than the alternatives offered either to the East or to the West—but to chart them in detail is the task of the social rather than the literary historian. If in some quarters (the universities, for example) the shift seemed to indicate a revival of religion, in the country as a whole it took the form of a mild scepticism about both politics and religion. Nonconformist Christianity had been an important force in the development of Left-wing thought in Britain; where Left-wing zeal flagged after the achievement of the welfare state, the religious impulse behind it seemed to flag too. Such religious revival as there has been in post-war Britain appears to have been confined to the better educated. Its symbol is not Billy Graham, the American evangelist whose carefully staged campaigns caused considerable temporary excitement in 1954 and 1955, but, say, C. S. Lewis, a literary scholar and critic of considerable brilliance and at the same time a highly sophisticated Christian apologist. The literature of this kind of religion has not been extensive—the theological thrillers of Charles Williams, the books of Lewis himself (a disciple of Williams in some respects) and (though this is perhaps a somewhat different sort of thing) the later work of Dorothy Sayers.

The concern with the Fall and Original Sin on the part of the neo-Christians is part of a wider awareness of the limitations of human nature: even those who angrily repudiate the notion that every individual is properly held guilty because of Adam's first sin will generally agree that man is an imperfect and fallible creature and it is not merely bad institutions or undesirable economic conditions that produce human evil. Poverty, squalor, mass unemployment, malnutrition and a great variety of diseases have been pretty much stamped out in Britain; the problems of 'teddy boys' and razor slashers and mail robberies remain, as do the larger problems of human selfishness and greed. If the decade after the Second World War did not show the bright iconoclasm of the decade after the First, and if there is nothing today quite like the despairing wit of *Chrome Yellow* or *Antic Hay*, there is nevertheless less optimism about human nature and political institutions than there was in the 1930s: a restrained and reasonably cheerful scepticism about the possibilities of man and his works is one mark of the early 1950s.

13

The Atomic Age, ushered in so spectacularly by the dropping of atomic bombs on Japan in 1945, has, of course, affected men's imagination, but not quite in the way that might have been expected. It was a great moral shock to most thinking people that the first proof of man's having uncovered one of the inmost secrets of the universe should have been the making and the using of an appalling weapon of mass destruction quite unprecedented in its indiscriminate lethal effects. The fear that science might end by producing a world in which life was too easy and all the virtues associated with effort and struggle would disappear (a fear voiced in Huxley's *Brave New World*) gave way to a more immediate fear that the scientist would end by destroying the world altogether. But the very awfulness of the prospect seemed to make it less real, and though the possibility of the destruction of the planet continued to agitate a number of people, the majority soon learned to shrug it off on the grounds that if it did happen there would be nobody left to worry about it, and if it did not the world would go on very much as it was. This again contributed to the restrained scepticism, not pessimistic nor yet very optimistic, that has marked the early 1950s.

All this was only indirectly reflected in literature. No great novels or plays dealing with the moral problems raised by the atom bomb have yet been written. But the mood of cautious reflection, of distrust of systems or panaceas, has been reflected in the retreat from the doctrinaire and the ideological and the concentration on particular human problems. If the First World War produced a suspicion of catchwords, the Second produced a suspicion of systems—all systems, those created by the idealistic Left as well as those perpetuated by the complacent Right. In the 1930s it was widely believed by the younger generation of writers that environment made man what he was; in the decade following the Second World War the general belief was rather that a stream can rise no higher than its source, and that the writer's first duty was to take a good look at the source. It was not so much that man's scientific knowledge had outstripped his ethical growth—that was an old charge; it was rather that man himself required a long, cool look. Psychology and sociology between them appeared in the 1930s to have explained the human animal. But now he was seen still to be obstinately mysterious as well as mysteriously obstinate.

On the popular level, the development of science fiction has been rapid and striking. The notion that inter-planetary travel will soon become commonplace appears to be widespread—one sphere, at least, where the belief in fast and inevitable progress survives. This seems to be linked with the idea that the only way to unite the nations of the world in true political federation is to bring them face to face with a common enemy from another planet. That is why the inhabitants of other planets (and that there are inhabitants of other planets appears to be an article of faith with the science fiction writer) are often shown as hostile. The view that other orders of rational creatures than our own earthly one should be as fatuously obsessed with warfare and destruction might strike one as rather far-fetched; but inter-planetary warfare is a means of projecting the unity of the world and of deflecting heroism away from intra-terrestial conflicts. Rocket ships and astronomy have become a major interest of the young on both sides of the Atlantic. Occasionally a serious moralist cashes in on this to tell a moral fable in terms of inter-planetary struggles; on the whole, however, the science fiction writers are out to tell adventure stories at a fairly simple level, with all the usual features of danger, suspense, and the eventual triumph of right over wrong.

More serious literary interest has been shown by the moral problems arising out of the secrecy imposed on scientists engaged in atomic research during a period of tension between Russian Communism and the West, and the genuine conflict of loyalties that may result. The cases of scientists who, out of purely idealistic motives, betrayed their country's atomic secrets to Russia have fascinated many. Rebecca West has made a special study of treason in the modern world, of which such betrayals are only one minor aspect; others have concentrated on the scientist's or the diplomat's problem, often with considerable sympathy though without illusions. The theme has, however, proved more intractable than might have been expected, and has not produced work of any great literary interest. This is perhaps surprising, because it is a theme with genuinely tragic implications, closely related to the problem of the man of goodwill whose very goodwill leads him to produce evil—the problem that Shakespeare treated in his handling of Brutus in *Julius Caesar*. Graham Greene's novel, *The Quiet American*, handles a theme of this kind, not in the context of science and security but from the point of view of one who sees moral idealism in politics often leading to all kinds of moral horrors. The modern British writer tends to be suspicious of moral innocence, sometimes because he looks back on the red 'thirties and sees innocent idealists supporting the cruelties of a Communist dictatorship out of the highest motives, and partly because he is suspicious of the simple black-and-white moral approach to international affairs which he sees represented by American diplomacy. In the case of Graham Greene, a more general concern with the ambiguities of human goodwill, which is a feature of many of his novels, complicates the issue. The difference between, say, Stephen Spender's play, *Trial of a Judge*, and Graham Greene's novel—quite apart from the question of how far the theme is fully realized in the texture of the work in each case—is largely one of individual temperament; but it is also a difference in period, and the former can stand for the late 1930s as the latter can for the early 1950s.

The present age has seen a steadily growing interest in American literature on the part of British writers. In poetry, mutual cross-fertilization has been going on ever since Pound and Eliot first came to London, and the fact that Eliot and Auden crossed the Atlantic in different directions—not to mention the further fact that the Americanized Auden was invited back to England as Professor of Poetry at Oxford— is sufficiently indicative of the state of affairs. The major movements in both poetry and criticism since 1912 or at least since 1920 have straddled the Atlantic. Sometimes a movement has crossed the Atlantic from Britain to America only to be re-imported by Britain later after it has suffered a sea-change. The later Yeats has had more influence on American than on English poets, and the critical work of Richards, Leavis and Empson has influenced American criticism to a greater degree than it has English. But the most significant development of all has been the recognition in Britain of the independence of American literature and the study of it as a foreign literature. Recognition of the foreignness of American literature was a prerequisite for its proper appreciation and for the fruitful use of American influence: so long as Englishmen regarded America as a bit of England gone wrong American literature was bound to be misread in England. American fiction, in particular, came to be appreciated for its lively rendering of a kind of society which had more raw vigour and surface colour than English society. Hemingway's exploration of the possibilities of heroism in the modern world was followed in Britain with considerable fascination, and, more belatedly, the social, moral and psychological jungles of Faulkner's Yoknapatawpha County were studied with wonder and admiration. The language in which the hero tells his story in Saul Bellow's *The Adventures of Augie March* (described by Angus Wilson as a 'strange mixture of American slang, literary allusion and poetry of the self-educated adventurer') or the unfamiliar setting against which J. D. Salinger projected some of the problems of adolescence in his *Catcher in the Rye* excited the English novelist, and led him sometimes to see his own art as stereotyped and jaded, so that discussions of the question 'Is the English. Novel in Decline?' came to be frequent. No great success has so far been achieved by serious English novelists in imitating American modes, but recognition of the originality and vitality of the American novel has affected the English literary atmosphere, certainly by the 1950s, if not earlier.

On the other hand, Continental influences have been surprisingly slight in the latter part of our period. In the 1930s the novels of Kafka and the poetry of Rilke had considerable influence. But Kafka, while he had a tremendous vogue, never really entered the English literary imagination, though some (Rex Warner and William Sansom, for example) have on occasion tried to imitate him. And Rilke's influence on modern English poetry, in spite or because of the renderings by Stephen Spender and J. B. Leishman, seems simply to have been the encouragement of vaguely elegiac rumination. In the late 1940s, when French Existentialism made such an impact on America, it met only with polite interest in Britain. French influence was of course important in the early work of Eliot, and lasted in some degree throughout the 1920s; Germany compelled the attention of younger writers in the 1930s—not only through Kafka and Rilke but directly, through physical contact, as Isherwood's Berlin stories show: Isherwood, Spender and Auden were all more interested in Germany than in France. After the rise of Hitler, of course, Germany was a horror story, and after the war it seemed for a time to be merely a vacuum. American influence was stronger than Continental European in the decade after the war ended.

Britain has a tendency to become more insular after periods

of crisis, and perhaps this is what happened in some degree after the Second World War. The war itself encouraged people to take an interest in their own threatened heritage and it cannot be an accident that since the war visiting old country houses has become a popular British pastime and that broadcasts on Roman Britain and similar subjects have proved immensely popular. When the remains of a Mithraic temple were revealed by excavation in 1955, enormous crowds of people flocked to examine them. And much recent poetry has been local and topographical. At the same time unprecedented numbers of people have been taking their holidays abroad. The restriction of the amount of currency that can be taken out of the country has meant that holiday makers on the Continent have represented a much wider range of social classes than ever before; a Continental trip is no longer the rich man's prerogative. Never before have so many parties of British schoolchildren been seen in Paris at Easter time. On the other hand, because of the impossibility of taking British currency into the dollar area, it is impossible for the ordinary tourist to visit America. This all adds up to a set of paradoxes: more trips to the Continent, less Continental influence on literature; virtually no trips to America, more American influence on literature. And a certain complacent insularity noticeable among those very intellectuals who used to be so internationally minded. But certain exceptions and qualifications must be made. The established writer is in fact one of the few classes of people who do find it possible to visit America in time of currency restriction, for he can give lectures or readings, and he probably has American royalties due to him. And if the British public as a whole is taking its holidays on the Continent to a greater degree than ever before, it is probable that the professional writer is doing so to a lesser degree than before. Perhaps this is attributable to the fact that the British intellectual today is on the whole less of a rebel than he has been for generations. He leaves it to the Philistines to travel in France and report how much better they order things there, while he stays at home and tries to distil the meaning of his own place and people.

One of the reasons why he stays at home may well be that he has not much money. The writer in Britain today, while he may make a reasonable living with the help of broadcasting and weekly journalism, is most unlikely to make much out of his books. Profits from poetry are negligible and from fiction are small. Harassed by income tax (which seems to many to fall unfairly on the free-lance writer), pushed down to a relatively lower place on the economic scale than he has known for generations, he is rarely able to give himself wholly to his art. The days of the novelist-prince are over. The novelist in Britain today, instead of being the lionized man of wealth that Scott or Dickens was able to become, is likely to be a schoolteacher, a university don, or even a business man; and even those writers who try to avoid taking another job find themselves spending more and more time writing broadcasts and journalism. It is, of course, a fine thing for the British writer that he has the BBC to turn to; in some respects it has proved itself the *deus ex machina* of the man of letters. But not every writer can adjust himself to that kind of work or even be certain of getting it. Most writers would prefer to be able to devote two or three years to, say, an important novel, with a generous advance on royalties from a publisher and a confidence that once the novel is published it will provide enough to live on at least for some little time. That state of affairs just does not exist in post-war Britain— not because the writer is less esteemed than he was, but because the whole social and economic picture has changed.

For a long time now there has been no standard means of recruitment into the literary profession. This has had some advantages: there are no pontificating literary dictators whose nod of approval must be obtained by a writer before he can be said to have set his foot on the ladder, nor are there one or two periodicals whose approval means success and disapproval failure. How and whether a man becomes a writer is today a matter of chance. Groups and coteries are fluctuating and unstable; publishers are cautious; standards are erratic. Indeed, on the economic and professional side the whole literary situation is confused and unpredictable. The long struggle upward from Grub Street, which progressed steadily throughout the eighteenth and nineteenth centuries, has ceased, and the next stage is obscure. The situation is complicated by the increasing separation between art and entertainment in our time. Entertainment—in films, television, radio—is now the best paid profession in the world. The lucky novelist who manages to sell a novel to Hollywood or even to make the best seller list has moved, willingly and consciously or not, from the realm of art to that of entertainment. Perhaps it is a pity that they should ever have been separated. That there are still bridges between them is a matter of hope for the optimists who see the artist eventually reconquering the realm of entertainment, and of despair for the pessimists who anticipate the reverse process.

CHAPTER II

POETRY

I

THE first half of the twentieth century saw a revolution in poetic taste in England comparable to that which occurred at the end of the seventeenth century or at the end of the eighteenth and the beginning of the nineteenth. The result of that revolution was the ousting of the view of poetry represented by Palgrave's *Golden Treasury* in favour of a poetic practice and a critical theory which exalted cerebral complexity, allusive suggestion, and precision of the individual image. The poet was no longer the sweet singer whose function was to render in mellifluous verse and a more or less conventional romantic imagery a self-indulged personal emotion; he was the explorer of experience who used language in order to build up rich patterns of meaning which, however impressive their immediate impact, required repeated close attention before they communicated themselves fully to the reader. A core of burning paradox was preferred to a gloss of surface beauty. It was not the function of poetry to pander to the languid dreams of a pampered sensibility, to revel in the sweetness of a cultivated nostalgia or the sad plangency of controlled self-pity. Tennyson's 'Break, break, break' and Arnold's 'Dover Beach' show, in very different ways, how Victorian poetry always tended to run to elegy. Eliot's *The Waste Land*, published in 1922, was worlds apart from that skilful alternation of worry and elegy which constituted Tennyson's *In Memoriam*. Complex, allusive, drawing on a great variety of both occidental and oriental myth and symbol, using abrupt contrasts and shifting counter-suggestions to help unfold the meaning, eliminating all conjunctive phrases or overt statements that might indicate the relation of one scene or situation to another, *The Waste Land* was both a demonstration and a manifesto of what the new poetry wanted to do and could do. Both seventeenth century metaphysical poetry and the nineteenth-century French symbolists contributed techniques and attitudes to the revolution. Bridges' publication of Gerard Manley Hopkins' poems in 1918 showed a poet eschewing the conventions of Victorian poetic statement and striving after a kind of poetic statement both precise and passionate, both profoundly felt and desperately accurate, even if this involved wresting language to a new and startling shape. It was the complete absence of any sign of laxness in Hopkins' poetry, the clear signs of words and rhythms having been bent to do their master's will, with no dependence at all on a general aura of 'poetic' feeling, that attracted the new poets to him after 1918; here was that 'unified sensibility', that fusion of thought and emotion, which Eliot had found in the metaphysicals and which he had found conspicuously lacking in most eighteenth- and nineteenth-century poetry as the result of a 'dissociation of sensibility' setting in in the latter part of the seventeenth century.

So the poetic revolution which began in the years immediately preceding the First World War, and which both produced and was further encouraged by *The Waste Land*, was in some sense a revolt against what might be called the Victorian Romantic tradition in favour of an older tradition in English poetry. Such a revolution was bound to bring with it an underestimation of romantic poetry, just as the Romantic Movement had brought an underestimation of Dryden and Pope, and the 'refining of our numbers' in the latter part of the seventeenth-century an underestimation of the metaphysicals. But it was not a wanton underestimation: the criticism that accompanied the poetic revolution put its finger unerringly on the weaknesses of romantic poetry, on its tendency to naïve confession, its preference for emotional softness, its combination of theatricality with prophetic solemnity, its narcissism. This is not to say that all English poetry from Wordsworth to Swinburne had these faults, but simply that during this period these were the faults into which poetry tended to fall when genius failed. And these were the faults which the *avant garde* poets of the early 1920s and even earlier were determined to avoid. 'The poet', wrote Eliot in 1917, 'has, not a "personality" to express, but a particular medium, which is only a medium and not a personality, in which impressions and experiences combine in peculiar and unexpected ways.' The function of poetry is not self-expression but the proper fusion of meaning in language. Further, we must note 'how completely any semi-ethical criterion of "sublimity" misses the mark. For it is not the "greatness", the intensity, of the emotions, the components, but the intensity of the artistic process, the pressure, so to speak, under which the fusion takes place, that counts.' But though poems are works of art, not pieces of emotional autobiography or rhetorical prophecy, the function of art is the exploration of experience, and poetry that lives merely in the world of words (as Eliot alleged Swinburne's poetry did) is as unsatisfactory as that which confuses 'art and the event'.

What had happened to English poetry can in some degree be illustrated by four quotations. Keats, in his sonnet 'When I have fears that I may cease to be', reflects on the possibility of his dying before he fully lived, and concludes:

> *then on the shore*
> *Of the wide world I stand alone, and think*
> *Till Love and Fame to nothingness do sink.*

Matthew Arnold, meditating by the melancholy surge of the sea (a favourite situation of the Victorian poet), reflects on the ebb of faith and concludes:

Ah, love, let us be true
To one another! for the world, which seems
To lie before us like a land of dreams,
So various, so beautiful, so new,
Hath really neither joy, nor love, nor light,
Nor certitude, nor peace, nor help for pain;
And we are here as on a darkling plain
Swept with confused alarms of struggle and flight,
Where ignorant armies clash by night.

Hopkins, struggling with a mood of spiritual nullity, ends:

O the mind, mind has mountains; cliffs of fall
Frightful, sheer, no-man-fathomed. Nor does long our small
Durance deal with that steep or deep. Here! creep,
Wretch, under a comfort serves in a whirlwind: all
Life death does end and each day dies with sleep.

Eliot, presenting in 'Gerontion' a complexly symbolic picture
of a way of life that has lost all meaning and value, concludes:

These with a thousand small deliberations
Protract the profit of their chilled delirium,
Excite the membrane, when the sense has cooled,
With pungent sauces, multiply variety
In a wilderness of mirrors. What will the spider do,
Suspend its operations, will the weevil
Delay? De Bailhache, Fresca, Mrs Cammel, whirled
Beyond the circuit of the shuddering Bear
In fractured atoms. Gull against the wind, in the windy straits
Of Belle Isle, or running on the Horn,
White feathers in the snow, the Gulf claims,
And an old man driven by the Trades
To a sleepy corner.
                              Tenants of the house,
Thoughts of a dry brain in a dry season.

Keats's sonnet represents what might be called the romantic
sensibility, meeting an unhappy situation by cultivating a

mood of bitter-sweet reverie. Arnold in 'Dover Beach' does very much the same, except that there are two people involved together in the emotional situation. Hopkins, on the other hand, is not cultivating a mood of pleasing sadness; he has hammered language into an exact and disturbing picture of that grim state of mind which is the subject of the poem. In Eliot's poem the poet's sensibility is not directly there at all; everything is projected dramatically through 'thoughts of a dry brain in a dry season' in a pattern of images, situations and suggestions which combine to create a symbolic picture of desiccation.

All this may suggest that the poetic revolution which took place roughly in the decade 1912 to 1922 was a revolt against the kind of romantic egotism which persisted throughout the nineteenth century. And yet, of course, not all nineteenth-century English poetry cultivated that strain. Keats was not always brooding by the sea; Browning wrote dramatic monologues; Tennyson frequently exercised his virtuosity out of an impulse of craftsmanship rather than self-pity. Further, there were English poets between Matthew Arnold and Eliot, and Eliot and his contemporaries could hardly be said to have been reacting against poets who flourished from fifty to a hundred years before. To the retrospective eye it does indeed seem as though the poetic revolution represented by *The Waste Land* was directed chiefly against the Romantic-Victorian tradition, the tradition which Palgrave stood for and which his *Golden Treasury* established firmly in the minds of generations of schoolteachers. The rebels themselves were conscious of the fact that the poetry of their own time represented the final ebb of that tradition; it seemed to them often exhausted and pallid, and the quiet nature poetry of the Georgians was construed by innovators like Ezra Pound— whose stay in London just before the First World War stirred things up enormously—as the timid and sapless work of uninspired amateurs. That the poetry of the so-called Georgians was less uniform than it appeared to those contemporaries who were seeking for a radically new kind of vitality in English poetry, and that such poets as Gordon Bottomley, Walter De la Mare, Lascelles Abercrombie, Harold Monro and Edward Thomas displayed at their best both power and individuality, does not alter the fact that each of these poets was content to de-limit or modify the poetic inheritance of the nineteenth century rather than abandon it in favour of a radically different approach. Masefield's rather self-conscious 'realism' in subject and vocabulary represented no new approach to the poet's medium: a few swear-words do not make a new poetic style—a fact which Masefield's early reviewers failed to appreciate—and neither did the appealing hymn-tune rhythms of Kipling, whose salt-water equivalent Masefield was at first taken to be. De la Mare is perhaps the last of the true romantic poets of England, brilliant in his own way, but it was not a way that pointed to new paths for English poetry. What Wilfred Owen and Isaac Rosenberg would have gone on to do if they had not been killed in the war is a barren speculation; both had restless and pioneering poetic minds, and Owen was to have a significant influence on the young poets of the 1930s, but they were of no direct influence on the first phase of the modern revolution.

The new movement began with a revolt against every kind of verbal imprecision and lushness. T. E. Hulme, the curious erratic critic and philosopher who was killed in the war in 1917, writing in the *New Age* from 1909 onwards, contrasted a sloppy romanticism with a precise and disciplined classicism. He advocated hardness and precision of imagery 'in order to get the exact curve of the thing' together with subtler and more flexible rhythms. From this—with Pound acting as midwife—was born Imagism, a movement which flourished briefly on both sides of the Atlantic. Its programme was limited enough—too limited indeed to produce in itself poetry of any real stature. Pound, who had come to Europe from his native America full of a passionate desire to 'make it new', had been exploring in his own impressionist way Provençal poetry, Greek and Latin lyric poetry, and (later, and sometimes through odd intermediaries) the classical poetry of China and Japan, and Hulme's neo-classicism appealed to his sense of craftsmanship and his feeling that English and American poetry wanted above all a new technical brilliance and verbal integrity. Writing from London, in December 1912, an account of the state of English poetry for the pioneer Chicago magazine *Poetry*, Pound said of the *Imagistes* (they used the French form of the word at first, and later became Imagists) that 'they are in opposition to the numerous and unassembled writers who busy themselves with dull and interminable effusions, and who seem to think that a man can write a good long poem before he learns to write a good short one, or even before he learns to produce a good single line'. F. S. Flint wrote for the March 1913 issue of *Poetry* a fuller statement of the aims of the Imagist movement. The three rules the Imagists observed, he said, were, first, 'direct treatment of the "thing"', secondly, 'to use absolutely no word that did not contribute to the presentation', and thirdly, 'to compose in sequence of the musical phrase, not in sequence of a metronome'. To Flint's account was added 'A Few Don'ts by an Imagiste' by Pound, which included such rules as, 'Use no superfluous word, no adjective, which does not reveal something', and 'Go in fear of abstractions'. The English Imagists found an organ in *The Egoist*, which included on its editorial staff Richard Aldington, who contributed imagist verse to its columns, as did Pound, H. D., Flint, J. G. Fletcher and others, British and American, including D. H. Lawrence, who found himself by accident *dans cette galère*, his poetry having been discovered to be imagist.

Clearly, Imagism was not enough. To use hard, dry and precise visual images might be sound enough advice to a generation seeking to restore cogency of idiom to a worn out poetic convention, but it is a very limited kind of poetry which can be made out of precise visual images only. In Pound's early poetry, Chinese influence helped to produce some very attractive imagist writing: but it is the patterning of groups of sharply etched visual scenes in terms of a larger poetic logic that produces the poems of any real stature among these. And though Eliot learned something from the Imagists, he was never content with merely the *justness* of his images, their visual accuracy; for him an image had to function as symbol as well as visual record, and the organization of the images within a poem was determined by a kind of poetic dialectic which was the most distinctive pioneering feature of Eliot's early work. For Eliot, an image draws its meaning not only by conveying the quality of the thing it denotes (as rock or sand conveys the quality of dryness) but also from its direct or oblique references to its earlier use in literature, religion or mythology and also from the pattern of meaning and suggestion set up cumulatively by the poem as it unfolds. Behind Eliot lay not only Imagism, but the metaphysical poets, Jacobean drama, the provocative ironies of Laforgue and the symbolic subtleties of Rimbaud and Verlaine, to name only a few influences. There lay, too, a deep suspicion of modern industrial civilization, a desire for classical discipline, and an interest in Sanskrit and Oriental philosophy, all of which were part of the atmosphere of Harvard University when he was a student there.

2

The rebels of the revolutionary decade were intent on restoring wit and cerebration to poetry. Grierson's great edition of Donne, published in 1912, came at just the right time to encourage the move towards the metaphysical poets, now esteemed for their toughness and complexity, their fusion of thought and passion. The pun returned to serious poetry for the first time since the seventeenth century: in the eighteenth century it had been scorned as 'low', and in the nineteenth it had been used almost exclusively in comic verse. The revival of the pun was not only an indication that for the new poets irony and even humour could co-exist with profundity and seriousness; it also reflected a concern with the 'ambivalence' of experience, with the paradoxes that lay at the heart of all significant human situations. In the 1930s, the younger American critics, bred in the new poetic tradition which saw Donne and Hopkins rather than Spenser and Tennyson as key figures in the history of English poetry, were to proclaim that the language of poetry is inevitably and essentially paradox, an oversimplification deriving from the practice and preferences of the revolutionary poets of the immediately preceding decades.

The movement was international. Pound, the gadfly who stung many poets into new activity, came from America and went on to Italy; Eliot, who soon became the central figure in the revolution, was an American who settled in England and became a British subject. Yeats, whose later poetry shows in its own remarkable way the influence of the new attitude, was an Irishman who never lost interest in or contact with the Anglo-Irish culture which bred him. The change in Yeats—attributable only partly to his having come temporarily under the influence of Pound and his friends—was most striking. He had begun as a dreamy romantic, seeking in a beautiful world of words compensation for the drabness of a world in which science had killed traditional values. 'I am very religious', he once wrote, 'and deprived by Huxley and Tyndall, whom I detested, of the simple-minded religion of my childhood, I had made a new religion, almost an infallible church of poetic tradition, of a fardel of stories, and of personages, and of emotions, inseparable from their first expression, passed on from generation to generation by poets and painters with some help from philosophers and theologians.'

The tone of his early poetry is languid and nostalgic:

> *The woods of Arcady are dead,*
> *And over is their antique joy;*
> *Of old the world on dreaming fed;*
> *Grey Truth is now her painted toy;*
> *Yet still she turns her restless head:*
> *But O, sick children of the world,*
> *Of all the many changing things*
> *In dreary dancing past us whirled,*
> *To the cracked tune that Chronos sings,*
> *Words alone are certain good.*

It is a far cry from this self-conscious romanticism to the complex magic of 'Byzantium' or the packed austerity of the Crazy Jane poems. Yeats's poetic career was in some respects the history of poetry in his own time.

This is not to say that Yeats passively reflected any new movement that arose. He worked out his poetic salvation in his own way and never at any period in his career did he lose the compelling individuality of his accent. At first he was concerned to combine, or counterpoint, the three focal points of his poetic imagination—Dublin, with its Irish nationalism in both politics and literature; Rosses, Sligo and other places in the West of Ireland with their peasant population nurtured on legend and folklore; and London, where the 'companions of the Cheshire Cheese' (who included Lionel Johnson, Ernest Dowson, John Davidson, among others) talked about poetry and cultivated aesthetic attitudes. From the London centre he got some vaguely pre-Raphaelite notions and some knowledge of the French Symbolists; from Sligo and Rosses he got earthiness and folklore and a racy dialect; from Dublin, especially in the 'lull in politics' that followed the death of Parnell, he got the sense of belonging to a national literary movement. If London suggested the woods of Arcady it was Sligo that made possible such a poem as 'The

Stolen Child', with its quiet precision of natural imagery, its use of country place-names and its theme from folklore. And it was Dublin literary circles that sent him to Standish O'Grady's *History of Ireland, Heroic Period*, where he found the great stories of the heroic age of Irish history, and to George Sigerson's and Douglas Hyde's translations of Gaelic poetry into 'that dialect which gets from Gaelic its syntax and keeps its still partly Tudor vocabulary'. So, when he dabbled in neo-Platonism and wrote of the Rose as the symbol of the idea of Beauty which suffers with man, he associated it with Irish heroic themes:

> *Red Rose, proud Rose, sad Rose of all my days!*
> *Come near me, when I sing the ancient ways:*
> *Cuchulain battling with the bitter tide;*
> *The Druid, grey, wood-nurtured, quiet eyed,*
> *Who cast round Fergus dreams, and ruin untold;* . . .

Meanwhile, he was searching for a mystical philosophy which could impose some order on experience and take the place of the orthodox religion which for him had been destroyed by Huxley and Tyndall. The story of Yeats's adventures among theosophists, mystics, spiritualists, hypnotists and other eccentric thinkers is strange enough; the surprising thing is that Yeats drew nourishment from them all, and the magical system which he eventually constructed for himself and described in his book, *A Vision*—it combined a system of magic, a philosophy of history and a philosophy of personality—was able to provide the central core of order in such great poems as 'The Second Coming' and 'Byzantium'. He had come a long way before he ever met Pound in London in 1912. In some of his early poems handling folk themes, he achieved by a careful counterpointing of contrasting pairs of images (such as human and faery, natural and artificial, domestic and wild, familiar and strange, modern and ancient, ephemeral and permanent) more suggestive patterns of meaning than might have been expected from such material. He was concerned from the beginning with opposites, with the dichotomy which he saw as central in experience; in his earlier poetry he explored the contrasts, while later he found poetic ways of resolving them or of subsuming them in a *tertium quid*.

For all the striking differences between Yeats's earlier and his later poetry, there was no sudden and violent change, but a continuous development. In 1906 he looked back on his earlier life and recorded how 'without knowing it, I had come to care for nothing but impersonal beauty'. He concluded that 'we should ascend out of common interests, the thoughts of the newspapers, or the market-place, of men of science, but only so far as we can carry the normal, passionate reasoning self, the personality as a whole'. This resolution to use the whole man in writing poetry was, of course, very much what Eliot was to resolve to do a few years later. In *In the Seven Woods*, published in 1904, he showed both new quietness and sharpness of phrase (as in 'The Old Men Admiring Themselves in the Water') and a new suppleness of rhythms, combining the formal with the colloquial (as in 'Adam's Curse'). And in *The Green Helmet and Other Poems*, published in 1910, he could write:

> *Though leaves are many, the root is one;*
> *Through all the lying days of my youth*
> *I swayed my leaves and flowers in the sun;*
> *Now I may wither into the truth.*

An unhappy love affair, and active practical interest in the Irish theatre to which he had been directed by Lady Gregory, gave a new dimension and a new reality to his verse. 'No Second Troy' combines high passion and bitterly scornful irony in a way that had not been seen in English poetry for generations. And the rueful note and flexible vigour of 'The Fascination of What's Difficult' take us a long way indeed from the woods of Arcady:

The fascination of what's difficult
Has dried the sap out of my veins and rent
Spontaneous joy and natural content
Out of my heart . . . .
          My curse on plays
That have to be set up in fifty ways,
On the day's war with every knave and dolt,
Theatre business, management of men. . . .

A gift for epigram emerges now, too, in such sharp little poems as 'On hearing that the students of our university have joined the agitation against immoral literature'. In *Responsibilities* (1914) we see the ironic and realistic strain further developed and sometimes combined with magical and symbolic elements in a new richness of meaning. 'To a Shade' is a poem of cold passion perfectly wrought; 'The Cold Heaven' is a symbolic vision, realized with remarkable power; in other poems of this collection he experiments with different uses of the refrain, a device he was soon to develop with remarkable skill. The combination of metaphysical wit and lapidary precision of style which marks so many of these 'middle' poems of Yeats is indicated clearly enough in the concluding stanza of 'To a Young Beauty', one of the poems in *The Wild Swans at Coole*:

> *I know what wages beauty gives,*
> *How hard a life her servant lives,*
> *Yet praise the winters gone:*
> *There is not a fool can call me friend,*
> *And I may dine at journey's end*
> *With Landor and with Donne.*

The ideal now is to write a poem 'as cold and passionate as the dawn'. At the same time he is developing that strain of 'occasional' poetry, with its finely controlled, flexible rhythms and its overtones of colloquial speech, that will later yield such poems as 'Among School Children' and 'Coole and Ballylee, 1931'.

Meanwhile, Yeats's search for a language of symbols went on. He had been from the beginning aware of the breakdown of traditional value patterns and their accompanying symbols, and continuously sought a poetic language which would have all the magical evocativeness of traditional romantic symbolism with greater power and an ability to shock rather than lull the reader into attention. His private myths do not always work; those dealing with Michael Robartes and Owen Aherne are sometimes tedious; but he taught himself to rely on the individual poetic expression for the meaning, so that in his best poems the meaning does not really refer outward to formulations outside the poem but presses disturbingly home by means of image, symbol and rhythm. He was also developing his notion of the aristocratic dance. Despising the middle-class 'Paudeens' with their philistinism and materialism, he went either above them or below them, to the ordered life of the country house or the free life of the beggar, to find a way of living that he could respect. He prayed for his daughter:

> *And may her bridegroom bring her to a house*
> *Where all's accustomed, ceremonious;*
> *For arrogance and hatred are the wares*
> *Peddled in the thoroughfares.*
> *How but in custom and in ceremony*
> *Are innocence and beauty born?*

The aristocratic life of custom and ceremony takes its place in the cosmic dance:

> *Labour is blossoming or dancing where*
> *The body is not bruised to pleasure soul,*
> *Nor beauty born out of its own despair,*
> *Nor blear-eyed wisdom out of midnight oil.*
> *O chestnut-tree, great-rooted blossomer,*

Are you the leaf, the blossom or the bole?
O body swayed to music, O brightening glance,
How can we know the dancer from the dance?

This is the final stanza of his poem 'Among School Children', which moves effortlessly from a quiet description of the poet visiting a school through carefully modulated memories and speculations to this culmination.

The Tower (1928) and *The Winding Stair* (1933) represent the mature late Yeats at his very best—a realist-symbolist-metaphysical poet with a positively uncanny power over words. The two Byzantium poems—'Sailing to Byzantium' and 'Byzantium'—distil their meaning into a quintessence, haunting the mind and probing the emotions as no English poet had done since the seventeenth century. The theme of both poems is the attempt to compensate for old age by moving away from the teeming world of biological growth and change to the timeless world of art and intellect, a world of golden artefacts. 'Byzantium' is also a poem about art, about the making of poems, about the relation of art and life. The poet subdues the flesh in the spirit, the world of nature is left behind for the 'glory of changeless metal', but even as he is astride the symbolic dolphin that carries him above the seething tide of human passion, that passion floods back: art is, after all, nourished by the very world of growth and change, of begetting and dying, that it wants to leave behind in its search for permanence; the spirit is based on the mire and blood:

Astraddle on the dolphin's mire and blood,
Spirit after spirit! The smithies break the flood,
The golden smithies of the Emperor!
Marbles of the dancing floor
Break bitter furies of complexity,
Those images that yet
Fresh images beget,
That dolphin-torn, that gong-tormented sea.

36

The patterns of symbolic meaning in 'Byzantium' are rich and rewarding; but the power of the poem is felt at once by the most casual reader long before he has developed any coherent interpretation of it.

Winding stairs, spinning tops, 'gyres', spirals of all kind, are important symbols in Yeats's later poetry; not only are they connected with his philosophy of history and personality they also serve as a means of resolving some of those dichotomies that had arrested him from the beginning. Life is a journey up a spiral staircase; as we grow older we cover the ground we have covered before, only higher up; as we look down the winding stairs below us we see the places where we were but no longer are, measuring our progress by the increased number of our absences. The journey is both repetitious and progressive; we both travel in a circle and go forward. To resolve the 'antinomies' of life we must be able to be on all parts of the circle's circumference at once. The circles get smaller as the winding stair spirals to its summit; at the top, where the circle diminishes to a point, we will be standing on a circle whose circumference is infinitely small, and thus be everywhere on it at the same time. But the tower is ruined at the top, and when we arrive at the summit we reach old age and death. The dance of life includes death. Outside time the antinomies are resolved:

> *All could be known or shown*
> *If Time were but gone.*

In the poems of *Words for Music Perhaps* Yeats explores the paradoxes of time and change, of growth and identity, of love and age, of madness and wisdom, by his mythopoeic handling of invented characters such as Crazy Jane and Jack the Journeyman. Crazy Jane is wiser than the Bishop, but the paradox goes deeper than that:

37

A woman can be proud and stiff
When on love intent;
But Love has pitched his mansion in
The place of excrement;
For nothing can be sole or whole
That has not been rent.

The difference between this way of presenting love in poetry and the way of, say, Shelley's 'Epipsychidion' is fundamental.

In his very last poems there is what might be called a symbolic gaiety, a controlled wildness, with magical refrains, popular ballad rhythms, trance-like projections of arrested motion, satirical, political and autobiographical themes all playing their part in a procession of uncannily brilliant lyrics. The year before his death he could write like this (in 'The Statues'):

When Pearse summoned Cuchulain to his side,
What stalked through the Post Office? What intellect
What calculation, number, measurement, replied?
We Irish, born into that ancient sect
But thrown upon this filthy modern tide
And by its formless spawning fury wrecked,
Climb to our proper dark, that we may trace
The lineament of a plummet-measured face.

At the same time he could write that trance-poem, both magical and realistic, 'Long-Legged Fly', and that powerful political ballad, with its haunting refrain, 'The Ghost of Roger Casement'.

Yeats's total achievement remains astonishing. Though the twentieth century poetic revolution had its effect on him and helped to change him from a belated romantic to an original metaphysical poet, his own poetic genius stands strangely solitary. The fact that he was Irish partly accounts for that; but even more important was his attitude to the world and to his art, which was, in a literal and not in a metaphorical romantic sense, that of a magician. His use of language was magical, not rhetorical or self-indulgent or merely musical: he gave new meaning to things by the way he named them.

3

Yeats was the giant of the first half of the twentieth century; no other poet in English during his time had his stature. Yet he remained in large degree aloof from what might be called the politics of literature. Though the changes in his style do owe something to the great shift in poetic taste which began in England about 1912, his individuality, his Irishness, his unique mythopoeic faculty, kept him in some degree an outsider. The man who was at the centre of English—and American—poetry from say, 1920 to 1930 was T. S. Eliot, who *was* involved in the politics of literature, whose criticism preached and practised the aims of the anti-romantic revolution, and whose poetry expressed much more directly than that of Yeats the mood of his generation. *The Waste Land* was central to its time in both theme and technique. The combination of mythical, anthropological, Christian and oriental imagery in order to find an effective poetic way of projecting poetically the modern dilemma, the construction of the poem by means of a series of dramatic episodes linked to each other by a profound emotional pattern rather than by any overt logic, the cunning variations on the main theme of physical and spiritual barrenness and frustration, the teasing allusiveness—all this was to become very much the way of the 'new poetry'; it was Eliot's eclectic myth-using rather than Yeats's personal myth-making that was to provide the model for a whole generation of poets.

Yeats's concern with order led him to construct a private myth of the world, Eliot's led him to a position which he once described as Royalist in politics, Anglo-Catholic in religion, and classical in literature. He sought order in tradition rather than in magical formulas invented by himself; he turned in-creasingly to the traditional Christian symbols of value and in his later poetry—from *Ash Wednesday* (1930) on—became more and more concerned with rendering in his own packed and allusive way some of the major themes of Christian ex-perience. The 'hard dry' images that Hulme had insisted on, the irony and ambivalence that the new poets got from Donne, the undertones of colloquial and realistic speech in the midst of the gravest and most formal utterance—all these Eliot kept in his religious poetry; but there is a new tone, too, which rings out with calm assurance in the *Four Quartets*. This is the tone of mystical peace, of brooding over the still centre, of moving through history not, as in *The Waste Land* and other early poems, to provide ironical con-trasts between past and present, but in order to find a way out of the temporal process altogether, an escape from time in the fleeting visionary glimpse of eternity. How can we 're-deem the time', how can we escape from its burden? If all time is contained in eternity, then it can never be redeemed:

> *Time present and time past*
> *Are both perhaps present in time future,*
> *And time future contained in time past.*
> *If all time is eternally present*
> *All time is unredeemable.*

The solution is to be found 'at the still point of the turning world'.

> *A condition of complete simplicity*
> *(Costing not less than everything)*
> *And all shall be well and*
> *All manner of thing shall be well*
> *When the tongues of flame are in-folded*
> *Into the crowned knot of fire*
> *And the fire and the rose are one.*

Eliot's search for the mystic centre started with *Ash Wednesday*, where he explored the dark night of the soul under the guidance of St John of the Cross, and achieved its most individual expression in the *Four Quartets*.

Though Eliot moved back to traditional Christian values while Yeats turned to a system he invented himself, his accent remained always his own. What stands out in Eliot's poetry from the beginning is his style and cunning; he imposes his own accent on language, and it is an original and a striking one. 'Prufrock' and 'Portrait of a Lady' are as striking today as they were in 1917: the manipulating of phrase, the handling of pauses, the counterpointing of colloquial and formal speech—these are technical triumphs, and they represent skills that have stayed with him steadily. We recognize them in *The Waste Land*, in the Ariel poems, in the *Four Quartets*, in all four of his plays. The tone changes often, the accent almost never. It is the accent of poetry held down—beaten down, one sometimes feels—to its most subdued, its least obvious pitch. Eliot never confuses poetry with what sounds like poetry, or with what casual readers might mistake for poetry. If he plays tricks, they are never the tricks of the pseudo-poet. There are no short cuts anywhere in his work, no complacent sinking back to the dead level of 'poetic' speech which seems to be poetic only because it is reminiscent of what popular thought takes poetry to be. Eliot sometimes fails by trying too hard to achieve certain effects by indirection—as he fails, in the view of some readers at least, at the end of *The Waste Land*—but he rarely fails by not trying hard enough, by not working at his craft. If his poetry sometimes runs down into artful prose, as in the beginning of the third part of 'Little Gidding', and sometimes bogs down in a mere stunt, as at the conclusion of 'Triumphal March', either defect is better for the art of poetry than the steady lapse into a too obvious pseudo-poetic accent, which so many poets sooner or later find hard to resist.

But Eliot remains a less great poet than Yeats. Though he is often brilliantly successful in rendering certain states of mind, certain moods, and in linking these states and these moods with history, with phases of human development, he is less impelled by sympathetic imagination than any other poet of his technical accomplishment who has written in English. His favourite theme is the sense of loss, and he handles it again and again in innumerable ways: the lost vision, the lost purpose, the lost meaning, the lost sense of fellowship, the lost sense of self—he pursues this theme from 'Prufrock' to *The Confidential Clerk* with remorseless penetration, and at his best he renders it with pitiless brilliance. His favourite solution is martyrdom. All his plays deal with martyrdom, and *Murder in the Cathedral* is the most successful because there martyrdom is made real and is given the proper religious impulse. In *Family Reunion*, Harry's quest for some undefined kind of self-sacrifice is purely verbal; it carries no conviction, it has no force or meaning in terms of the human situation. And Celia's martyrdom in *The Cocktail Party* has seemed to many unrealized and meaningless. Perhaps *The Cocktail Party* is in a sense the best clue to Eliot's deficiencies in human understanding and sympathy. The technical skill with which he manoeuvres poetry to the brink of prose without letting it fall over is certainly remarkable (and very much in line with his whole technical achievement), but the theme— that there is no choice between an unconvincing martyrdom and a penitential acceptance of routine—shows a strange paucity of imagination. If you can't get yourself crucified, at least be nice to your wife, is an odd enough theme for a poetic drama (as is the theme of *The Confidential Clerk*, that if you aren't a genius you'd better be content to do what your father did—*if* you are sure who your father really was), but when it is accompanied by the deliberate identification of the socially trivial and the spiritually significant (as in the dual role of Julia, for example) it suggests an ironic contempt for the whole human species, and that is a peculiar attitude for a religious poet. Whatever the other themes in *The Cocktail Party*—the Alcestis parallel and the resurrection motif—they are lost in this central desiccation.

Against this can be set the fact that *Ash Wednesday* and the *Four Quartets* handle impressively the theme of spiritual recovery and refreshment. They are certainly impressive groups of poems, and there is a kind of quiet grace blowing through *Ash Wednesday* which is particularly appealing; but even here, though in much less degree, to be sure, than in *The Cocktail Party*, the choice is between extremes, and there seems to be little interest in man as an ordinary fellow creature. The satirical Eliot of the early poems and the pilgrim Eliot of the middle and later poems both show this impatience with the potentialities of human imagination and human value, with such virtues as compassion, with such achievements as the innocent delight in the seasons or the tragic winning through to understanding through suffering. The possibilities of human love he shows no interest in: he has neither Shakespeare's relish of his fellow men nor Keats's feeling for the tangibilities of life and sensation nor Yeats's exultation in the clashing paradoxes of the human situation. Or at least he appears to study to repress these things in his poetry, though we do find them forcing their way through occasionally. On the whole, the attitude to life is that of Sir Henry Harcourt-Reilly of *The Cocktail Party*, and no man has the right to behave towards his fellows as Sir Henry does.

It is this combination of poetic skill and integrity with lack of interest in the vast middle ground of human experience—in all that lies between Apeneck Sweeney and the saint or martyr—that gives Eliot's poetry its unmistakable stamp. Of his stature as an artist in words, a renovator of the English poetic dialect, a cunning craftsman, a master of style, there can be no doubt whatsoever, and it is these aspects of his work that made him so influential among his younger contemporaries.

His astringency was of course necessary and salutary; but astringency of style need not imply severe limitation of human understanding and sympathy. The next generation of poets was to strive, not often with complete success, to remedy this deficiency. W. H. Auden, who, like every poet of his generation, learned much from Eliot, could write like this:

> *Lay your sleeping head, my love,*
> *Human on my faithless arm;*
> *Time and fever burn away*
> *Individual beauty from*
> *Thoughtful children, and the grave*
> *Proves the child ephemeral:*
> *But in my arms till break of day*
> *Let the living creature lie,*
> *Mortal, guilty, but to me*
> *The entirely beautiful.*

The acceptance of man as imperfect, we sometimes feel, should be possible at least occasionally for every poet. Auden's poem gives the other side of the sordid seduction of the typist by 'the young man carbuncular' in Part III of *The Waste Land*, and in its own way it, too, is true.

4

Early in the 1930s it looked as though a new school of English poets, led by W. H. Auden, was to make a new use of the technical achievements of Pound and Eliot and the example of Hopkins. Cecil Day Lewis—who, with Stephen Spender, seemed to constitute the remainder of the Auden school—wrote in 1934, in *A Hope for Poetry*: 'Post-war poetry was born amongst the ruins. Its immediate ancestors are Hopkins, Owen and Eliot.' Owen contributed only a certain kind of ironical under-statement and his use of alliterative assonance; the contributions of Hopkins and Eliot were more central and permanent. But in fact the post-war poetry which Day Lewis wrote about so confidently in 1934 was not as he saw it, a way out of the Waste Land led by a small group of forward-looking young men who, using techniques derived from the metaphysical poets, from Hopkins and from Eliot, and exhibiting a new social consciousness and a new awareness of ways to cure modern barrenness derived from both Marx and Freud, appealed 'above all for the creation of a society in which the real and living contact between man and man may again become possible'. Though they shared for a time common ideas and a common idiom, the group's homogeneity proved to be illusory. The most original and the most poetically exciting was W. H. Auden, and when he settled in America shortly before the Second World War the group rapidly disintegrated—or rather, it was seen never to have been a real group at all, but only a number of poets of about the same age and with the same kind of educational background, with varying degrees of talent and very different poetic personalities.

Nevertheless, it is worth inquiring what it was that made them appear to be a coherent group to their first readers. It was partly their reinterpretation of the Waste Land. For Eliot, the Waste Land came more and more to be a symbol of a state of spiritual desiccation; for these younger poets, growing up after the First World War, taking their first adult look at England to find it wasting under economic depression and mass unemployment, oppressively aware of the immense chasm between the patterns of upper class behaviour taught in the English Public Schools and taken for granted at the older universities and the depressing realities of English social life—for such men, the Waste Land was a real physical state and also a psychological condition. The Waste Land of the early Auden is not a symbolic myth but a geographical reality:

Get there if you can and see the land you once were proud to own
Though the roads have almost vanished and the expresses never run:

Smokeless chimneys, damaged bridges, rotting wharves and choked
  canals,
Tramlines buckled, smashed trucks lying on their side across the
  rails; . . .

But Auden is less concerned with describing this country than
with diagnosing its trouble:

> *Go home, now, stranger, proud of your young stock,*
> *Stranger, turn back again, frustrate and vexed:*
> *This land, cut off, will not communicate,*
> *Be no accessory content to one*
> *Aimless for faces rather there than here.*
> *Beams from your car may cross a bedroom wall,*
> *They wake no sleeper; . . .*

He searches continually for symbols that will project his diagnosis. Sometimes he sees England as full of invalids and
hypochondriacs who need to be pulled out of their bath chairs
and given proper psychological treatment. Sometimes it is
'death of the old gang' that is necessary. The sense of immi-
nent crisis is pervasive in his earliest poetry:

> *Where lights and wine are set*
> *For supper by the lake,*
> *But leaders must migrate:*
> *'Leave for Cape Wrath tonight',*
> *And the host after waiting*
> *Must quench the lamps and pass*
> *Alive into the house.*

The 'private faces in public places' that Auden introduced
into his early poetry did not arise from any attempt to press
private reading into the service of a public culture, as with
Eliot, or from a personal mythology, as with Yeats: it was a

measure of his uncertainty about his symbols and about the area of reference which he could take for granted. Something odd had happened to English poetry when poets were compelled to use as public symbols the Christian names of their personal friends. But Auden had the vitality, the sheer poetic exuberance, to be able to impose his own authentic accent on all he touched. His bewildering use of imagery drawn from English public school life, his ambivalent metaphors from military manoeuvres and mountain climbing, his clinical obsessions and his psychological jargon, his private jokes and sudden clowning—all these were often bewildering; but they looked like the beginnings of a significant new poetic style. He drew on the jogging impromptus of Skelton and the movement of Middle English alliterative verse to provide new kinds of life for his poems. Music hall, folk ballad and jazz lyric were other elements he brought into his verse, particularly after he settled in America. He seemed to be well on the way to developing an excitingly rich poetic idiom.

He has never quite fulfilled the expectations he aroused, though he has written some of the best lyrics of our time. He rapidly shed his psychologico-economic diagnosis of the troubles of the time, and with it went some of his more irritating English public school imagery. He became more meditative, more concerned with archetypal images and situations, more religious in tone and feeling and eventually more specifically Christian. At the same time his gift for light verse and his taste for clowning both developed steadily, and one was presented with the odd spectacle of a religious poet with an irresistible impulse to make jokes. Puns and ironic overtones had been restored to serious English poetry by the revolution of 1912 to 1922, but Auden's impulse to clown seems to have little to do with the desire to complicate the texture of one's verse by such devices—sometimes it seems to be an almost hysterical outburst. At other times he would display a mere cleverness with patterns of symbolic meaning which perhaps

47

derived from his hobnobbing with the American 'New Criticism'. Some of the light verse he published after the Second World War is admirable of its kind: 'Under Which Lyre', the Phi Beta Kappa Poem at Harvard, 1946, is both clever and funny. Of his serious poetry—which continued to constitute the main bulk of his verse—his best were those grave and quiet lyrics where he projected a simple emotional situation with a certain amount of intellectual complication but keeping the thought geared to the emotion by the shape of the verse (as in 'Lay your sleeping head, my love') or such reflective poems as 'Musée des Beaux Arts' and 'At the Grave of Henry James'. By this time he was an American poet, however, and even though American and English poetry had been developing along similar lines since Eliot first started writing, some significant differences remained, and the American Auden, while he never altogether lost his English accent and his English kind of music hall comedy, belongs to American poetry.

Meanwhile, his former companions developed in their own way. Stephen Spender had begun very much under Auden's influence, but had shown from the beginning a preference for simpler lyrical modes and a much less complicated sensibility. In his earliest phase he expressed a simple Left-wing concern with the state of society in a verse that could be naïve to the point of crudity:

oh young men oh young comrades
it is too late now to stay in those houses
your fathers built where they built you to build to breed money on
money.

Spender lacked metaphysical wit, and his poetry is both less complex and less exciting than Auden's; but from the beginning he could show a quiet control in descriptive or confessional verse that has its own appeal:

I think continually of those who were truly great.
Who, from the womb, remembered the soul's history
Through corridors of light where the hours are suns,
Endless and singing.

His moods of compassion and confession could lead to embarrassing naïveté, and also to the subdued success of such a poem as 'An Elementary School Class Room in a Slum':

Far far from gusty waves, these children's faces.
Like rootless weeds the torn hair round their paleness.
The tall girl with her weighed-down head. The paper-
seeming boy with rat's eyes. The stunted unlucky heir
Of twisted bones, reciting a father's gnarled disease,
His lesson from his desk. At back of the dim class,
One unnoted, sweet and young: his eyes live in a dream
Of squirrels' game, in tree room, other than this. . . .

Spender's range is limited. After he had outgrown his rather shrill imitation of Auden he cultivated his own quiet autobiographical style, as unlike Auden's really as any modern poetry could be, and equally unlike Eliot:

What I expected was
Thunder, fighting,
Long struggles with men
And climbing.
After continual straining
I should grow strong;
Then the rocks would shake
And I should rest long.

What I had not foreseen
Was the gradual day
Weakening the will
Leaking the brightness away,

49

The lack of good to touch
The fading of body and soul
Like smoke before wind
Corrupt, unsubstantial. . . .

Cecil Day Lewis fell easily—too easily—into the Auden
manner in his earliest poetry, in which we often cannot help
feeling that he is simply aping a style:

Make no mistake, this is where you get off,
Sue with her suckling, Cyril with his cough,
Bert with a blazer and a safety-razor,
Old John Braddleum and Terence the toff.
And now, may I ask, have you made any plans?
You can't go further along these lines.

By the time Day Lewis settled down to a style of his own he
was seen to be perhaps the least adventurous of the three who
started out as rebels of the 1930s. Not for him the flaming
paradox of packed and ambivalent suggestion; he requires
time and space to unfold himself; his craftsmanship, though
often considerable, is much more conventional than, say,
Auden's. Discursive poetry is not much to mid-twentieth century taste, and Day Lewis's reflective and reminiscent poems,
his almost (at times) Victorian diction fairly quickly lost
him his place among the pioneers. His eclecticism, variety
and general competence as a craftsman have led him to become what might be called the academic poet of our time.
The fact that he was elected Professor of Poetry at Oxford
seems symbolic and appropriate, as is the broadcasting of his
rendering of Virgil over the BBC. His shorter poems, often
self-questioning statements in which recollection of past
experience and speculation on the future of the poet's personal relationships and emotions are quietly combined, are
sometimes more Georgian than contemporary in tone: the
imagery is predominantly rural and English, the tone elegiac,

the questioning personal yet abstract. No single poem seems representative of his peculiar talents, because his talents are so evenly dispersed over so wide a range, spreading wide rather than running deep. But this stanza, which opens his poem 'Buzzards over Castle Hill', has neither Auden's sparkle nor Spender's compassionate egotism; its technique is open-worked and its style verging on the pedestrian; but it has its own quiet force:

> *A world seems to end at the top of this hill.*
> *Across it, clouds and thistle-clocks fly,*
> *And ragged hedges are running down from the sky,*
> *As though the wild had begun to spill*
> *Over a rampart soon to be drowned*
> *With all its guards of domesticated ground.*

Only in the relatively free rhythms of the third and sixth lines do we get even the slightest whisper of the poetic revolution of 1912 to 1922.

Louis MacNeice was another of the poets who first emerged in the early 1930s, though he was never closely associated, at least by the critics, with the Auden-Spender-Day Lewis trio. He has cultivated a deliberately ironical dry flatness of statement which can be most effective in poetry of social comment or urban observation (as in 'Sunday Morning', 'Morning Sun' and 'Birmingham'). Like Day Lewis, he lacks the burning centre, but he never sounds Victorian, as Day Lewis sometimes does, and of the new elements brought into English poetry by the anti-romantic revolution he has deliberately selected the colloquial-ironical rather than the complex-metaphysical. A carefully controlled melancholy underlies much of his poetry; he has a sombre sense of modern life, of its tragi-comedies and futilities, and above all of the sadness that underlies all modern attempts to recapture, in memories of youth or by sudden emotion when listening to a street singer or watching a landscape, a sense of significance in daily living. His best poetry has always been fairly low-pressured, sardonic in a subdued manner; with an occasional burst of wild Celtic irony. He droops often enough; but the very unpretentiousness has its own appeal:

In doggerel and stout let me honour this country
Though the air is so soft that it smudges the words
And herds of great clouds find the gaps in the fences
Of chance preconceptions and foam-quoits on rock-points
At once hit and miss, hit and miss. . . .

5

In the late 1930s, the tendency was to see the anti-romantic revolution of the preceding decade, dominated by Eliot, as having given way to a younger generation of Left-wing poets who learned their technique from Hopkins, Eliot and a variety of miscellaneous sources from Skelton to the modern music-hall. But the pattern was much more complicated than that. In the first place, there were many individual poets who cannot be fitted into this map. The brittle and exhibitionist verbal patterns of Edith Sitwell, brilliant in their way but somehow lacking in fullness and depth of poetic utterance— a highly-coloured surface art of remarkable virtuosity—continued well into the 1930s, though her later poetry showed her striving for a simpler and deeper human note. The exhibitionist brilliance of some of her earlier poetry led some critics to dismiss her as a publicity-seeking clown, but this was unjust and imperceptive. For even her most stylized work shows not only an uncanny eye for the arresting image but an ability to place the image so that it unexpectedly illuminates an area of human passion. Sometimes she repeats herself, or the pressure drops too low, or the pattern of meaning seems too wantonly contrived. But she has the true poet's respect for the uncanny power of words and for the source of that power in the elemental depths of human consciousness. And the tone and texture of her poetry are often strikingly original. The humorous, mythological, casual yet cosmic poems of Robert Graves, with their highly individual use of folk elements and original handling of traditional metrical forms, show a poetic sensibility almost belligerently at variance with all the contemporary poetic schools. The Byronic satire and heavy-languaged descriptive verse of Roy Campbell, with his unfashionable sonority of diction, represent the work of an equally belligerent but less profoundly talented outsider. Geoffrey Grigson, whose periodical *New Verse* was hospitable to many of the new poets of the 1930s, preached an almost imagist precision and objectivity and in his own verse cultivated an ascetic verbal restraint. In Cambridge, William Empson, having pondered with I. A. Richards the nature of meaning and the possibilities of non-referential ambiguities, produced his own kind of subtle patterns of meaning which turned out more often than might have been expected to be both teasing and haunting.

Then there were new movements and programmes—short-lived, most of them, and appearing with bewildering rapidity in the years immediately preceding the outbreak of the Second World War. A short-lived Surrealist review started—belatedly enough—in 1936, but the Surrealist movement, though it had its influence on David Gascoyne and other young poets of the 1930s, was never strong in England. The Apocalypse movement, founded in 1938 by Henry Treece, G. S. Fraser and J. F. Hendry, was rather vaguely in favour of myth and liberation. These poets rebelled against the political and social poetry of the early 1930s, with its reporting on the state of England (though the poets who had done so had ceased doing this by then anyway) and praised myth and the free exercise of the imagination. It looked for a short while as though a new Romantic Movement was about to arise, after nearly thirty years of anti-romanticism among the *avant garde;* but though Surrealism, D. H. Lawrence,

Kafka, and other 'liberating' agents were announced as influences, and two anthologies (*The New Apocalypse* in 1939 and *The White Horseman* in 1941) of this kind of poetry duly appeared, when the smoke had cleared away it was plain that the movement had been ill thought out and was unproductive as a movement. Two poets, however, stood out to illustrate in different ways what the 'liberation' of the late 1930s was leading to. They were George Barker and Dylan Thomas.

While Auden and his followers faced the crumbling world of the 1930s by devising a poetic diagnosis in which both a rhetorical and a prophetic purpose was implicit, George Barker, appearing as a poet first in 1935, quietly identified himself with the crumbling parts and produced a poetry that was at once lyrical and (in feeling at least) tragic. Barker did not address the world, but preferred to make himself a symbol of it. He was not, as so many of his contemporaries in 1935 were, a poet speaking to a generation about itself: he embodied rather than confronted all those aspects of that generation that were worth speaking to or about. His poetry was dramatic rather than didactic, lyrical rather than rhetorical, tragic rather than revolutionary. The opening poem of his first volume sounds a distinctive note at once:

> *Pallid the mirages, the palaces*
> *Appearing brilliant on the mountain tops, pale*
> *The whispering sibilant fields and pale*
> *The phantasmal countenances female*
> *Haunting our progress: in all climactic places*
> *Appear the brilliant the distraught the pallid faces*

The title of this poem is 'The Amazons', and the poet is not addressing them: he is haunted by them. The excessive dependence on adjectives in the verse just quoted is largely corrected in his later poetry, though sometimes at the expense of a wild abstraction that is not wholly convincing:

Meeting a monster of mourning wherever I go
Who crosses me at morning and evening also,
For whom are you miserable I ask and he murmurs
I am miserable for innumerable man: for him
Who wanders through Woolworth's gazing at tin stars;
I mourn the maternal future tense, Time's mother,
Who has him in her lap, and I mourn also her,
Time whose dial face flashes with scars.

'I mourn for the maternal future tense' is both too proposi-
tional and too abstract. He did better in the long poem entitled 'Vision of England '38', which conveys as much comment and protest as any of the more rhetorical or diagnostic
poems of the early Auden without ever losing the pure lyrical
tone. The rhythm and some of the references—as well as the
title itself—suggest *Piers Plowman*, but it is only a suggestion,
only a reminder of the old English peasant behind all, an
anchor to earth, defining and sharpening the meaning. The
poem, while in many ways impressive, is not wholly successful: often the symbols are trotted out too readily, almost
mechanically, and occasionally the perspective changes awk-
wardly from the grand vision to the petty exposure. It is in
his twenty *Pacific Sonnets* that Barker showed that he had been
able to contrive a form to control and organize his explosive
inward utterance. It was clear that what his poetry required
was not a more prosaic statement but a shape to hold together his centrifugal insights. The first sonnet opens with a
great expanding utterance:

> *Between the wall of China and my heart*
> *O exile is . . .*

which contracts immediately into less reverberating statements, but the echoes of the initial cry sound through the
poem so that an otherwise banal line like

> *I speak of things nearest to my heart*

takes its place properly in the pattern of the whole.

The 'three memorial sonnets for two young men lost overboard in a storm in mid-Pacific' show Hopkins' influence on this excited, personal verse:

> *The seagull, spreadeagled, splayed on the wind*
> *Span backward shrieking, belly facing upward,*
> *Fled backward with a gimlet in his heart*
> *To see the two youths swimming hand in hand*
> *Through green eternity. O swept overboard*
> *Not could the thirtyfoot jaws them part,*
> *Or the flouncing skirts that swept them over*
> *Separate what death pronounced was love . . .*

Sometimes the texture of the verse is much simpler, as in another of the *Pacific Sonnets:*

> *Those whom I may not meet pester me now*
> *Like dogs I lost seem leaping at my breast,*
> *But lost, lost across space, found in a daydream*
> *Only, or foundered in the floundering west*
> *Go under whispering messages that blow*
> *Over the world that pester me with home . . .*

But the passionate imperative utterance was more congenial to Barker, as is made abundantly clear in his *Sacred and Secular Elegies:*

> *. . . Now answer History with a marvellous golden yes*
> *As she steps up asking all possible questions; . . .*

Or consider the conclusion of the fourth Sacred Elegy:

> *Thanatos, thanatos! the labourer, dropping his lever,*
> *Hides the black letter close to his heart and goes,*
> *Thanatos, thanatos, home for the day and for ever.*
> *Crying, from the conch of Venus the emergent Eros*
> *Breaks free, bursts from the heart of the lover . . .*

This has power, an urgent personal compulsion. Yet Barker has never gone beyond this to integrate his talents into a wholly satisfying poetic complexity. The merely ecstatic, the wild, the hallucinatory cry, often take control, and the poet is left at the mercy of his devices.

The American magazine of verse, *Poetry*, devoted an issue in March 1947 to what it called 'Post-war Romanticism in England'. It looked, from the other side of the Atlantic, as though there was a new tendency in English poetry which could be so described. The Second World War had produced neither Rupert Brookes nor Siegfried Sassoons—neither patriotic poets hailing the struggle nor angry pacifist poets satirizing war—but had apparently resulted in a general trend towards introspective and self-exploratory lyric verse. *Poetry* printed in its special romantic number poems by Henry Treece, Vernon Watkins, Kathleen Raine, J. F. Hendry, among others, and articles on George Barker and Dylan Thomas who were regarded as having had a decisive influence on the new trend. Less than ten years later, the perspective has changed: but we can still recognize that both Hulme's 'hard, dry' image and the tight cerebration which Eliot brought into English poetry had not, for many poets at least, the prestige they once had. While Empsonian verse was still written and Empson himself was producing some of his best work and influencing another new generation, the main movement in the late 1940s seemed to be towards the visionary, with Blake rather than Donne the presiding genius.

Dylan Thomas, though he certainly did influence some of his contemporaries, was never part of this movement to the degree that it was once thought. In his all too brief lifetime he was regularly taken to represent the antithesis of Eliot and of the cerebral orderliness of the 1920s and the 1930s, an example of a wild and whirling irresponsibility. 'Thomas discovered poetry on his hand like blood, and screamed aloud', wrote the American poet and critic, Kenneth Rexroth, who also said of the first English reaction to Thomas that 'it was as though something had escaped that had been locked up in Wild Wales since the Synod of Whitby, and was clanking its chains and yammering in the Rectory drawing room'. Some later critics reversed this judgment in some degree, to discuss his poems as texts for exposition, ignoring the rhyme-scheme and the complicated verbal and visual patterning to concentrate solely on the intellectual implications of the images. The truth is that Thomas was neither a whirling romantic nor a metaphysical imagist, but a poet who used pattern and metaphor in a complex craftsmanship in order to create a ritual of celebration. He saw life as a continuous process, saw the workings of biology as a magical transformation producing unity out of diversity, the generations linked with one another and man linked with nature. Again and again in his early poems he sought for a poetic ritual to celebrate this unity:

> Before I knocked and flesh let enter,
> With liquid hands tapped on the womb,
> I who was shapeless as the water
> That shaped the Jordan near my home
> Was brother to Mnetha's daughter
> And sister to the fathering worm.

Or again:

> The force that through the green fuse drives the flower
> Drives my green age; that blasts the roots of trees
> Is my destroyer.

And most clearly of all:

> This bread I break was once the oat,
> This wine upon a foreign tree
> Plunged in its fruit;
> Man in the day or wind at night
> Laid the crops low, broke the grape's joy. . . .

This flesh you break, this blood you let
Make desolation in the vein,
Were oat and grape
Born of the sensual root and sap;
My wine you drink, my bread you snap.

Man is locked in a round of identities; the beginning of growth is also the first movement towards death, the beginning of love is the first move towards procreation, which in turn moves towards new growth, and the only way out of time's squirrel-cage is to embrace the unity of man with nature, of the generations with each other, of the divine with the human, of life with death, to see the glory and the wonder of it. If we ignore the cosmic round to seize the moment when we think we have it, we are both deluded and doomed:

I see the boys of summer in their ruin
Lay the gold tithings barren,
Setting no store by harvest, freeze the soils;
There in their heat the winter floods
Of frozen loves they fetch their girls,
And drown the cargoed apples in their tides.

Those boys of light are curdlers in their folly,
Sour the boiling honey; . . .

This is from an early poem; and several of these early poems strike this note—the note of doom in the midst of present pleasure, for concealed in each moment lie change and death. Thomas did not rush towards the celebration of unity in all life and all time which later became an important theme of comfort for him; he moved to it through disillusion and experiment. The force that drives the flower and tree to full burgeoning and then to death would destroy him also. Only later came the realization that such destruction is not destruction, but a guarantee of immortality, of perpetual life in a cosmic eternity:

And death shall have no dominion.
Dead men naked they shall be one
With the man in the wind and the west moon;
When their bones are picked clean and the clean bones gone,
They shall have stars at elbow and foot;
Though they go mad they shall be sane,
Though they sink through the sea they shall rise again;
Though lovers be lost love shall not,
And death shall have no dominion.

It is this thought that sounds the note of triumph in 'Ceremony after a Fire Raid' and which provides the comfort in 'A Refusal to Mourn the Death, by Fire, of a Child in London'.

'A Refusal to Mourn' illustrates not only a characteristic theme of what might be called the middle Thomas, but also a characteristic way of handling the theme. The poem is ritualistic in tone; its dominant images are sacramental; and the cunningly contrived rise and fall of the cadence of each stanza adds to the note of formal ceremony. There are four stanzas, the first two and one line of the third containing a single sentence which swells out to an impressive surge of meaning. Then, after a pause, the final stanza makes a concluding ritual statement, an antiphonal chant answering the first three stanzas. The paraphrasable meaning of the poem is simple enough: it is that never, until the end of the world and the final return of all things to their primal elements, will the poet distort the meaning of the child's death by mourning. One dies but once, and through that death becomes reunited with the timeless unity of things. But the paraphrasable meaning is not. of course, the meaning of the poem, which is expanded at each point through a deliberately sacramental imagery while at the same time the emotion is controlled and organized by the cadences of the stanza. The first stanza and a half describe the end of the world as a return from differentiated identity to elemental unity:

Never until the mankind making
Bird bead and flower
Fathering and all humbling darkness
Tells with silence the last light breaking
And the still hour
Is come of the sea tumbling in harness

And I must enter again the round
Zion of the water bead
And the synagogue of the ear of corn
Shall I let pray the shadow of a sound
Or sow my salt seed
In the least valley of sackcloth to mourn

The majesty and burning of the child's death. . . .

There is no obscurity here, to anybody who knows Thomas's
idiom. We have only to recall 'This bread I break was once
the oat' to realize the significance of the first three lines of the
second stanza. The water bead and the ear of corn are symbolic primal elements, to which all return at the end. '*Zion*
of the water bead' and '*synagogue* of the ear of corn' increase
the sacramental suggestions. It is a kind of imagery of which
Thomas is very fond (one finds it in many other of his poems,
e.g., 'the parables of sunlight' in 'Poem in October' and his
use of Adam and Christ in his early work). He says 'synagogue' rather than 'church' because he wants to shock the
reader into attention to the sacramental meaning: a more
everyday religious word might pass by as a conventional
poetic image, but 'synagogue' attracts our attention at once;
it has no meaning other than its literal one, and therefore can
be used freshly in a non-literal way.

Thomas's earlier poems often fail by being too closely
packed with metaphor suggestive of identity. Words like
'Adam', 'Christ', 'ghost', 'worm', 'womb', phrases like 'the
mouth of time', 'death's feather', 'beach of flesh', 'hatching

hair', 'half-tracked thigh', abound, and though each has its orderly place in the poem the reader often feels dulled by the continuous impact of repeated words of this kind. The sonnet-sequence, 'Altarwise by owl-light' contains some fascinating identifying imagery (suggesting the identity of man with Christ, of creation with death, of history with the present), but it is altogether too closely packed, too dense, to come across effectively. The opening is almost a self-parody:

> *Altarwise by owl-light in the half-way house*
> *The gentleman lay graveward with his furies;*
> *Abaddon in the hangnail cracked from Adam,*
> *And, from his fork, a dog among the fairies,*
> *The atlas-eater with a jaw for news,*
> *Bit out the mandrake with tomorrow's scream. . . .*

The careful explicator will be able to produce informative glosses on each of these phrases, but the fact remains that the poem is congested with its metaphors, and the reader is left with a feeling of oppression. A fair number of Thomas's earlier poems are obscure for this reason. It is not the obscurity of free association or of references to private reading, but an obscurity which results from an attempt to pack too much into a short space, to make every comma tell, as it were. With his continuous emphasis on birth, pre-natal life, the relation of parent to child, growth, the relation of body and spirit, of life to death, of human and animal to vegetable, and similar themes, and his constant search for devices to celebrate these and identify them with each other, he pushes into service every word, every myth, every Biblical, Freudian or folk image, which might help in building up the total pattern of meaning.

Thomas progressed from those poems in which his techniques of identification are sometimes carried too far, through a period of 'occasional' verse in which he focussed his general notions on particular incidents and situations to give a grave and formal ceremonial poetry ('A Refusal to Mourn', 'Do not go gentle into that good night', 'On the Marriage of a Virgin', etc.) to a period of more limpid, open-worked poetry in which instead of endeavouring to leap outside time into a pantheistic cosmos beyond the dimensions, he accepts time and change and uses memory as an elegiac device ('Poem in October', 'Fern Hill', 'Over Sir John's Hill', 'Poem on his Birthday'). But these divisions are not strictly chronological, nor do they take account of all the kinds of verse he was writing. There is, for example, 'A Winter's Tale', a 'middle' poem which handles a universal folk theme with a quiet beauty that results from perfect control of the imagery.

Another remarkable poem, which does not quite fit into this three-fold classification, is 'Vision and Prayer', a finely wrought pattern-poem in two parts of six stanzas each. In no other poem has Thomas so successfully handled the theme of the identity of himself, everyman and Christ. He imagines himself addressing the unborn Christ, who, in his mother's womb, seems separated from himself by a 'wall thin as a wren's bone'. The infant in the next room replies, explaining that it is his destiny to storm out across the partition that separates man from God, and the poet identifies himself with the glory and suffering of Christ's redemptive career. The first part of the poem blazes to a conclusion with a vision of triumph and pain of Christ's death. The second movement begins in a slow, hushed, almost muttering cadence: the poet prays that Christ remain in the womb, for men are indifferent and wanton and not worth redemption. Let the splendour of Christ's martyrdom remain unrevealed: 'May the crimson/ Sun spin a grave grey/ And the colour of gray/ Stream upon his martyrdom.' But as he ends this sad prayer the sun of God blazes forth and takes up the poet in its lightning. 'The sun roars at the prayer's end.' This is a very different kind of religious poetry from *Ash Wednesday* or the *Four Quartets;* and the difference between Eliot's and Thomas's religious verse can stand for the gap between the new classicism of the 1920s and the new romanticism of the late 1930s and the 1940s.

A more significant difference between Eliot and Thomas, however, is that Thomas was by instinct a popular poet:

> *Not for the proud man apart*
> *From the raging moon I write*
> *On these spendthrift pages*
> *Nor for the towering dead*
> *With their nightingales and psalms*
> *But for the lovers, their arms*
> *Round the griefs of the ages,*
> *Who pay no praise or wages*
> *Nor heed my craft or art.*

He enjoyed reading his own poetry to large, popular audiences, and he had considerable success as a writer for the radio (notably in his play, *Under Milk Wood*). He dazzled his generation, and on his sudden and premature death in 1954 a wave of emotion swept over both Britain and America of a kind that the death of a poet in modern times very rarely evokes. The reaction was inevitable: critics soon arose to write Thomas off as a Welsh magician who produced fancy rhetorical gush and fooled both himself and his readers into thinking it magnificent poetry. The charge is altogether unjust. Although it is true that Thomas's range was severely limited, that (especially in his earlier poems) he overdid a handful of images and phrases to the point of parodying himself, and that many of his poems are clotted with an excess of parallel-seeking metaphors, yet his best poems are quite remarkable achievements, with a power and a beauty and an individuality of accent not easily found in any period. In some sense he spoke for his generation as the younger Eliot had spoken for his. Yet he had no lessons to teach others, as Pound and Eliot had. He was not leading a poetic revolution, but finding a style to fit his own vision. His influence was on the whole not happy; very few were able to catch his accent with any success, and those who tried and failed only did harm to their master's reputation.

It is a mistake, too, to see poets such as Barker and Thomas as representing a new romanticism aiming at the overthrow of the school of Eliot. The Eliot revolution has proved permanent; even if later poets have, as was inevitable, chosen other themes and other techniques, none of any stature has totally abandoned the cerebral discipline or renounced the intellectual toughness in the midst of passionate feeling which the revolution of 1912 to 1920 brought back into English poetry. There has been no return to James Elroy Flecker or Swinburne or Tennyson or Shelley. Hopkins remains an influence still, as do the seventeenth-century poets, and, perhaps surprisingly, Wordsworth in his more meditative and speculative moods. Blake, too, seems to be exerting some influence on the younger poets: the search for a language of symbols which Yeats began is still going on. A certain visionary bareness can be seen in some contemporary poetry: Kathleen Raine, for example, in moving from Donne to Blake, has increasingly aimed at the calm and lucid vision, gaining force from a balanced intentness rather than a powerful initial impact. The trend in the mid-1950s seems to be all towards quietness. Laurie Lee's 'Milkmaid' presents a quiet version of Wordsworth's solitary reaper:

> *The girl's far treble, muted to the heat,*
> *calls like a fainting bird across the fields,*
> *to where her flock lies panting for her voice,*
> *their black horns buried deep in marigolds. . . .*

> *the girl dreams milk within her body's field,*
> *and hears, far off, her muted children cry.*

Norman Nicholson gazes with calm intentness on natural objects until they yield their vision:

Yet I, even I, have heard the angels speak,
I, who never learned the liturgical tongue,
Who cannot read the written revelation,
Walking at night on the shingle, waking at dawn in the straw,
I have seen long spears of lightning lance at my eyes,
And felt the words, pricked out with fire,
Notched in my bones and burning in my body.

Lawrence Durrell has increasingly cultivated a reflective-descriptive poetry, most successful when dealing with his favourite eastern Mediterranean scenes:

For look. The mauve street is swallowed
And the bats have begun to stitch slowly.
At the stable door the carpenter's three sons
Bend over a bucket of burning shavings
Warming their inwardness and quite unearthly
As the candle marking time begins.

Topographical poetry is popular. James Kirkup describes a painting, a glass of water, a piece of sculpture, as well as 'Chelsea Embankment' or 'London Spring' in order to move from description to reflection. This kind of poetry is Wordsworthian in a sense. The quiet precision of John Clare, too, has had its influence in recent poetry. But the metaphysical twist is never wholly lost: this is not descriptive poetry with a moral, but a distillation of symbols out of a visual surface—or that is what it aims at. The poet does not reflect about what he has described; he lets the description generate the reflection. The younger poets are quiet, controlled, careful: the danger today is timidity, lack of excitement, a tendency to sink into mere observation or meditation.

Meanwhile a remarkable poetic movement had developed in Scotland. The Scottish poet had for a long time been facing special problems of his own. Scots as a full-blooded literary language ceased to exist in the seventeenth century. The migration of King James VI of Scotland to England in 1603 to become James I of England, taking with him a group of his court poets; the prestige and achievement of Elizabethan English poetry; the disappearance of an independent Scottish parliament in 1707; the development by the beginning of the eighteenth century of a situation in which educated Scotsmen wrote in English (which they learned at school) and spoke a broad Scots—these were some of the factors which destroyed the Scots literary language, which had flourished so vigorously in the Middle Ages. A healthy literary language is nourished by ordinary speech while reaching out towards a richness of vocabulary and towards various kinds of resonance and stylization which would never be found in the ordinary spoken language. When the spoken language and the literary language become wholly divorced, the former degenerates into a series of regional dialects. It was the fate of Scots (originally a northern form of English but later a literary language of its own in the light of its native achievements and traditions) to be forced after the seventeenth century from a literary language into a series of regional dialects, in which rustic poets wrote sentimental local verse. Even the achievement of Robert Fergusson and Robert Burns could not really arrest this movement; indeed, Burns's magnificent exploitation of the rustic folk tradition, while a great achievement in itself, proved to have a harmful effect on Scots poetry, for it encouraged an affected rusticity and discouraged poets writing in Scots dialect from coming to grips with the realities of Scottish life after the Industrial Revolution. Scots verse in the nineteenth century, drawing

on an escapist caricature of Burns, became contentedly ver-
nacular, exploiting with pathos, whimsicality, sentimentality,
nostalgia or dialect humour selected aspects of an idealized
Scottish rustic life. The 'kailyard' school of Scottish poetry as
of Scottish fiction dealt in facile emotional stereotypes with a
monstrously sentimentalized rural Scotland. As J. H. Millar
expressed it over fifty years ago, 'the land was plangent with
the sobs of grown men, vainly endeavouring to stifle their
emotion by an elaborate affectation of "peching" and "hoast-
ing".'

George Douglas Brown's novel, *The House with the Green
Shutters*, published in 1901, was an effective blow against the
sentimentalization of Scottish village life, in favour of a grim
realism; but the plight of the Scottish dialect poet was too
deep to be cured by simple shock treatment. In any case,
Brown's work represented a protest, not a clearly thought-
out literary programme. By narrowing their subject matter,
by concentrating on the single emotional situation, some dialect poets managed to write some single poems of integrity
and even distinction; among the work of Violet Jacob, Mar-
ion Angus and Helen Cruikshank (is it significant that all
three are women?) there are some highly effective poems; but
dialect poetry is limited by its very nature. A poet must use a
language in which the whole man can speak. From the time
of James Thomson (of *The Seasons*) if not of Drummond of
Hawthornden it was generally assumed that that language
was English for Scotsmen as for Englishmen. Yet English has
remained in some degree an artificial language for Scotsmen,
most of whom speak some kind of Scots dialect in childhood
and only learn standard English at school. If this were simply
a matter of pronunciation the situation would be no different
from what it is in any rural district of England, but it is more
than that, it involves vocabulary and also the way in which
language is felt. Further, there is a standard upper-class English pronunciation not used at all in Scotland except by the

tiny minority of Scots educated in English public schools. A Scottish poet, unlike the prose writer, may wish to use some kind of Scots speech because he wants to bring into service his deepest feelings about language. But, if he is a real poet, he will also want to use a language in which the whole man can speak. His deepest feelings about language may lead him to reject standard English, while on the other hand the necessity for using a language which can speak for the whole man will lead him to reject a regional dialect, for a regional dialect is not a full literary language. He is thus caught in an impossible dilemma.

It is as an escape from this dilemma that the 'Lallans' movement has developed in modern Scotland. This movement, revolting against the conception of Scots as a number of regional dialects to be used in comic or sentimental verse, has gone 'back to Dunbar', back to the golden age of Scottish poetry in the fifteenth century when Scots was used more richly and variously than it has ever been used since, and seeks to bring together elements from Middle Scots, from modern Scottish dialects, and from English, to form again a rich and subtle literary language. Such a language is bound to be synthetic—as Dunbar's was, and indeed as Fergusson's and Burns's was (for both Fergusson and Burns combined elements from other regional dialects and from older Scots with their native regional dialects and with contemporary English to produce their poetic tongue)—but 'synthetic' is not a term of abuse: it is applicable to any literary language in the making. And modern literary Scots, its defenders argue, is a full literary language in the making, as the language of Wyatt and Surrey and the English 'courtly makers' of the sixteenth century was an English poetic language in the making.

The modern writer of Lallans maintains that he has all of earlier Scots, all of Scotland's regional dialects, and all of English at his disposal. He uses standard English where he needs it, but he also has at his disposal words that English cannot give him. Monosyllables like 'busk', 'blate', 'steek', 'bield', 'deave', have no English equivalent in poetic force, nor have expressions such as 'ill-gushioned', 'disjeskit', 'undeemous', 'eident', 'fusionless', 'yowtherin', 'yowdendrift', 'forfarn'. Words of Germanic weight such as 'thole' (endure) and 'wale' (choose) survive in Scots which have been lost in English, and Scots has too words from the French such as 'lourd', 'aumrie', 'bien'. 'Aiblins' has poetic overtones that 'perhaps' lacks, 'eild' is an expressive word for 'age' which English has lost, 'yirdit' is not the same as 'buried', 'glaur' is not 'dirt', 'watergaw' is different from 'rainbow', and 'kyths' ('appears', 'makes itself known') makes contact with an expressive Germanic root which survives in modern English only in 'kith' and 'uncouth'. Scots preserves many older English words which modern English has lost —the sceptical reader might look through the Oxford English Dictionary and see how many words, no longer used in English, are marked 'Now *Sc.*'—and thus it maintains more contact with Anglo-Saxon than modern English does. An 'on-ding' (of rain or snow) represents a use of language which German maintains and which English once had but has no more. At the same time there are French, and Norse, and (though not as many as might be thought) Gaelic elements which add their own potentialities to Scots. It is considerations such as these that have moved the modern Lallans poets.

The pioneer of the modern Scottish Renaissance is Hugh MacDiarmid (pen name of Christopher Murray Grieve). He provided the programme, the focus, and the models. In the 1920s his lyric and other poetry in synthetic Scots and his flaming rebellious utterance about the plight of his country made him the most exciting and challenging force to have appeared in Scottish culture for a long time. With wit, energy, and a magnificent lack of any fear of contradicting himself, he played the part of modern Scotland's great rebel in art, politics, economics, education and philosophy, never compromising on any issue but standing forth grandiosely as an international, republican, communist Scottish nationalist with an epic scorn for what he called 'the whole gang of high mucky-mucks, famous fatheads, old wives of both sexes, stuffed shirts, hollow men with headpieces stuffed with straw, bird-wits, lookers-under-beds, trained seals, creeping Jesuses, Scots Wha Ha'evers, village idiots, policemen, leaders of white-mouse factions and noted connoisseurs of bread and butter, glorified gangsters, and what "Billy" Phelps calls Medlar Novelists (the medlar being a fruit that becomes rotten before it is ripe), Commercial Calvinists, makers of "noises like a turnip", and all the touts and toadies and lick-spittles of the English Ascendancy, and their infernal women-folk, and all their skunkoil skulduggery'. He deplored the English influences on Scottish life and letters and sought to restore to Scotland an indigenous civilization which would nevertheless be international in its outlook and world-wide in its associations. He saw the essential genius of Scotland (Lowland and Highland alike) as primary Gaelic (Celtic), and he saw the Gaelic genius as one aspect of a many-sided 'whole' response to life of which modern capitalism was wholly incapable.

But it is his poetry that matters. Of this the most popular and the most influential has been his shorter lyrics in synthetic Scots. In many of these MacDiarmid exploits any English vocabulary he needs and adds the subtleties and precisions which words peculiar to Scots can contribute. Consider the contribution of the purely Scots words to a poem such as this:

> *Lourd on my hert as winter lies*
> *The state that Scotland's in the day,*
> *Spring to the North has aye come slow*
> *But noo dour winter's like to stay*
>   *For guid,*
>   *And no' for guid!*

O wae's me on the weary days
When it is scarce grey licht at noon;
It maun be a' the stupid folk
Diffusin' their dullness roon' and roon'
    Like soot,
    That keeps the sunlicht oot.

Nae wonder if I think I see
A lichter shadow than the neist
I'm fain to cry: 'The dawn, the dawn!
I see it brakin' in the East',
    But ah
    —It's juist mair snaw!

There are three strata of vocabulary here. There are the words which Scots shares with English (and they are in the majority); there are words, such as 'lourd' (heavy) which Scots got from French or which, more generally, illustrate the broader basis of Scots ('dour' 'aye'); and there are words, similar to those in English but spelled and pronounced differently, such as 'hert' for English 'heart' and 'licht' for English 'light'. (It might be remarked here that MacDiarmid's use of apostrophes in words like 'diffusin' ' or 'roon' ' is objected to by the younger Lallans poets on the grounds that the apostrophe suggests that the final *g* or *d* is dropped through some dialectical pecularity or is in some way a deviation from the norm, whereas in fact it represents a norm of its own.)

MacDiarmid's vocabulary can be much more complex than this; sometimes his coined and borrowed words are employed with an almost humorous brilliance to achieve effects which simply cannot be achieved in standard English, as in the magnificent (and untranslatable) *Water Music*:

    Archin' here and arrachin' there,
    Allevolie or allemand,
    Whiles appliable, whiles areird,
    The polysemous poem's planned.

Lively, louch, atweesh, atween,
Auchimuty or aspate,
Threidin' through the averins
Or bightsome in the aftergait.

Or barmybrined or barritchfu'
Or rinnin' like an attercap,
Or shinin' like an Atchison,
Wi' a blare or wi' a bawp. . . .

Brent on or boutgate or beschacht,
Bellwaverin' or borne-heid,
They mimp and primp, or bick and birr,
Dillay-dally or show speed. . . .

This is, of course, quite different from Lewis Carroll nonsense verse; every word here has a precise meaning, and the poem is untranslatable only because meaning, sound and movement are so intimately linked that any attempt to separate them destroys what the poem says.

Different kinds of effects can be achieved by different proportions of English and Scots words, or of Modern Scottish dialect words and words taken from Middle Scots. One of the most perfect examples of what synthetic Scots can achieve is 'The Eemis Stane' ('The Insecure Stone'):

I' the how-dumb-deid o' the cauld hairst nicht
The warl' like an eemis stane
Wags i' the lift;
An' my eerie memories fa'
Like a yowdendrift.

Like a yowdendrift, so's I couldna read
The words cut oot i' the stane
Had the fug o' fame
An' history's hazelraw
No' yirdit thaim.

73

A literal rendering of this into English sounds very flat: 'In the very dead of the cold harvest night the world, like an insecure stone, sways in the sky; and my eerie memories fall like a swirl of blown snow. Like a swirl of blown snow so that I cannot read the words cut in the stone even if the moss of fame and history's lichen had not buried them.' The central image is that of a tottering tombstone with its inscription obliterated by time, but it is the choice of language that gives the peculiar force to the 'conceit' at the heart of the poem.

Another side of MacDiarmid is revealed in his long poem, or poem-sequence, *A Drunk Man Looks at the Thistle*, perhaps his most brilliant sustained work. This is a satiric poem about modern Scotland, in which the homely and the fantastic, the popular and the learned, the reverent and the blasphemous, the tender and the cruel, are juxtaposed with deliberately explosive intention. The clash of imagery is more violent than in Eliot's *Waste Land*, and has a different function. The light by which the poem moves is moonlight, and moonlight is effectively linked not only with the slightly unfamiliar appearance of the natural world in the eyes of the drunken speaker but also with the meditative strain in the poem, the constant urge to work things out, the stumbling towards the inner meaning of things. The constant shift from meditation to comic satire, with its deliberate incongruities and the resulting shock of recognition, is made dramatically appropriate by the situation in which the speaker is presented. It is, after all, a drunk man speaking, and drunkenness serves for MacDiarmid the same purpose which the dream served for the mediaeval poet. The logic of dreams and the logic of drunkenness are similar; both give poetic probability to those violent transitions of mood and *tempo* which play such an important part in giving life to the poem as a whole. For this is a dramatic poem, and the ebb and flow of drunken speculation, interspersed with physical observations as the drunk man's eye falls on some part of his environment and with

concrete memories as they rise unbidden in the uninhibited
mind, weave a dramatic whole as the poem moves forward to
its superb lyrical conclusion punctuated with the final dry
parenthesis:

> *Yet ha'e I Silence left, the croon o' a'.*
>
> *No' her, wha on the hills langsyne I saw*
> *Liftin' a foreheid o' perpetual snaw.*
>
> *No' her, wha in the how-dumb-deid o' nicht*
> *Kyths, like Eternity in Time's despite.*
>
> *No' her, withooten shape, wha's name is Daith,*
> *No' Him, unkennable abies* to faith.*
>
> *—God whom, gin e'er He saw a man, 'ud be*
> *E'en mair dumfooner'd at the sicht than he.*
>
> *—But Him, whom nocht in man or Deity,*
> *Or Daith or Dreid or Laneliness can touch,*
> *Wha's deed owre often and has seen owre much.*
>
> *O I ha'e Silence left,*
>
> > *—'And weel ye micht',*
> *Say Jean'll say, 'efter sic a nicht!'*

The vocabulary here is quieter and less violently 'synthetic' than in some other parts of the poem where MacDiarmid
ransacks Middle Scots and other sources to find the arresting
word:

> *In wi' your gruntle then, puir wheengin' saul*
> *Lap up the ugsome aidle wi' the lave,*
> *What gin it's your ain vomit that you swill*
> *And frae Life's gantin' and unfaddomed grave?*

* Except.

Or:

> *What gin the gorded fullyery on hie*
> *And a' the fanerels o' the michty ship*
> *Gi'e back mair licht than fa's upon them ev'n*
> *Gin sic black ingangs haud us in their grip?*

('Gruntle', pig's snout; 'wheengin',' complaining; 'aidle', foul slop; 'gin', if; 'lave', rest, others; 'gantin',' gaping; 'gorded fullyery', frosted foliage; 'fanerels', accessories; 'ingangs', intestines; 'haud', hold.)

The power of this vocabulary speaks for itself: there is no other way of getting this kind of effect. True, a vocabulary of this sort if used merely to weave pallid ingenuities can sound monstrously artificial. A stream can rise no higher than its source, and a poet's vocabulary can do no more than the scope of his talent will allow. This is what makes nonsense of arguments about the proper language for a Scots poet. The proof of the pudding is in the eating, and the best language is that which *works*.

The drunkenness of the hero is part of the dramatic scheme of the poem; it also provides a justification of that special kind of exuberance in which MacDiarmid has always delighted. The concern with Scotland is passionate but never jingoistic; the exaggerated terms in which it is expressed derive from the drunkard's expansiveness. There is no offence in his grotesque pictures of other nationalities; it is all part of the slight distortion of perspective which he employs in order to compel the reader's attention. Distortion and exaggeration constitute the norm of much of the idiom of *A Drunk Man*, just as they do in, say, Dante's *Inferno*. But MacDiarmid's is a profane and irreverent Inferno, deliberately profane and irreverent in order to test the staying power of the stereotypes of thought and diction which he is concerned to expose.

Scotland, the central theme of the poem, is treated in two

different ways. At some points it is the microcosm of the world, and problems of life and death, of the progress of civilization, of fate and destiny, are illustrated with reference to Scotland:

And as at sicna times am I,
I wad ha'e Scotland to my eye
Until I saw a timeless flame
Tak' Auchtermuchty for a name,
And kent that Ecclefechan stood
As pairt o' an eternal mood.

At other points Scotland is not a microcosm of all history and geography, but a little country fixed in time and space, bound to a specific destiny, with its own special problems and its own special faults. This characteristic shifting of perspective illustrates on the one hand MacDiarmid's passionate concern with the regeneration of his own country and on the other that concern with what man has made of man in every part of this planet which leads him to search constantly for parallels to and illustrations of the Scottish predicament. For all its ironic severity about modern Scotland, *A Drunk Man* is not a hopeless poem; time and again the poet seeks refreshment in the recollection of physical sensation, and the challenging beauties of the physical world, the glories of sensation, remain. The silence invoked at the end is not the silence of the inanimate world or of death, but the silence of the man who has lost speech in experience.

MacDiarmid's later poetry has more often been in English, an argumentative ratiocinative verse, with an enormous range of allusions, references and quotations, which frequently builds up cumulatively a complex and exciting pattern of meaning, and sometimes falls down into congested argument or mere cataloguing. This side of MacDiarmid's work has never aroused the enthusiasm which his lyrical poems in Scots have aroused, but it is of great interest, and often reveals the innermost structure of the man's thought and sensibility (if one is content to wait for the cumulative pattern of meaning to unfold) as nothing else of his has done. More influential has been his critical position, turning firmly against the degenerate sentimentalization of the Burns tradition, with its 'couthy' and 'pawky' verse and its false Burns cult, to draw attention to the achievement of the mediaeval Scottish 'makars'. It is because the mediaeval 'makars' used Scots as a full literary language, a medium in which the whole man could speak, that such a poet as William Dunbar has exercised so important an influence on the Scottish Renaissance. A complete Scots must be synthetic, and a synthetic Scots must include archaisms.

The younger Scottish poets who took MacDiarmid's advice and turned to a Scots diction made up of elements from Middle Scots as well as from different regional dialects of modern spoken Scots have often proved more devoted to this Lallans (which is the name they have given to this synthetic language) than their master. They no longer use present participle endings in -in' as MacDiarmid, but substitute the Middle Scots form -an. So Alexander Scott, translating the Anglo-Saxon poem, *The Wanderer*, begins:

> *Aften he prays for mercy, the lanelie man,*
> *mercy o God, albeid wi a murnan hert*
> *amang the loweran seas for lang and lang*
> *he maun steer wi 's hands the icecauld swaws,*
> *stravaigan exile's straths; the wierd can never be skailit!*

The attempt to standardize Lallans has not, however, been wholly successful. Words first revived from Middle Scots by MacDiarmid are used over and over again by younger poets (e.g. 'cramasie', crimson; 'jizzen', childbed; 'yirdit', buried), often quite inorganically. And the necessity of drawing on older forms has often produced words which sound (and sometimes are) mock-antique, like Sydney Goodsir Smith's 'glamorie', 'lemanrie', 'wanhope' and others. Sydney Smith has a genuine lyrical gift and has produced some poems which haunt the ear and the mind in a remarkable way; but his range is very limited and his touch with language sometimes uncertain. A synthetic language must be used at a very high temperature if its elements are to fuse properly, and much Lallans poetry today reads like exercises in translation into a dead language. To escape this obvious danger, the Lallans poets have tended to concentrate on the emotional moment: indeed, one of Sydney Smith's poems is entitled 'The Moment':

> *The gaslicht flichtered on the stair,*
> *The streaman cobbles black wi rain,*
> *I held the auld world's glamorie there*
> *—And aa the grienan years were lain.*

('Grienan', yearning; 'aa' is the modern Lallans poet's spelling of the Scots for 'all', earlier spelt *a'*.) Concentration on the emotional moment has sometimes resulted in sentimentality —and a sentimental poem is not less sentimental for being expressed in a difficult vocabulary. And so the paradox arises that Lallans, developed as a language for Scottish poetry in order to enable the whole man to speak, has had to cultivate on occasion an excessive emotionalism, a narrow concentration on one phase of experience, in order to prevent its language from sounding artificial. MacDiarmid himself, in his earlier lyrics, was able to solve this problem magnificently, but his followers have not always been able to do so. Sydney Goodsir Smith's 'The Winter o the Hert' cannot really stand beside MacDiarmid's 'Lourd on my hert as winter lies'. The former poem opens:

> *O, the rain that rains upo the toun*
> *Greits in the hert o me,*
> *And the swaw that dings upo the shore*
> *Is the tempest that has fiefit me.*

And it concludes:

> *Ice buds like perls frae the ryce**,
> *Teardraps shairp as traitorie—*
> *Spring, haste ye til this caudrife airt,*
> *This winter i the hert o me.*

This is mere self-indulgence compared with MacDiarmid's sharply individualized poem (quoted on pp. 71–2) with its fine sardonic ending,

> *But ah*
> *—It's juist mair snaw!*

Smith often salts his poetry with a wild humour or an extravagant bohemian self-mockery, which sometimes comes off and sometimes does not. MacDiarmid's equally wild humour reminds one of Dunbar and Villon and Skelton, the Goliardic tradition of the Middle Ages, the 'flyting' tradition of mediaeval Scotland, or the humanist polemics of Renaissance Europe. But that of the younger poets often suggests nineteenth-century romantic bohemianism. Yet the Lallans movement flourishes, and keeps attracting younger Scottish poets. If it is to have a real future, education in Scotland will have to undergo some serious changes and a genuine effort will have to be made to train an audience for synthetic Scots. The future of Lallans, in fact, lies with the Scottish schools.

Not all Scottish poets—not even all those who have remained in Scotland and have considered themselves as contributing to Scottish literature—have accepted MacDiarmid's thesis about Lallans; some have considered English their proper and natural language, in which they can express whatever is peculiarly Scottish in their sensibility more effectively than in a contrived language made up partly of modern rural dialect speech and partly of Middle Scots. The most

* Branch.

distinguished of the non-Lallans modern Scottish poets is
Edwin Muir, a critic of integrity and discernment and a poet
of limited range but of remarkable stature. Muir comes from
Orkney, which is in the Scandinavian and not in either the
Celtic or the Lowland Scots orbit of Scottish culture, and
this may have affected his view of Scottish literary history
and cultural needs (as MacDiarmid claims that it has done).
But whatever the reason, English is for him the natural
speech for poetry, and he uses it with power and individuality.
He does not, however, seem to belong to any of the main
streams of modern English poetry. His poetry, lucid yet symbolic, contemplative yet exciting, phrased with a quiet precision yet full of echoing overtones of meaning, seems to have
by-passed alike nineteenth-century romanticism and the
Eliot revolution; nor is it in the least eighteenth-century in
flavour; its tone is more like that of the gentler metaphysicals
—Vaughan, perhaps, or Traherne—yet Muir's is a different
sort of quietness:

> *I see myself sometimes, an old old man*
> *Who has walked so long with time as time's true servant,*
> *That he's grown strange to me—who was once myself—*
> *Almost as strange as time, and yet familiar*
> *With old man's staff and legendary cloak,*
> *For see, it is I, it is I. And I return*
> *So altered, so adopted, to the house*
> *Of my own life. There all the doors stand open*
> *Perpetually, and the rooms ring with sweet voices,*
> *And there my long life's seasons sound their changes,*
> *Childhood and youth and manhood all together,*
> *And welcome waits, and not a room but is*
> *My own, beloved and longed for. . . .*
> *And yet I cannot enter, for all within*
> *Rises before me there, rises against me,*
> *A sweet and terrible labyrinth of longing,*
> *So that I turn aside and take the road*
> *That always, early or late, runs on before.*

Muir's is a poetry of dreams, visions, mystical promptings and questionings. He has become increasingly a religious poet, but not in any conventional sense: he sees the numinous in the every day, using symbols often deliberately stark. Though sometimes reminiscent of Eliot's later poetry, Muir's is really very different from Eliot's; he does not use, as Eliot does, imagery and situations drawn from the Christian liturgical and mystical traditions: he distils meaning from the incidents he describes by the quiet intentness of the writing. From the beginning he has been obsessed with time and the escape from time:

> *Sometimes I see, caught in a snare,*
> *One with a foolish lovely face,*
> *Who stands with scattered moon-struck air*
> *Alone, in a wild woody place. . . .*
>
> *For still she smiles, and does not know*
> *Her feet are in the snaring lime.*
> *He who entrapped her long ago.*
> *And kills her, is unpitying Time.*

He waits for the moment of double vision, when behind the appearance he sees the reality:

> *Those lumbering horses in the steady plough,*
> *On the bare field—I wonder, why, just now,*
> *They seemed terrible, so wild and strange,*
> *Like magic power on the stony grange. . . .*

That fine poem 'Adam's Dream' deals with Time and the Fall, but quite concretely, in a tone at once colloquial and magical. The concreteness is achieved by relating every mood or idea to a set of incidents, which are narrated in that tone of controlled precision so characteristic of Muir. Place as well as time is important for him, geography as well as history. He writes about historical events as they are both inside and out-side time, and in their symbolic relation to place. And 'The Animals' begins:

> *They do not live in the world,*
> *Are not in time and space.*
> *From birth to death hurled*
> *No word do they have, not one*
> *To plant a foot upon,*
> *Were never in any place.*

And it concludes:

> *But these have never trod*
> *Twice the familiar track,*
> *Never never turned back*
> *Into the memoried day*
> *All is new and near*
> *In the unchanging Here*
> *On the fifth great day of God,*
> *That shall remain the same,*
> *Never shall pass away.*

> *On the sixth day we came.*

The theme, the method, the tone, are all characteristic of Muir. There is a faint suggestion of the later Yeats about the poem, but it is only a suggestion. Muir is one of the most individual poets of our time. He lacks range and amplitude, but there is a complexity both of thought and feeling behind his surface simplicity, and within his chosen limits he has produced poetry of great force and beauty.

Muir has achieved distinction as a poet relatively late in life. A younger Scottish poet, who also writes in English, if not with Muir's individuality and distinction then certainly with poise and skill, is Norman McCaig; but even he was born in 1910 and did not become known as a poet until he was well into his forties. McCaig's tone is, like Muir's, deliberately quiet, but he manipulates ideas (with an almost metaphysical touch) where Muir distils them. And there are younger English-writing Scottish poets of some accomplishment. All, however, cultivate a small plot: it seems that the Scottish poet today, whether writing in Lallans or in English, must drastically restrict his field of operations if he is to retain his integrity—and restriction is not always a guarantee of that. But perhaps this is a feature of poetry in England, too, sign of the lack of poetic adventurousness in the middle of the twentieth century.

CHAPTER III

FICTION

I

THE English novel grew up and matured as a patterning of imagined events against a clearly realized social background; it was, in the eighteenth and nineteenth centuries, what might be called a public instrument, taking its view of what was significant in human behaviour from the accepted pattern of public belief and arranging its plot in terms of events whose significance would be agreed on by author and reader. Robinson Crusoe, on finding himself alone on his island, did not seek to exploit his loneliness by omphaloskepsis or by meditating on the relation between the individual and the universe: his task was to re-create in this distant isolation the skeleton at least of the civilization he had left behind him—complete with umbrella. For the English novel depended on society, and on public agreement about what, among the multifarious details of daily life, was worth picking out as significant. What was significant was what altered a social relationship—love and marriage, quarrelling and reconciliation, gain or loss of money or of social status. You could, of course, criticize society, but you did so by showing how social convention did not in fact lead to that generally approved practical morality which it professed to foster. You could explore the relation between spontaneity of feeling and social convention, as Jane Austen did, or the relation between gentility and morality, as Thackeray did, or the effect of industrial society on private character, as Dickens did, or investigate the possibilities of self-knowledge and vocation in a context of society at work, as George Eliot did, but in every case the plot would be carried forward by public symbols. And in every case society is *there*, to be taken account of and accepted as a basic fact about human life even when the author wishes to alter it or attack it. Marriage, as the accepted resolution of a situation involving the love of two people of opposite sex, becomes the appropriate symbol of the happy ending where two such persons are concerned. If the twentieth-century novelist has more often preferred to regard marriage less as a happy ending than as an uncertain beginning, that is simply one of innumerable indications of the shift in direction of the modern novel. The novelist in the last forty years or so has lacked that stable background of public belief in the light of which he could select critical events in the behaviour of his characters in the confident knowledge that his readers, too, would see them as critical. What is significant in human behaviour to him is more likely to depend on his own sensibility than on the pattern of belief provided by his age.

The end of the novel as a public instrument, caused by the disintegration (or the novelist's sense of disintegration) of the background of public belief is one of the major facts about modern literature. 'To believe that your impressions hold good for others', Virginia Woolf once wrote, discussing Jane Austen, 'is to be released from the cramp and confinement of personality'. If, speaking very generally, we can say that the earlier English novel is always, directly or obliquely, about the relation between gentility and morality, then the corresponding theme for the modern novel would be the relation between loneliness and love. Individual sensibilities have to come to terms with each other somehow, and the most that can be achieved (if indeed even that can be achieved) is, in E. M. Forster's terms, the 'little society' as opposed to the 'great society'. For Forster, as for D. H. Lawrence, the 'great society' is always the enemy: it is not a question of how to reform the great society—'O, reform it altogether'. Lawrence's concern was with how individuals could fully realize themselves as individuals as a preliminary to making true contact with the 'otherness' of other individuals. And that kind of problem has nothing to do with society at large. When Dickens wants to show how a mechanical utilitarianism can impose a false, mechanical picture on experience and stultify true vitality, he gives us, in *Hard Times*, a social picture in which the characters are arranged on class lines and where the remedy is seen as the readjustment of the social system through individual benevolence. But when Lawrence gives us, in *Lady Chatterley's Lover*, a picture of true and vital experience breaking through the mechanical conventions which destroy real human contacts, the social symbols are transmuted into personal sexual symbols, and the social problem resolves itself wholly into the personal one.

The modern novelist has been faced by two major problems, one moral and one psychological. The moral one concerns the value of experience: what is significant in experience and how can one show that it is so? The psychological problem concerns the nature of consciousness, and its relation to time. Modern psychology has made it increasingly difficult for the novelist to think of consciousness as moving in a straight chronological line from one point to the next. He tends rather to see it as altogether fluid, existing simultaneously at several different levels. To those who look at consciousness in this way (and it is a question of modes of thinking rather than of better or worse ways) the presentation of a story in a straight chronological line becomes unsatisfactory and unreal. People are what they are because of what they have been; the present moment is an unreal abstraction, there is only the continuous flow of the 'already' into the 'not yet'; consciousness itself is a continuous blend of retrospect and anticipation, and time is Bergson's *durée* rather than a series of discrete chronological points. We *are* our memories, and to describe us truthfully at any given moment means to say everything about our past. Memory is no longer regarded as a device for looking back on what has been left behind, but as an integral part of consciousness and personality.

Each of these two problems, the moral and the psychological, has had its own effect on the technique of the novel. Those novelists who, like Virginia Woolf, have been particularly sensitive to the disintegration of the public background of belief and who have been concerned with rendering experience in terms of private sensibility ('What is meant by reality?' Mrs Woolf asked in a lecture in 1928. 'It would seem to be something very erratic, very undependable—now to be found in a dusty road, now in a scrap of newspaper in the street, now in a daffodil in the sun. It lights up a group in a room and stamps some casual saying. . . .') have had to find technical devices for convincing the reader, as he reads, of the truth of their own sense of significance. And this means, among other things, borrowing some of the techniques of lyrical poetry. Consciousness in operation, the 'stream of consciousness' rendered with almost poetic force, creates a pattern of values as it moves. The novelist thus claims complete omniscience and moves at once right inside the characters' minds. The long journey from the-novel-pretending-to-be-history to the-novel-as-the-work-of-the-omniscient-imagination has finally been completed. In the early days of the novel, the author had to pretend that he was writing history (as Defoe did) or at least show how he came to be in possession of the 'facts' he was narrating. But as the novel flourished and developed, the necessity for the author's disguising his imagination as factual knowledge grew less and less, and the 'stream of consciousness' novel marks its final and total disappearance. (Today, indeed, people are more likely to write history as fiction than to write fiction as history.) This means, too, that the modern novelist finds no need of the stately porches with which older novelists used to open their novels. The 'Two travellers might have been seen' opening, which was designed to put the reader in the position of co-spectator of the action with the narrator, with the plot itself unfolding in such a way that whatever was significant always manifested itself in some overt gesture or action—this method gave way to a more immediate plunging *in medias res*. The reviewing stand technique, where author and reader stood side by side taking the salute, as it were, of the characters as they deployed themselves below, gave way to a method which involved presentation from the inside. In this kind of novel a character's change in mood, marked externally by a sigh or a flicker of an eyelid or perhaps by nothing externally perceptible at all, might be more significant than his running off with a friend's wife or his decision to marry or his loss of a fortune. Further, in this kind of novel the writer does not need to bring his main characters through a series of testing circumstances before their true potentialities can be revealed: everything about a character is always there, *in posse*, at some level of his consciousness, and by probing depth-wise rather than proceeding lengthwise the author can reveal it.

If consciousness is a constant flow of retrospect into anticipation and the individual's reaction to any given situation is determined by the sum of his past experiences, then everyone is in some sense a prisoner of his own individuality. And if 'reality' itself is, as Virginia Woolf saw it, a matter of personal impression rather than public systematization, then real communication between individuals is difficult if not impossible. So again the theme becomes the relation of loneliness to love: how is love possible in a world of lonely, imprisoned consciousnesses, each unique, each determined by its private history? The only older novelist who was concerned —indeed, obsessed—by this theme was Laurence Sterne, whose *Life and Opinions of Tristram Shandy* is a curiously modern book, both in its handling of character and in its treatment of time. Sterne had learned from John Locke a lesson similar to that which modern novelists have learned from modern psychologists—that the private train of association colours the individual mind and constitutes a barrier to effective human intercourse. Uncle Toby talks about his theory of fortification and Walter Shandy interprets his remarks in the light of his own obsession with nomenclature, and Walter talks about names while Toby takes him to be referring to the theory of fortification. But for Sterne, simple affection can spark across this gulf, and love solves the problem posed by psychology. For the modern writer, no such simple solution is possible, for he is likely to regard love as a form of selfishness or at least as something much more complicated and problematical than simple affection between two persons. For Lawrence, true love begins with the lovers' recognition of each other's true separateness, while Virginia Woolf's Mrs Dalloway rejected Peter Walsh, the man she really loved, because she was afraid that his possessive love would infringe on her own personality.

We must preserve the integrity of our private selves yet we must make contact with others. Mrs Dalloway is going to give a party: parties bring people together, help them to escape from their essential loneliness. But do they provide real escape from loneliness, or do we feel lonelier still in a crowd? If you are driven completely into your private world you go mad, as Septimus Warren Smith goes mad in the novel—or rather you go mad if, having sunk into your private world, representatives of crude conventionality think that they can bring you back by imposing on you their unreal 'social' norms. So Warren Smith is driven to suicide by Dr Holmes. Perhaps death is the only ultimate solution, since in death one went out of the prison of self and became part of everything:

> ... did it matter that she must inevitably cease completely; all this must go on without her; did she resent it;

or did it not become consoling to believe that death ended absolutely? but that somehow in the streets of London, on the ebb and flow of things, here, there, she survived, Peter survived, lived in each other, she being part, she was positive, of the trees at home; of the house there, ugly, rambling all to bits and pieces as it was; part of people she had never met; being laid out like a mist between the people she knew best, who lifted her on their branches as she had seen the trees lift the mist, but it spread ever so far, her life, herself. . . .

This is the reverse of A. E. Housman's view:

> *When we two are spilt on air,*
> *Long we shall be strangers there.*

To be spilt on air is to be redeemed from the prison-house of self. Yet it is to be dead—a desperate enough solution.

Towards the end of the novel Mrs Dalloway watches through the window the old lady across the street as she goes upstairs to bed. We see each other through glass (a symbol used also in *To the Lighthouse*), the invisible obstacle that comes between individuals. 'She parted the curtains; she looked. Oh, but how surprising!—in the room opposite the old lady stared straight at her! She was going to bed.' So Yeats 'climbed up the narrow winding stair to bed', moving up the spiral staircase of life to the top of the tower, where all stages exist simultaneously. That is Byzantium, the changeless world of art. But in life you never reach it: the tower is ruined at the top. When you get there, you are dead.

So for the living it is the moment that counts, the realized point of experience wrested from flux. The sword, Excalibur-like, coming up from the neutral flat of the waters, the upraised hand, arresting, the lighthouse rising up from the sea—these are Virginia Woolf's images for the assertion of the moment in spite of flux, the lonely realization of self in spite of company. Mrs Dalloway ends with the sentence: 'For there she was.' And *To the Lighthouse* ends with Mr Ramsay and his children arriving at the lighthouse, while at the same moment, on shore, Lily Briscoe realizes her vision and completes her painting. We escape from the flux to realize the moment, and from the moment to lose ourselves in the flux.

> *The smithies break the flood,*
> *The golden smithies of the Emperor!*

Art conquers the flux, but the flux wins in the end:

> *. . . Those images that yet*
> *Fresh images beget*
> *That dolphin-torn, that gong-tormented sea.*

In seeing these characteristically modern themes in Virginia Woolf we must not, of course, forget the important technical aspects of her work. She devised a method both of rendering the new view of consciousness and of coping with the problem of making a private view of significance convincing to the reader. In *Mrs Dalloway*, for example, she deals with the events of a single day, but by exploring the way in which retrospect colours present consciousness, in which the past conditions the present within the mind and emotions of the individual, she reveals all that is relevant about the past of her principal characters. And by the imagery and rhythms of her prose she achieves, almost lyrically, a distillation of meaning that the reader accepts both as important and as moving, within the novel.

Virginia Woolf saw Galsworthy, Bennett and Wells as 'materialists' because they were concerned with presenting life as though the public pattern of significance still existed and everything significant in individual experience could be expressed in terms of a man's relation to social institutions such as marriage, property or a deliberate change of physical environment. One cannot say that the 'materialists' are wrong; theirs is a perfectly legitimate mode of presenting reality; but we can say that by remaining insensitive to important shifts in sensibility in their own time they cut themselves off from the possibility of rendering impressively the profounder spirit of their own age. And it can be argued that only through such a rendering can the artist achieve true universality. Certainly the most memorable novels of our time have been written with a consciousness of the two modern problems, the moral and the psychological.

James Joyce solved the problem of selection and significance in his own way. Instead of using quasi-poetic techniques for making a private view of reality persuasive to the reader while he reads, he sought a method of presenting a limited tract of time and space as microcosm, as a small scale model of the whole of human life, to which all attitudes were possible, depending on your point of view. In *Ulysses* he tells the story of a group of people on one day in Dublin, and arranges his material and employs language in such a way that it becomes a symbolic picture of all of human history, which is simultaneously tragic and comic, heroic and trivial, magnificent and dreary. What is significant in human life, what kind of incident should the novelist select as of importance? The older novelist answered this question by reference to a publicly agreed, socially exhibited, standard; a writer like Virginia Woolf took her private sense of the significant and found ways of making it convincing to the reader; but Joyce solved the problem in a more original manner: everything is significant in human life, he seems to be saying, and by the same token nothing is significant—it all depends on how you look at it. And if you can cultivate a sufficiently multiple vision, and find a way of presenting that vision, you can conceive a wholly new kind of comedy, the comedy of multiple identity. Leopold Bloom, the rather seedy advertisement canvasser in Dublin, plodding around Dublin on his trivial and shabby business, is also Ulysses, the adventurer, the hero, husband of Penelope, lover of Calypso, wanderer and home lover, brave warrior and cunning schemer. Bloom, too, an Irish Jew, is both of Dublin and not of Dublin, both a member of his community and an exile; his humane curiosity shows him as the Baconian scientist, concerned with 'the relief of man's estate', while his relative lack of formal education and the streak of vulgarity in him shows him simultaneously as the anti-scientist, the prey of popular half-truths; he is admirable and lovable and at the same time disgusting. By contriving a series of symbolic overtones which sound continually and in a highly complex fashion throughout the novel, Joyce relates his hero not only to Ulysses but to Shakespeare, Jesus, the Wandering Jew, and numerous other characters in history and literature, good and bad, high and low. And the other characters in the novel, though in a lesser degree, are similarly expanded. This is not to deny the value of life, for if Joyce depresses the heroic to the level of the trivial he also raises the trivial to the level of the heroic, and as the bulk of daily living is trivial, the result is, as it were, a net gain for daily living.

It has more than once been argued that *Ulysses* demonstrates a religious sense of evil, which is one of the keys to the meaning of the book. But the view of the novel here suggested would repudiate that interpretation as based on a profound misinterpretation of what Joyce is doing. The comedy of life for Joyce lies in its microcosmic aspect: everything is in a sense everything else; 'all is all' as Stephen Dedalus asserts in the library scene. Yet this tremendous expansion of meaning, achieved by style (which shifts continually, to express different attitudes to the same or similar things), comes from a realistic base, unlike *Finnegans Wake*, where the symbolic superstructure is the whole novel. And this realistic base in *Ulysses* is lively and entertaining in its own right, constituting an unforgettable picture of Dublin life in the early part of the present century. Further, in his concern to expand Bloom into a great inclusive character, Joyce does not lose sight of that modern problem which I have called the relation of loneliness to love. Every man is eternally lonely, and we see in Joyce (as, in a different way, we see in Sterne) the tragic gap between man's inner self, revealed to us through the 'stream of consciousness' technique, and the self which he presents to his neighbour and companions. That contrast is emphasized again and again in *Ulysses*, and not only with respect to Bloom. All men are exiles. But all men belong to a community as well. In Bloom himself the paradox of the exile who belongs is sharply defined, whereas in various other characters it is often only suggested. Men achieve contact by social ritual, notably in the public house. The raised glass is the symbol of contact; and it is significant that the pub, and the group drinking in the pub, recur again and again in *Ulysses*. It is equally significant that when we see Bloom drinking, it is a modest glass of burgundy, consumed alone, that he drinks. For Bloom the social gesture is indulged in privately: he is the exile, and when he joins the social group (to which he belongs yet does not belong) he does not drink with the others.

The concept of the microcosm is thus for Joyce the solution to the first of the two problems facing the modern novelist. The second problem, the rendering of consciousness in a new relation to time, he solves very much as Virginia Woolf does in *Mrs Dalloway*—by restricting his surface action to a short period of time and working backwards through exploring the past within the present consciousness of his characters. Thus we know Leopold Bloom perhaps more completely than we know any other character in fiction, even though the overt action in which he is concerned occupies less than twenty-four hours. Joyce employs the 'interior monologue' more consistently and with less intervention on the author's part than any other major writer.

There are other aspects of *Ulysses* which are equally impressive. The character of Stephen Dedalus, the potential artist moving in a world of insensitive vulgarians—an alienated man in a different sense than Bloom—is both important in the total design of the novel and significant in its own right. In spite of his alienation, arising largely from his desire to cultivate the aloofness and impersonality of the artist, Stephen belongs to his environment as Bloom does not belong and he moves for the most part in an atmosphere of conviviality. The novel opens with three episodes involving Stephen—we see him first in the Martello tower with his companions, the Rabelaisian Mulligan and the prim English Haines; then we see him at work, teaching in the school and talking to the headmaster to whom he offers his resignation; and thirdly we see him alone, walking along the beach, with his restless scholastic mind sorting and categorizing his observations. He is haunted by feelings of guilt about his dead mother and by Hamlet-like thoughts which help to isolate him from his kind. Bloom, whom we first see in the fourth episode but who from now on remains the central figure, is also haunted—by thought of his dead infant son, of his father who committed suicide, of his Jewish background, of his wife's infidelity—and the streams of consciousness of the two so different men interweave in subtle counterpoint long before they actually meet, in the fourteenth episode. In the great 'night-town' scene, where the exhausted Bloom looks after the drunken Stephen and finally sees in him, symbolically, the image of his dead son, the father-son motif (which involves not only Ulysses and Telemachus, but also Hamlet and his father and many other literary and theological themes) is resolved, and the concluding section of the book, where Bloom takes Stephen home and gives him cocoa and the offer of a bed (he accepts the former but refuses the latter), contains all kinds of ritual overtones involving the reconciliation of opposites and the possibility of sacramental identification of oneself with someone else (the theme of loneliness and love at a new level). And Molly Bloom's final soliloquy, bringing together her experiences as woman with a vulgar sensuality which is the guarantee that life will keep going, grounds all in pragmatic acquiescence. Life is what it is, and is to be accepted. It is multifarious and monstrous and ordinary and terrible and heroic and trivial at the same time, but it remains interesting and important and worth attending to, for in any one part of it all of it is contained.

The expansion of *Ulysses* into microcosm, the providing of symbolic overtones of meaning for every literal action, is achieved with remarkable virtuosity, not only through sheer skill in the handling of language, but by the deft use of allusion and suggestion, references to the other arts (and especially a cunning and continuous use of music) and the use of devices, such as the vice-regal procession in the tenth episode, for the presentation of different streams of action simultaneously.

Joyce is the most perfect example of the modern 'alienation of the artist'. The view that the artist does not belong to society, that the rules applicable to men in society do not apply to him because he is outside and different in virtue of his being an artist, is a modern one, arising in the latter part of the nineteenth century as part of the war between the artist and the Philistine which Puritan middle-class civilization made inevitable. But Joyce related it to the artist's need for objectivity, and that need for objectivity was in turn bound up with his solution of the problem of selection and significance: if you were objective enough, the problem disappeared, not because you had any illusions about the possibility of a scientific naturalism, but because to the objective man everything was both significant and insignificant. The career of the artist as exile falls into four parts. First, in *Dubliners*, Joyce produced a group of short stories describing the atmosphere of the country from which he had to escape before he could feel really free as an artist. 'My intention', he wrote to Grant Richards, 'was to write a chapter of the moral history of my country and I chose Dublin for the scene because that city seemed to me the centre of paralysis . . . I have written it for the most part in a style of scrupulous meanness.' Secondly, in *A Portrait of the Artist as a Young Man*, he gave an account of the development of the potential artist as implying the development of the exile. Thirdly, the artist having fully developed, he recreated in *Ulysses* the life he left behind and presented it as a microcosm of all human life. Finally, in *Finnegans Wake*, he abandoned the realistic base of *Ulysses* and by a continuously symbolic and complexly punning use of language sought to achieve directly an evocation of all human history.

Dubliners, for all its studied neutrality, is not written in the style of 'scrupulous meanness' that Joyce professed to employ in it. The rhythms of his prose are carefully modulated and convey a powerful effect. In one of the stories, 'Araby', a small boy has been waiting impatiently all week for a bazaar, which his imagination has built up as something splendid and glorious. When the day comes, his uncle, with whom he lives and on whom he depends for getting money to go to the bazaar, comes home very late, somewhat drunk. The bazaar is almost over by the time the boy gets the money and makes his way to the hall in a deserted suburban train. The hall is almost empty, and as he walks slowly down the middle someone begins to turn out the lights. The bazaar was over. 'Gazing up into the darkness I saw myself as a creature driven and derided by vanity; and my eyes burned with anguish and anger.' The rhythms of this concluding sentence are an expansion of the Horatian 'Tendens Venfranos in agros, aut Lacedaemonium Tarentum' of the same kind that Dr Johnson could use so effectively: 'The shepherd in Virgil grew at last acquainted with Love, and found him a native of the rocks.' Or, more elaborately, 'Is not a Patron, my Lord, one who looks with unconcern on a man struggling for life in the water, and, when he has reached ground, encumbers him with help?' At the end of 'Ivy Day in the Committee Room', a perfect rendering of the dreariness of Irish local politics after the death of Parnell, the various shabby characters meet and talk in the dismal committee room and finally one of them recites a bad sentimental poem about Parnell. The story concludes: 'Mr Crofton said that it was a very fine piece of writing.' The simple cadence of that artfully artless sentence comments like a sigh on the story which it concludes. And 'The Dead', the most elaborate and the longest of all the stories, which was written some time after the others and stands rather apart from them as a larger symbolic comment on Ireland, ends with one of the most perfectly cadenced pieces of prose in the language.

In the *Portrait* the prose is varied with great skill and beauty, but never for its own sake, always to provide the proper medium for the presentation of a particular stage in the growing up of the hero, who, as he moves from childhood to manhood, learns his own destiny as artist and as exile. School, with its sights and sounds and smells and emotions; home, with the political squabbling summed up so magnificently in the great Christmas dinner scene where there is a fight about Parnell and the Church and Mr Casey, the guest, breaks down, to the terror and wonder of the watching Stephen:

> Mr Casey, freeing his arms from his holders, suddenly bowed his head on his hands with a sob of pain.
> —Poor Parnell! he cried loudly. My dead king!
> He sobbed loudly and bitterly.
> Stephen, raising his terrorstricken face, saw that his father's eyes were full of tears.

Stephen is tied by family, country and religion, but one by one he looses himself from those ties to discover his true vocation in the free and uncommitted life of the artist. The

Church was the greatest rival to the world of art: it, too, promised loneliness and power. But he understood at last that 'he was destined to learn his own wisdom apart from others or to learn the wisdom of others himself wandering among the snares of the world'. And so the Artist is born. The climax of the book comes soon after Stephen's realization of his true destiny. He is wandering alone by the shore, 'alone and young and wilful and wildhearted, alone amid a waste of wild air and brackish water and the seaharvest of shells and tangle and veiled grey sunlight and gayclad lightclad figures of children and girls and voices childish and girlish in the air'. He sees a girl standing in midstream, 'alone and still, gazing out to sea', and he contemplates her, intently, frankly, without desire or ulterior motive of any kind: he is relishing the artist's perception of life. And as he looks, joy overcomes him:

—Heavenly God! cried Stephen's soul, in an outburst of profane joy.

It is profane joy, the artist's joy in life.

But the life which he joys to contemplate as an artist cannot be lived by him as a man. Once Stephen has recognized his destiny, the shedding of his other loyalties proceeds apace. He is haunted by the seagulls flying overhead in the evening sky. They symbolize escape for the artist, escape from the cramping environment where other claims on his loyalty oppress him. Like the Greek Daedalus who made the labyrinth for King Minos and afterwards made wings to enable him to escape across the sea from that tyrannous king, Stephen Dedalus seeks to escape from the labyrinth of Dublin life and claims. Daedalus, too, was the first craftsman, 'old artificer'. As epigraph to the book Joyce had quoted a line from Ovid's description of Daedalus's construction of the labyrinth: 'Et ignotas animum dimittit in artes', 'and he set his mind to unknown arts'; so Joyce would set his mind to enlarge the boundaries of the art of the writer. And if Stephen Dedalus's surname is that of the old artificer, his Christian name is that of the first Christian martyr: the artist is both craftsman and martyr.

So Stephen, in the latter part of the *Portrait*, works out his theory of the artist as exile. 'The artist, like the God of creation, remains within or behind or beyond or above his handiwork, invisible, refined out of existence, indifferent, paring his fingernails'. When his friend Cranly tries to persuade him to accept the claim of his people and religion and cross-examines him about his ethics, Stephen bursts out:

> You have asked me what I would do and what I would not do. I will tell you what I will do and what I will not do. I will not serve that in which I no longer believe, whether it call itself my home, my fatherland, or my church: and I will try to express myself in some mode of life or art as freely as I can, using for my defence the only arms I allow myself to use—silence, exile, and cunning. . . .
>
> — Alone, quite alone. You have no fear of that. And you know what that word means. Not only to be separate from all others but to have not even one friend.
>
> — I will take the risk, said Stephen.

A Portrait of the Artist as a Young Man is thus an important document in the history of the artist as exile as well as a remarkable work of art in its own right. Combining the naturalistic and the symbolist traditions, Joyce found a solution to the problems of the literary artist in his time which, although it has features in common with the solutions found by other writers, remains unique and in a quite literal sense inimitable. The enormously complex aesthetic apparatus required to expand the realistic 'slice of life' into the symbolic microcosm works admirably in *Ulysses*, where the liveliness of the framework picture of Dublin life compels our interest until further readings have yielded more and more meaning; but it can be questioned whether it works in *Finnegans Wake*, where the law of diminishing returns begins to apply and the enormous exegetical effort required to find the line of meaning (to say nothing of the various other levels of significance) cannot be expected of any reader who is not a lifetime devotee of the work. The influence of Joyce on modern writers has been fragmentary; they have learned from him the use of certain technical devices, certain ways of resolving particular problems in construction or presentation, but nobody has adopted his general approach or his full method. He was a lonely genius, who followed up the implications of his own method with such startling rigour that he left no road that way for others to follow.

A word should be said about Joyce's use of language, which follows inevitably from his purpose of trying to take all possible points of view simultaneously. More and more the pun becomes the norm of artistic expression, since the artist for Joyce is by definition the man who must say several things at once. Further, in a work like *Ulysses* and, to a greater degree *Finnegans Wake*, the complex symbolic pattern demands that the reader should be made continuously aware of echoes and correspondences which link character with character, situation with situation, and word with word. This again is achieved partly by complex puns and by invented 'portmanteau' words. One sometimes feels with Joyce that his real ambition was to find one word so enormously packed with counterpointed meanings that it said in one vast, reverberating pun everything that could ever be said about human experience from every possible point of view and at every level of consciousness. Failing that, he was driven to extend his novels further and further in an attempt to achieve the total interlock of meanings. It is not surprising that Joyce's astonishing verbal inventiveness has had little influence on subsequent novelists. This kind of re-creation of language out of the parts of the existing language depends for its effectiveness on the fact that the existing language is there, a series of verbal units to be manipulated and played about with; but if everybody manipulated and played about with the units of meaning in this way the stable verbal units of meaning would disappear, and the whole possibility of literary expression would disappear with it. This perhaps illustrates the element of self-frustration in Joyce's view of art and in his later literary practice. But it is not to deny his unique and extraordinary genius.

2

The problem of what to do with new knowledge has always presented itself to the writer after a burst of philosophical or scientific activity. 'The new philosophy calls all in doubt', John Donne had exclaimed, and the post-Victorian poets and novelists have often expressed a similar perplexity. New psychological knowledge posed problems for novelists concerned with the presentation of character; it also troubled those who were concerned with the moral pattern of their work. We now know, or we think we know, so much about psychological conditioning, about the psychosomatic aspects of illness, about the effect of childhood frustrations on adult vices, that we are in danger of being unable to pass any moral judgment on individuals. This man committed rape or murder, but we know that he saw something terrible in the woodshed when he was three, was brought up in a slum without orange juice and cod-liver oil, was bullied by a drunken stepfather, had his emotions and instincts warped in this way or that: how, then, can we blame him for what he was eventually driven to do? *Tout comprendre, c'est tout pardonner*, says the French proverb; to know all is to forgive all. But to forgive all is to make it impossible to write the *Divina Commedia* or *Paradise Lost*. If we knew all about the inhibitions of King Claudius's childhood, we could not make him the villain of a tragedy. If we knew all Iago's psychological history, we might be tempted to spend all our sympathy on him rather than on Othello. And it did not take even that much psychology to make the Romantics turn Milton's Satan into a hero. If our moral judgments of men are to be dissolved in psychological understanding, we can no longer pattern a tragedy or create any significant work of art with a human situation as its subject matter. Certainly a behaviourist psychology—using this term in its widest sense—leaves little room for an appraisal of personality as such, and without an appraisal of personality as such, why should Hamlet's death be any more significant than that of Polonius?

What are we to do with our knowledge? The early novels of Aldous Huxley are obsessed with this problem. Knowledge destroys value. We believe that we have a vision of ultimate reality, until we learn that it is all glandular, that every emotional conviction of value can be explained away physiologically. An operation on the frontal lobes of the brain can completely change a man's personality; what a man is may be determined by the way the doctor delivered him as an infant or an accidental fall in childhood. There is no value, only irresponsible accident, and if we have emotional conviction of value, we are simply old fashioned as well as deluded. Theodore Gumbril, the disillusioned schoolmaster of *Antic Hay*, meditates as follows in the school chapel:

> No, but seriously, Gumbril reminded himself, the problem was very troublesome indeed. God as a sense of warmth about the heart, God as exultation, God as tears in the eyes, God as a rush of power or thought—that was all right. But God as truth, God as $2+2=4$—that wasn't so clearly all right. Was there any chance of their being the same? Were there bridges, to join the two worlds?

Gumbril decided that there were not, and therein lay his dilemma. Or again, take the description of the concert in the third chapter of *Point Counter Point*:

Pongileoni's blowing and the scraping of the anonymous fiddlers had shaken the air in the great hall, had set the glass of the windows looking on to it vibrating; and this in turn had shaken the air in Lord Edward's apartment on the further side. The shaking air rattled Lord Edward's *membrana tympani;* the interlocked *malleus, incus,* and stirrup bones were set in motion so as to agitate the membrane of the oval window and raise an infinitesimal storm in the fluid of the labyrinth. The hairy endings of the auditory nerve shuddered like weeds in a rough sea; a vast number of obscure miracles were performed in the brain, and Lord Edward ecstatically whispered 'Bach!'

God as a sense of warmth about the heart as opposed to God as $2+2=4$; music as a series of sound waves impinging on a physiological organism and music as something significant and moving—these are expressed by Huxley as irreconcilable alternatives. Both explanations seem to be true, yet each seems to deny the other. If the dilemma is posed in this way, the only solution would seem to be either complete scepticism or complete irrationality, and neither scepticism nor irrationality can provide a proper environment for great art. Huxley's early novels are witty fables designed to illustrate this dilemma; he takes us on a conducted tour of dried up wells, sources of value which no longer yield anything because the curse of knowledge has struck them: we know too much about how they came to be what they are.

What are we to do with our knowledge? The question is not always a despairing one. Huxley's observation about music was not new. Shakespeare's Benedick, in *Much Ado About Nothing*, remarks in an ironic moment: 'Is it not strange that sheeps' guts should hale souls out of men's bodies?' Unlike Huxley, Shakespeare was not tortured by this perception: he included it dramatically as one element in the complex and paradoxical nature of things, so that it enriches rather than frustrates his picture of human values in action.

It is thus not merely the possession of the knowledge that causes the dilemma: it is the failure of contemporary civilization to provide a context within which all knowledge can fall into a pattern and the most contradictory elements can be resolved in a higher unity. The problem becomes part of the larger problem of modern man's search for a tradition and the desperate appeal to anthropology and private myth-making to help to provide such a tradition. Eliot used Jessie Weston's *From Ritual to Romance* to provide the mythological groundwork of *The Waste Land*, and Yeats, collecting oddities of human thought from the Cabala to Madame Blavatsky, constructed with what he found a strange personal mythology which served also as a philosophy of history and an interpretation of human character—and, most important of all, a scaffolding from which to build poems in which opposites are being continually reconciled.

What are we to do with our knowledge? Use it for 'the relief of man's estate', to help us adapt to our environment and to adapt our environment to us? But adaptation itself has its dangers. Bernard Shaw, who was committed by his view of evolution to a belief in the virtue of willed adaptation, had at the same time an emotional sympathy with the man who rebelled against his environment rather than adapted himself to it. He was thus torn between the hero as rebel and the hero as adapter (which explains such characters as the munitions manufacturer in *Major Barbara*, who is hero only in the sense that he brilliantly adapted himself to competitive capitalist civilization). And Huxley, again, realized that if we pursue the ideal of adaptation far enough and move much farther in the direction in which modern technological civilization seems to be going, all moral effort will be eliminated from life and the possibilities of heroism of any kind will cease to exist. For heroism becomes impossible under conditions of perfect adaptation. What one might call the Salvation Army view of morality—fight the good fight—is deeply rooted in Christian civilization. The struggle against temptation, the battle between good and evil within the soul (Prudentius' *Psychomachia*), the achievement of self-mastery—all this becomes otiose in a state of perfect adaptation. As Mustapha Mond tells the Savage in Huxley's *Brave New World*:

'. . . civilization has absolutely no need of nobility or heroism. These things are symptoms of political inefficiency. In a properly organized society like ours, nobody has any opportunities for being noble or heroic. Conditions have got to be thoroughly unstable before the occasion can arise. Where there are wars, where there are divided allegiances, where there are temptations to be resisted, objects of love to be fought for or defended—there, obviously, nobility and heroism have some sense. But there aren't any wars nowadays. The greatest care is taken to prevent you from loving anyone too much. There's no such thing as a divided allegiance; you're so conditioned that you can't help doing what you ought to do. And what you ought to do is on the whole so pleasant, so many of the natural impulses are allowed free play, that there really aren't any temptations to resist.'

God and poetry and danger and freedom become unnecessary and even meaningless when the Baconian ideal has been realized; they are all replaced by comfort. But the Savage is not satisfied:

'But I don't want comfort. I want God, I want poetry, I want real danger, I want freedom, I want goodness. I want sin.'

'In fact,' said Mustapha Mond, 'you're claiming the right to be unhappy.'

'All right, then,' said the Savage defiantly. 'I'm claiming the right to be unhappy.'

'Not to mention the right to grow old and ugly and impotent; the right to have syphilis and cancer; the right to have too little to eat; the right to be lousy; the right to live in constant apprehension of what may happen tomorrow; the right to catch typhoid; the right to be tortured by unspeakable pains of every kind.'

There was a long silence.

'I claim them all,' said the Savage at last.

Mustapha Mond shrugged his shoulders. 'You're welcome,' he said.

This is, of course, a melodramatic and not wholly logical presentation of the dilemma; the possibilities of moral effort are not dependent on the prevalence of syphilis and typhoid. But they *are* dependent on the existence of an imperfect world, a world in which there are difficulties to be overcome and dangers to be confronted. It is the old problem that Milton faced in *Paradise Lost*. Prelapsarian life in the Garden of Eden could accommodate only a very passive kind of virtue, in which Milton himself was not really interested. Only after the Fall, in the postlapsarian struggle to bridge the gap between the real and the ideal, is a life of true moral effort possible, though far from easy; so the Fall was therefore a good thing. 'I cannot praise a fugitive and cloistered virtue, unexercised and unbreathed.'

This leads directly to the problem of the hero in the modern novel. No man is a hero to his valet—or to his psychoanalyst. If we come too close to our hero his heroism dissolves. And if the conditions of social life are such that initiative or endurance or physical courage are unnecessary or even silly, then the old-fashioned hero becomes the modern fool. We can trace the transition from hero to fool quite easily. Don Quixote, standing between the feudal period and a more modern commercial age, is the great transitional figure, the hero as fool, and a fool for whom we retain a certain admiration. He seeks the 'crowded hour of glorious life' in a civilization which does not go in for that sort of thing. As we leave the feudal age further and further behind and move through commercial towards industrial civilization, we note the emergence of a new kind of hero, the prudential hero, of whom Robinson Crusoe is the first important example in English literature (unless Bunyan's Christian be allowed that claim, in a rather different sense). The hero whose motives are prudential rather than selfless, or who seeks safety rather than glory, can never appeal to the imagination as the older species of hero could, and Romantic attempts to revive the older hero provide interesting testimony to man's reluctance to accept prudence as an ideal. But Scott, who is generally thought of as the founder of the romantic historical novel, was really concerned, in his best novels (which deal with the immediate past of his own country, a period of transition from a feudal into a commercial society) with charting the inevitable progress of the new hero. Baillie Nicol Jarvie, the Glasgow merchant who flourishes by trading with the West Indies, is the true hero of *Rob Roy*, not the theatrical freebooter whose world is already over and who survives into the modern world only as a rather shabby bandit. In Scott's novels dealing with seventeenth- and eighteenth-century Scotland, the knight is sadly modulated into the antiquary and the clash of arms gives way to pedantic argument about heraldry. The true heroism of *The Heart of Midlothian* lies in the humble struggle for survival, while the older heroic ideal has become a dreary business of smuggling and robbery. And in *Redgauntlet* the little band of belated Jacobites are dismissed with friendly contempt by King George's representative as not to be taken seriously; the background of the novel is full of lawyers and business men, with whom the future lies.

But the prudential hero is found out by the Victorians as a hypocrite or a villain, and the modern novelist has returned to the hero as fool without Cervantes' affectionate undertones. One might call such a character the anti-hero. The early novels of Huxley present him often, and he is a staple figure in the novels of Evelyn Waugh. This kind of anti-hero is related to the hero as victim whom we find in Samuel Butler's *Way of All Flesh*. But we are asked to laugh at him— as we laugh at Paul Pennyfeather in Waugh's *Decline and Fall* —rather than to pity him, even though the laughter has masochistic overtones. Idealism emerges as mere ignorance, innocence as a dangerous lack of sophistication which makes the virtuous anti-hero the complacent tool of sophisticated vice, as Paul Pennyfeather finds himself (without knowing what it is all about) organizing the white slave traffic. If you try behaving like an old-fashioned hero, as the hero of *Men at Arms* does when he goes on an unauthorized and dangerous private raid on the enemy coast, you will find yourself court-martialled and demoted. And unhappy accidents never produce tragedy, but the bitter farce of *A Handful of Dust*. This can be hilariously funny in the hands of a witty and skilful writer like Evelyn Waugh. Interest is sustained by a gallery of nostalgic eccentrics who are sometimes funny (like Apthorne in *Men at Arms*) and sometimes pathetic. Sometimes, even, these nostalgic figures rise to a sad dignity, for they are pale shadows of the lost hero, with no place in the modern world. We feel this most in *Brideshead Revisited*, in whose first chapter the nostalgic note swells out as never before in Waugh's novels. Here the cruelly farcical coincidences of many of the earlier novels give way to suggestions of a lost world lying dimly behind the feverish gestures of value-less modern life. Religion, the old Catholic religion, is presented in Waugh's later novels not as a living source of spiritual values which can redeem the modern waste land, but as what might perhaps be called the stiff upper lip of the soul; it gives the believer dignity of bearing, like wearing evening dress in the jungle. Thus religion provides aristocratic gestures to shore against the ruins. This is an odd use of religion in fiction, but perhaps no odder than the more serious use of it made by Graham Greene, another Catholic novelist, who seems concerned to show the essential incompatibility between human decency and theological virtue: the decent thing is, literally, damnable, or, if it is not absolutely damnable it is (like the hero's behaviour in *The Heart of the Matter*) only doubtfully exempted. The problem of human values is, for Greene, essentially the question of good and evil (rather than of right and wrong) and this cannot be solved on a humanist standard. The problems which bothered the early Huxley and which were exploited with cynical comedy by the early Waugh were problems raised by scientific humanism; you get rid of scientific humanism and you get rid of the problems. That was cutting the Gordian knot with a vengeance.

The presentation of the anti-hero in modern English satiric fiction is often complicated by the process of psychological understanding. If too much psychological understanding destroys a hero's heroism, it also destroy's a villain's villainy, and sometimes one is left with a character who is half laughed at, half wept over, like the principal character in Angus Wilson's *Hemlock and After*, a novel which sets out as satire and ends as diagnosis. Knowledge brings its own kind of sympathy, and too much knowledge can destroy the picture of the victim as a man from an alien and intolerable world, a picture which is essential for true satire.

One way out of these problems is frankly to take the hero as clown, and present him, in an amoral context, as thriving through comic coincidence, on the follies and stupidities and hollowness of others. This kind of clowning, anarchist comedy can be very funny and very appealing at first reading, but one wonders afterwards whether the world created by the novelist is really amenable to such treatment. Other novels deal with the déclassé intellectual, who is sometimes shown making a series of attempts, always ultimately unsuccessful, to contract out of society altogether and achieve a complete 'neutrality' with reference to other people and to the claims which they might make. The English novel, which in its early days was so concerned with—one might even say obsessed by—class, has at last reached the point where it seeks to escape altogether from everything that the word suggests.

3

Virginia Woolf's verdict on those of her contemporaries she called the 'materialists' has on the whole been vindicated by time. Wells we admire for his understanding of the humours of lower middle-class character in such a work as *Mr Polly* and we may appreciate, too, the inventiveness and dramatic quality of some of his scientific fiction; but he appears from the perspective of the mid-1950s to be a man of enormous talent in a variety of ways rather than a literary artist of major significance. Arnold Bennett we respect for the workmanship and the vivid documentary appeal of such a novel as *The Old Wives' Tale* or (in a rather different way) *Riceyman Steps*, but he was clearly not a major genius. Galsworthy's reputation as a novelist has not been sustained; for though his humane curiosity about men and his solid sense of character of the English middle class did give some reality to his novels, the lack of any consistent ability to body forth his vision of men in fully realized concrete particulars (seen so disastrously in the character of Irene in *The Man of Property*, who is not a character but a piece of arty nonsense) is manifest when we read him now, though parts of the Forsyte series do retain their appeal. The best of the novelists writing in the early 1920s—when Virginia Woolf was formulating her criticism of her contemporaries—were (apart from Mrs Woolf herself) Conrad, Joyce, Lawrence and (perhaps in a more limited way) Ford Madox Ford. Of these, Conrad belonged to an older generation and had already produced all his best work (much of which was done before or early in the First World War). The Conrad who has survived as a great novelist is not the Conrad hailed in his own day—the romantic Conrad, the picturesque, inscrutable, polychromatic exploiter of the call of the sea and of the unknown, but the subtler and more profound Conrad of the 'middle' novels and stories, the Conrad of *Nostromo, The Secret Agent, Under Western Eyes* and *Chance*. It is the novelist of moral exploration and discovery presented through particularized detail of character and action rather than the cultivator of misty attitudes about inscrutability and darkness who is still read and admired, the novelist, in fact, whom F. R. Leavis so effectively presents in his chapter on Conrad in *The Great Tradition*.

D. H. Lawrence's reputation as a novelist has risen steadily since his death, and if we cannot altogether accept Dr Leavis's estimate here, it is not because we do not concede Lawrence's genius but because that estimate, placing him among the supreme geniuses of English fiction and far above any other twentieth-century novelist, seems to ignore, almost wilfully, Lawrence's real limitations. That Lawrence had a powerful original vision of life and that this vision enabled him to use the novel not as the quasi-realistic social-cum-psychological fable it had been for so long but as a symbolic and poetic presentation of the underlying realities of individual life and of human relations, is unquestionable. Further his ability to make his symbolic action startling in its inward and penetrating reality, and to combine the most precisely observed detail of human gesture or the natural world with his poetic sense of the underlying meaning of things—this is a great gift and shows a great novelist. Yet it can hardly be denied that side by side with this brilliant gift for combined particularization and symbolic interpretation there is an embarrassing murkiness, a feverish and obsessive iteration of symbols of personal preoccupations which are not properly integrated into the story as told. This partly accounts for the failure of some of the central scenes in even his best novels. What, for example, is the meaning of the incidents that take place at the end of Chapter XV (entitled 'The

Bitterness of Ecstasy') of *The Rainbow*? Ursula and Skebrensky have some sort of tremendous crisis, which finishes their
relationship for ever. It is symbolized by Ursula's compulsive
desire to lie on her back and look at the moon and by the
particular way she accepts Skebrensky's love-making. A tear
rolls from her eye as she lies looking at the moon; Skebrensky
retreats, afraid; they are 'like two dead people'. When they
meet later he asks, 'Have you done with me' and she replies,
'It isn't me. You have done with me—we have done with
each other.' The reader who has followed the novel with
excitement and admiration up to this point is left baffled and
irritated. It would be most unfair to stress this side of Lawrence, for his virtues are unique and impressive; but the fact
remains that something of this sort occurs at some point in
every one of his novels. That perhaps is one reason why his
short stories are often so much more perfectly done—within
the limited compass of the short story he felt less temptation
to implicate *all* of his notions about human relations, however
imperfectly worked into the realized fabric of the story some
of them might be. Lawrence's short stories are very properly
now esteemed as containing his finest work. Of his novels,
The Rainbow and *Women in Love* are his most sustained successful works, but even these have some striking flaws. One
forgives the flaws for the sake of the genius which is overwhelming, but one cannot forget them, for they leap out at
the reader.

Lawrence was a prophet as well as a poet and novelist, and
those who take his prophecy literally and agree with it may
be less disturbed by the passages of murky rhetoric ('suave
loins of darkness') and unassimilated symbolism which are
found in his novels. Other readers may feel that these flaws
are the inevitable price an artist must pay if he is also a
prophet. The violence of Lawrence's apprehension of his
vision, and the whole crockery-throwing aspect of his view of
life and love ('Look, we have come through!') were both

liberating and dangerous. If it seems ungenerous to stress the dangers in the face of the unquestionably liberating genius, one can only insist that art must be redeemed from the irrelevant claims of personality, and that too many defences as well as adverse criticisms of Lawrence have been based on their confusion. When the murk and the unassimilated excitement comes into the novels, it must be condemned, not welcomed as an illustration of the vitality of the author's personality. But if that is the price we have to pay for the Lawrentian genius, we pay it gladly. The last word about him must always be that he was a great and original writer who brought a new kind of poetic imagination to English fiction.

4

The tradition of sensibility in the English novel, so firmly established by Virginia Woolf, has been followed, if not developed, by a number of skilful professional novelists, many of them women. In the short story, Katherine Mansfield, whose work in the 1920s was hailed by many critics as showing a delicacy of emotional perception comparable to that of Tchekov but whose reputation has not worn as well as that of Virginia Woolf, has had less influence; the individuality of her vision made her stories almost too personal and so in a sense unavailable as models or inspiration. Yet her influence can, too, be discerned in a general way in the stream of 'sensitive' novels and stories which has continued since the 1920s. Technically, the period since the 1920s has been one of consolidation. The frontiers of the art of fiction have not been extended during the last quarter of a century. But much skilful and interesting work has been done.

Elizabeth Bowen is one of the most talented of the novelists working in what might very loosely be called the tradition of sensibility (though she herself has reservations about the use of the term with reference to her novels). Her best, though not her most ambitious, novels are probably *The House in Paris* and *The Death of the Heart*. In the former there is an adroit use of the technique of revealing bit by bit the history of human passion which lies behind the puzzling situation with which the reader is at first confronted (the way this is done is somewhat reminiscent of *The Ballad and the Source*, by Rosamond Lehmann, another woman novelist in the tradition, though in some ways more solidly anchored in social fact). Miss Bowen has not only a gift for rendering states of mind with quiet precision; she is also concerned with local atmosphere, with place and with weather, and her novels contain many memorable scenes in which mood, region and climate effectively interpenetrate and interpret each other. *The Death of the Heart* brings into the open a theme which is implicit in much of her writing, both novels and short stories: all the main characters are portrayed as victims of each other, of the conventions they live by, of compulsions whose origins they do not understand, of the adult's fear of living fully and the child's fear of not living fully. The moral, which is never stated but only more delicately suggested, seems to be that in order to be livable, life has to be suppressed, to be emptied. It is only by the death of the heart that we can survive at all. No such view is, of course, being *advocated* by the author; but we can say that this deeply tragic insight (antithetical to the Lawrentian insight) is her comment on life in a certain phase of our civilization, or perhaps of any civilization.

A novelist who can be said to have in some respects created a tradition of her own is Ivy Compton-Burnett, who constructs her terrifying novels almost entirely out of dialogue. The novels are terrifying because of the studied calm with which the facts about human cruelty and selfishness are revealed. The conversation which carries on the action and reveals bit by bit the disturbing truths about the characters is carried on with a poised stylization. Miss Burnett deals in closed societies, families whose mutual tormentings are covered by the most polite and conventional outward behaviour. Yet the same thing that covers the evil also reveals it, and it is the contrast between the tone of the conversation and what is actually said or indicated that gives the novels their uncanny power. The plots themselves are for the most part highly melodramatic, though this fact is obscured for the casual reader by the calm surface of the dialogue; but the novels have none of the poetic justice which traditional melodrama goes in for: the mutual destructiveness of men and women, the battening on the weak by the self-assertive and the unscrupulous and the exploitation of 'servants' by 'masters' (and everyone in Miss Compton-Burnett's novels is, symbolically if not literally, either a master or a servant) goes on until the end. It is a dark vision of life, conveyed through the medium of delicate and witty entertainment.

Miss Compton-Burnett is an eccentric among modern English novelists, and it is the eccentrics in this period of technical consolidation who have kept the novel lively and interesting. Another eccentric, of a very different kind, is Henry Green, whose novels, with their unusual titles—*Loving, Living, Nothing, Concluding, Back*—have a cultivated naïveté which enables them to by-pass many of the problems discussed in the first part of this section. Green looks at life as if for the first time, and the result is a strange and often effective primitivism. His naïveté is, of course, highly sophisticated (if one may be paradoxical); it is, that is to say, a pose deliberately assumed for technical purposes. The result is impressive, a picture of human beings in action seen freshly, with a gaze of quizzical wonder.

Nevertheless, the problems discussed in the first part of this section continue to haunt the modern novelist. The theme of the isolation of the individual, with all the ambiguities of love and loneliness, which we found in Joyce and Virginia Woolf, is found today in those novelists who (like Antonia

White in *Beyond the Glass* and P. H. Newby in *The Retreat*) are concerned with madness or at least with that impairment of reason which drives the individual into a world that cannot be shared on any terms with others. And L. P. Hartley's *The Go-Between*, the story of a child moving in an adult world and interpreting its signs so as to build up a pattern of meaning which is in fact far removed from that seen by those who actually make the signs, is his most explicit of a series of novels all of which deal in some degree with the interaction of public and private worlds and the difficulties or the impossibility of sharing sensibility.

At the moment of writing, in the mid-1950s, the English novel seems on the whole to be in the hands of competent but unexciting professionals. Critics are arguing about whether as a literary form it is exhausted or not. But it is dangerous to try to predict the future course of any branch of literature. One can only express the hope that, with the radio serial and various kinds of television programme taking over the more superficial functions of fiction as entertainment, the novelist may find a clearer field for the further development of the novel as a real art form.

CHAPTER IV

CRITICAL AND GENERAL PROSE

I

LITERARY criticism has assumed an importance and a stature in the present age beyond anything it had achieved earlier. Some of the most original and creative minds on both sides of the Atlantic have devoted themselves to it; it has become a serious 'discipline' in its own right, no longer a branch of philosophy or of general aesthetics, nor, on the other hand, the genial discursiveness of leisured gentlemen. The demonstration of the nature, differentiating features, and peculiar value of a work of literary art, the meticulous analysis of the individual poem or novel or play in order to reveal its unique structure and pattern of meaning, as well as the larger purpose of showing how both creative literature and discriminating criticism are central to a civilization, are all features of modern criticism. One of the reasons for the increased importance of the critic is to be found in the present state of literary culture, with its division of readers into highbrows, middlebrows and lowbrows and the ever-widening gap between the general reader and qualified expert. The anti-romantic poetic revolution was accompanied from the start by a formidable barrage of criticism and has ever since been both guided and interpreted by important critical pronouncements. And the concern to maintain standards in an industrial civilization in which the making and marketing of works of art (or alleged works of art) is part of a free enterprise economy, the problems of best sellers and coterie writers, of 'classics and commercials', of the artist and the philistine, have come to characterize literary criticisms more and more ever since Matthew Arnold attacked the philistines in his *Culture and Anarchy*. Arnold, indeed, has been a potent force in one area of modern criticism, as even the titles of such books as F. R. Leavis's *Mass Civilization and Minority Culture* or Leavis and Thompson's *Culture and Environment* suggest. At the same time the increasing claims of science and new psychological knowledge have led such critics as I. A. Richards to attempt a complete reformulation of literary value in the light of the kind of meaning involved in the literary as distinct from the scientific use of language.

The Victorian legacy to modern criticism was rich but confused. Literature as self-expression, literature as exemplified psychological understanding (a view illustrated in Bradley on Shakespeare), literature as in some vague way a substitute for religion (as in Arnold and Pater), literature as anything treated with emotional conviction—these were some of the popular views which came into the twentieth century from the nineteenth. As for method, the impressionistic discursiveness of Lamb, the autobiographical gusto of Hazlitt, the biographical method exemplified by the 'English Men of Letters' series, the gentleman-and-scholar urbanity of such academic critics as Quiller-Couch, Saintsbury and Raleigh, have all been in greater or less degree repudiated by modern critics in favour of a more rigorous and more analytic procedure. The amateur note, so long the characteristic of English criticism, has given way to a professional and even technical specialization which has produced the same kind of division between 'popular' and 'serious' criticism as has developed in creative literature. Much modern criticism has, in fact, deliberately minimized the distinction between critical and creative writing. Eliot, writing in 1923 on 'The Function of Criticism', remarked: 'Probably . . . the larger part of the labour of an author in composing his work is critical labour; the labour of sifting, combining, constructing, expunging, correcting, testing: this frightful toil is as much critical as corrective.

I maintain even that the criticism employed by a trained and skilled writer on his own work is the most vital, the highest kind of criticism; and . . . that some creative writers are superior to others solely because their critical faculty is superior.' This remark can be set beside Eliot's statement that 'the poet has, not a "personality" to express, but a particular medium, which is only a medium and not a personality, in which expressions and experiences combine in peculiar and unexpected ways' to illustrate the tone and intention of much modern criticism.

On the whole, then, modern criticism (both English and American) has repudiated its nineteenth-century legacy in favour of something both less impressionistic and less academic. For impressionism and academicism are the two opposite poles from which the modern critic flees equally. Impressionism is the discussion of a work of art in terms of autobiographical chat about the state of mind it produces in the reader, while academicism includes both the amassing of factual details about works and their authors which have no relevance for the evaluation of those works and the determination to enjoy and admire everything produced in the past, however minor and indeed however bad, because it represents some phase in the history of literature and of literary taste. One result of the repudiation of impressionism is that criticism has become less merely descriptive and more sternly normative, while the insistence that scholarship is not criticism has led to a more firmly drawn division between those two activities than was earlier thought necessary. Further, the discussion of literature in the context of the history of ideas, as a key to the thought of the past (as Sir Herbert Grierson in some degree discusses it in his *Cross-Currents in English Literature of the Seventeenth Century* and as is still done in much university teaching), has given way to a tendency to treat every work as though it were contemporary and anonymous, concentrating on its 'timeless' meaning and value. This is not to say that historical criticism is dead—there are few finer examples of it than Humphrey House's *The Dickens World*, which illuminates Dickens's novels by placing them in the context of the social history of their time—or that English scholarship has not continued to grow to sometimes unwieldy proportions; but it does mean that evaluative criticism, scrutinizing individual works of literary art and carefully assessing their literary worth, has increasingly become a separate discipline from literary scholarship and literary history.

The forces that precipitated the anti-romantic revolution in poetry also lie behind one of the principal movements in modern criticism. T. E. Hulme, in his essay on 'Romanticism and Classicism' (written in 1913 but not published until 1924) wrote:

> I object even to the best of the romantics. I object still more to the receptive attitude. I object to the sloppiness which doesn't consider that a poem is a poem unless it is moaning or whining about something or other. . . . The thing has got so bad now that a poem which is all dry and hard, a properly classical poem, would not be considered poetry at all. How many people now can lay their hands on their hearts and say they like either Horace or Pope? They feel a kind of chill when they read them.
>
> The dry hardness which you get in the classics is absolutely repugnant to them. Poetry that isn't damp isn't poetry at all. They cannot see that accurate description is a legitimate object of verse. Verse to them always means a bringing in of some of the emotions that are grouped round the word infinite.

Hulme went on to develop a view in which aesthetic, religious and political attitudes are carefully lined up into opposing pairs. The starting point is a position which he outlined in an article in *The New Age*, in December 1915:

> I do think that there is a certain general state of mind which has lasted from the Renaissance till now, with what

is, in reality, very little variation. . . . It is perhaps enough to say that, taking at first the form of the 'humanities', it has in its degeneracy taken the form of a belief in 'Progress' and the rest of it. It was in its way a fairly consistent system, but it is probably at the moment breaking up. . . . I feel, myself, a repugnance towards the *Weltanschauung* (as distinct from the technical part) of all philosophy since the Renaissance. In comparison with what I can vaguely call the religious attitude, it seems to be trivial.

Later in the same article he declared that it was 'the business of every honest man to clean the world of these sloppy dregs of the Renaissance'. These dregs include not only the nineteenth-century view of progress but also the romantic Rousseauistic position that 'man is by nature wonderful, of unlimited powers, and if hitherto he has not appeared so, it is because of external obstacles and fetters, which it should be the main business of social politics to remove'. Against this Hulme set his own view (which Eliot was soon to adopt also) 'the conviction that man is by nature bad or limited, and can consequently only accomplish anything of value by disciplines, ethical, heroic or political. In other words, it believes in Original Sin.' He concludes: 'We may define Romantics, then, as all those who do not believe in the Fall of Man.'

This position will be familiar to many from Eliot's criticism, for it was from Hulme that Eliot got much of his critical and general thought. We understand, too, the sources of Eliot's classicism in literature, royalism in politics, and Anglo-Catholicism in religion (to paraphrase his own famous description of his position) when we examine the pairs of opposites which Hulme lines up. For Hulme, there is classicism (good) and romanticism (bad), abstract or geometrical art (good) and naturalistic art (bad), the religious attitude (good) and humanism (bad), belief in original sin (good) and confidence in man (bad), hard, clear precise images (good) and the emotional and soft (bad), fancy (good) and imagination (bad), the mediaeval (good), the Renaissance view (bad), discipline (good) and self-expression (bad), dictatorship or at least royalism (good) and democracy (bad). To disentangle the arguments used by Hulme to arrive at these somewhat surprising collocations would be a thankless task; suffice it to note here that these *are* the collocations, and that they explain a great deal in the attitude of T. S. Eliot.

One does not, of course, have to accept Hulme's position on history, religion and politics in order to agree with his view of classicism, and many poets and critics were influenced, directly or indirectly, by his definition and advocacy of classicism without following him on other matters. As we have seen, the Imagist movement, which has left a permanent legacy to modern poetry, was largely the result of the application of Hulme's views on the poetic image by Pound and others. The suspicion of self-expression in literary theory and practice, the emphasis on discipline, order, pattern, and the interest in abstract art (in the sense of non-naturalistic) have all left their mark on modern literature. And the optimistic humanism which had underlain so much earlier literary criticism was now effectively challenged.

The claims of the artist's medium now came to be considered more important than the claims of his personality. 'The progress of an artist is a continual self-sacrifice, a continual extinction of personality', wrote Eliot. And again: 'Honest criticism and sensitive appreciation are directed not upon the poet but upon the poetry.' 'It is not the "greatness", the intensity, of the emotions, the components, but the intensity of the artistic process, the pressure, so to speak, under which the fusion takes place, that counts.' 'There are many people who appreciate the expression of sincere emotion in verse, and there is a smaller number of people who can appreciate technical excellence. But very few know when there is expression of *significant* emotion, emotion which has its life in the poem and not in the history of the poet. The emotion of art is impersonal.' These remarks of Eliot's are not only linked to his own poetic practice (e.g. the deliberate dramatic objectivity of 'Prufrock' or 'Gerontion'); they are also part of the modern drive against the 'vatic' view of poetry, the view that the poet is a wiser man and a profounder thinker than his fellows and that in his verse he communicates his deep wisdom. As W. H. Auden wrote in 1948:

'Why do you want to write poetry?' If the young man answers: 'I have important things to say,' then he is not a poet. If he answers: 'I like hanging around words listening to what they say,' then maybe he is going to be a poet.'

This is not the Swinburnian view of language as something to be exploited by the poet for incantatory qualities and general emotional suggestiveness, though it may at first sound like that. It is really very different. Poetry for Auden is 'a game of knowledge, a bringing to consciousness, by naming them, of emotions and their hidden relationships'. Poetic language is exploratory and cognitive: it reveals the nature of reality by the way it embodies it in words; and the poet begins by brooding over the potentialities of language as an art medium. The complex patterns of meaning built up by the words the poet uses are not to be judged by the degree to which they reflect directly the poet's emotional state or arouse a vague emotional response in the reader, still less by the degree to which they 'inspire' the reader to adopt noble attitudes; their function is to give a new meaning, both more precise and more subtle, to the experience they describe. And craftsmanship always comes first—not nobility of soul, or emotional sensitivity, or an ability to think beautiful thoughts.

This frontal attack on what might be considered the Victorian commonplaces of poetic criticism was also an attempt to take criticism out of the hands of laymen and confine it to the professionals. Of course, not all modern poets and critics since Eliot's early critical essays have adopted this view; far from it; but the view has been an important one in the last thirty years or so and has produced significant changes in the practice and criticism of poetry and in the way in which literature is taught at the universities. The gap between amateur and professional which has been widening since about 1920 has become an important feature of the modern cultural scene. Auden once pointed out that if we want to see what the majority of ordinary people consider poetry to be, we have only to look at the 'In memoriam' columns of newspapers, where crudely versified platitudes about life and death and immortality seem regularly to comfort thousands. Tennyson would no doubt have objected to such verses because of their crude versification and the platitudinousness of their thought, but neither he nor his readers would have quarrelled with the general position on the nature and function of poetry which they implied—they would only have asked for more melodious versification and more arresting sentiments. The modern view that Tennyson was essentially a verse craftsman of a high order who was forced into the prophetic role by the spirit of the age and thus did violence to his genius reflects the modern suspicion of the prophetic view of poetry. And the gap that exists today between those who appreciate the verses in newspaper 'In memoriam' columns and those who hold the kind of view represented by the quotations from Eliot or Auden given above is indicative of the cleavage that exists between the serious professional and the 'ordinary reader'. It may well be true, as some modern critics have argued, that the truly perceptive readers of great literature have been a small minority in any age; but universal literacy and the resulting mass production of certain kinds of reading matter pose very special problems in the modern world. Homer and Sophocles and Shakespeare were not esteemed and preserved through the generations because subtle literary critics had formally demonstrated their excellence, but because a people's taste almost unconsciously built them into the fabric of their culture. Modern criticism, faced with the problems posed by universal education in an industrial civilization, has tried to replace this unconscious process by careful discrimination and appraisal carried out by a tiny minority in the interests of their civilization. That is one reason why the modern critic considers his function to be central to civilization: he cannot count on any automatic process of winnowing in the present state of affairs.

The attack on literature as mere self-expression, which is implicit in so much of Hulme and Eliot, and is found in America in the criticism of Irving Babbitt and later, led to a revaluation of the place of convention in art. In his essay on 'Four Elizabethan Dramatists' (1924) Eliot cited the case of the ballet dancer as the type of the artist: 'In the ballet only that is left to the actor which is properly the actor's art. The general movements are set for him. There are only limited movements that one can make, only a limited degree of emotion that he can express. He is not called upon for his personality. . . . The advantages of convention for an actor are precisely similar to its advantages for an author. No artist produces great art by a deliberate attempt to express his personality. He expresses his personality indirectly through concentrating upon a task which is a task in the same sense as the making of an efficient engine or the turning of a jug or a table-leg.' Convention, on this view, is not deadening, as it was to the Romantics, but liberating. And stylization becomes an important artistic device. Interest in the Japanese 'Nō' play and other forms of stylized art developed at the same time as the new anti-romantic criticism developed, and it bore fruitful results in Yeats's theory of the mask and his more stylized verse plays.

Hulme's anti-romanticism and his plea for an impersonal discipline and precision in art would not in itself have been

able to provide a sufficiently rich aesthetic to achieve anything of lasting significance in the creative field. His own
thought was often confused and self-contradictory, and he is
much more important in the history of criticism as a catalyst
than as a systematic thinker in his own right. The Imagist
movement, which sprang in some degree from Hulme's theories, was too limited in scope to change the face of English
poetry; what was needed was a more complex view of poetry
which could employ Hulme's view of the poetic image in a
richer context. This was provided in large measure by the
new view of the place of intellect in poetry—a view most
adequately represented, once again, by Eliot, in his essay
on 'The Metaphysical Poets' (1921). 'Tennyson and Browning are poets, and they think; but they do not feel their
thought as immediately as the odour of a rose. A thought to
Donne was an experience; it modified his sensibility.' Eliot
went on to develop his now famous theory about 'dissociation of sensibility'. This dissociation, he maintained, developed some time in the seventeenth century, helped by the
influence of Milton and Dryden. As a result, poets were no
longer able to fuse thought and emotion in the way which
Donne did so effectively; and eighteenth- and nineteenth-
century poetry is either reflective or emotional, expressing
either thought or feeling, but rarely both fused together. If the
current of English poetry had descended in a direct line from
the metaphysical poets of the seventeenth century, he argued,
all would have been well. But as it did not, it is the modern
poet's duty to restore the unified sensibility and the fusion
of metaphysical wit with passion, to English verse. A unified
poetic sensibility confronting the complexities of modern
civilization is bound to produce a more difficult poetry than
had been written in the eighteenth or nineteenth centuries.
'The poet must become more and more comprehensive, more
allusive, more direct, in order to force, to dislocate if necessary, language into meaning.' This argument is linked also

to the modern view that it is the duty of the poet to re-charge with meaning the exhausted English poetic vocabulary. The Romantic-Victorian tradition had eventually worn out and thinned down the English poetic language so that meaning and suggestion became blunted and over-generalized. Words had to be bullied, twisted, forcibly shaped into powerful new instruments. Laforgue and Corbière had done this for French poetry, Eliot claimed, as the English metaphysicals had done it for an earlier phase of English poetry. And other critics soon arose to point out that Gerard Manley Hopkins had done exactly this: by his idiosyncratic handling of language, his placing of old words in startling new contexts, his powerful new rhythms and verbal patterns, he reinvigorated the English poetic tongue. Obscurity at first reading is perfectly acceptable provided that the whole meaning of the poem 'explodes' (the term is Hopkins's) once the obscurities have been cleared up. A superficial clarity may be the result of depending too heavily on shop-worn words and idioms which *appear* to have a poetic meaning but which in fact on repeated and careful reading can be seen to lack all precision and individuality. The cliché and the appeal to what I. A. Richards has called 'the stock response' have been especially fought against by modern criticism.

The result of all this was a new view of the English poetic tradition, with Donne more important than Spenser and Hopkins than Tennyson. Again, not everyone even among the 'professionals' accepted this view, but more and more it became the view of the serious forward-looking poets and critics. It was, as we have seen, closely bound up with the poetic revolution discussed in the section on poetry. In America, the re-writing of English literary history was undertaken with brisk over-simplification in such a book as Cleanth Brooks's *Modern Poetry and the Tradition* (1939), which exalts every poet in the 'symbolist-metaphysical' tradition and depresses those who are not. This came at the end of two decades of vigorous critical discussion, and represented a text-book formulation of the new position. Such a formulation was bound to have great influence, and it has radically affected the teaching of English at American universities. It should be noted, however, that this re-writing of English literary history is a critical and not a historical movement: none of these critics actually write literary history, but they suggest who ought to be dethroned and who elevated. The modern movement is, indeed, fundamentally anti-historical as it is anti-biographical. Works of literature are independent, individual, self-existing works of art, to be discussed, analysed, appraised as specific works of art, not as illustrations of the history of ideas or of the biography of the writer. The tendency is to discuss poems and not poets. The older 'bio-critical' approach, where the author's life and his works were treated as mutually illuminating, was largely abandoned. And thus in addition to the ever-widening gap between professional and layman there developed a gap between scholar and critic, warfare between whom has been one of the features of the modern literary scene.

2

The Hulme-Eliot tradition in criticism has not been directly concerned with the fundamental aesthetic question of the value of literature; it has concentrated rather on meticulous descriptive analysis of individual works of literary art in order to demonstrate how the true literary craftsman operates. But another current in modern criticism has been more immediately concerned with the question of value. The claims of history and of science had been steadily establishing themselves throughout the nineteenth century. Early in that century Thomas Love Peacock had declared that 'poetry was the mental rattle that awakened the attention of intellect in the infancy of civil society; but for the maturity of mind to make a serious business of the playthings of childhood, is as absurd as for a grown man to rub his gums with coral, and cry to be charmed asleep by the jingle of silver bells'. This had stimulated Shelley's Platonic *Defence of Poetry*, and—more significantly from the modern point of view—it was this sort of attitude which led Matthew Arnold in 1879 to distingush poetry from historical and scientific discourse. 'Our religion has materialized itself in the fact, in the supposed fact; it has attached its emotion to the fact, and now the fact is failing it. But for poetry the idea is everything; the rest is a world of illusion, of divine illusion. Poetry attaches its emotion to the idea; the idea *is* the fact.' In *Science and Poetry*, published in 1926, I. A. Richards quoted Peacock to illustrate a point of view which he felt was widespread and required refuting, and quoted Arnold in order to illustrate the lines on which the refutation could best be conducted. Poetry, Richards argued, does not deal with historical or scientific fact; it deals with 'pseudo-statements' and 'a pseudo-statement is "true" if it suits and serves some attitude or links together attitudes which on other grounds are desirable. This kind of truth is so opposed to scientific truth that it is a pity to use so similar a word, but at present it is difficult to avoid the malpractice'.

Richards' view of the nature and value of poetry had been more fully developed in his *Principles of Literary Criticism* (1924), in which he first constructed a *general* theory of value and then showed how poetry was valuable in the light of that theory. His general theory could be called a psychological utilitarianism. 'Anything is valuable that satisfies an appetency', and therefore the most valuable state for a human being to be in is that which involves the satisfaction of the greatest number of appetencies consistent with the least number of frustrations of other appetencies. A subtly balanced organization of impulses becomes the ideal; anything which helps to achieve such an organization is thus of value. Poetry arises out of such a balanced state in the poet, and its function is to communicate that state to the reader. A successful poem indicated not that 'God's in his heaven, all's right with the world', but that 'all's well with the nervous system'.

This is, of course, a gross over-simplification of Richards' complex and ingenious argument, but it does at least make clear that Richards' concern in this early phase of his critical career was to demonstrate the value of poetry by showing how it arose from and communicated a state of psychological health, a finely balanced organization of the nervous system, which was a basic human value. (It should be noted that Richards' psychological humanism embraces ethics, too, for what is good is what produces value, and a concept of value is arrived at through the harmonizing of functions within the organism.) But if a poem is valuable as communicating the poet's valuable inner organization, how does that communication take place? In order to answer this question, Richards had to investigate the whole problem of meaning. In fact he had cleared the ground on this question before writing his *Principles of Literary Criticism*, in the pioneer study of semantics he wrote together with C. K. Ogden—*The Meaning of Meaning*, published in 1923. Here the authors drew an important distinction between the way in which words are employed in scientific and other factual writing and the way in which the poet uses them. 'A poem . . . has no concern with limited and directed reference. *It tells us, or should tell us, nothing.* It has a different, though an equally important and far more vital function—to use an evocative term in connection with an evocative matter. What it does, or should do, is to induce a fitting attitude to experience.' Poetry thus differs from science both in its objective—to perpetuate and communicate a valuable state of psychological adjustment—and in the kind of meaning it attributes to words, which is 'emotive' rather than 'scientific' or 'referential'. The investigation of the problem of meaning and communication had in turn directed Richards to the study of perception in order to explain the initial processes in reading and to discuss the nature of 'signs' and the other elements involved in communication. Semantics has become an increasingly important aspect of modern criticism ever since.

The careful study of the different kinds of meaning involved in different ways of handling language led inevitably to a close examination of the whole problem of reading (a problem which had continued to fascinate Richards in his later work). Many—perhaps most—people misunderstand the nature and value of poetry, and indeed of imaginative literature in general, because they read it as something else. Mere literacy is not enough; by itself it can do more harm than good. More and more critics came to insist that only the properly qualified reader can read a poem with true understanding and appreciation. The study of what Richards called 'emotive' meaning (though Richards' theory of emotive meaning has been criticized by some later semanticists) involves a much closer and more sensitive reading of literary texts than had generally been thought necessary. Richards himself illustrated some of the ways of tackling the problem of full and sensitive reading of poems in his influential *Practical Criticism* (1929). The Hulme-Eliot critical tradition, with its insistence on the importance of following the details of the artist's craftsmanship in meticulous detail, had encouraged rigorous analytic criticism. And now, from a quite different direction, came a further impetus to the same kind of analytic rigour. It is therefore not surprising that modern criticism should be characterized by the subtlest analytic procedures and that the more relaxed and discursive discourse of much nineteenth- and early twentieth-century criticism, with its large use of generalizations, should have been bitterly fought against by the liveliest critics of the present age.

Psychology has come into modern criticism in other ways

besides the psychological utilitarianism of Richards's *Principles* and the theories of perception that lay behind the study of semantics. Freudian theories gave a new impetus to the kind of criticism which uses psychology in order to investigate the creative process either in general or in partitular authors. This kind of investigation (as in Herbert Read's *Wordsworth*, for example) is not in the main track of modern criticism, which on the whole is anti-biographical. Nevertheless a great deal of psychologizing has gone on among writers of biographies as well as among those interested in such questions as the 'maladjustment' or the 'alienation' of the artist. In so far as this kind of use of psychology is criticism, it is genetic and not evaluative criticism; that is, it does not attempt to assess the value of individual literary works *as* literary works but tries rather to show either how the artist in general tends to proceed, or, more usefully, how this particular artist came to write in this particular way. Genetic criticism, both psychological and sociological, has been a significant though not a central mode of modern critical thinking. Explanation of origins in terms of psychological or sociological causation has continued to attract a number of interesting minds. In the Left-wing 1930s, the sociological and the economic kind of causal explanation often came together in a rather vague Marxist way, but England produced no permanently valuable Marxist criticism. Even Christopher Cauldwell's *Illusion and Reality*, which created such a stir when it first appeared in 1937, is immature and fragmentary, and it is now more often regarded as a historical phenomenon than as an illuminating work of genetic criticism.

Psychology has come into modern criticism in a third way —the study of myth and symbol. Here Jung rather than Freud is often the influence, direct or indirect. Maud Bodkin's *Archetypal Patterns in Poetry* (1934) proved a popular and influental work, while the series of studies published by G. Wilson Knight, beginning with *The Wheel of Fire* in 1930, has popularized a view of Shakespeare's plays which regards each play 'as a visionary unit bound to obey none but its own self-imposed laws' and sees the most significant feature of a work of imaginative literature in the pattern of meaning that is woven by the implications of image and symbol as they recur with varying degrees of explicitness throughout the total poem or play. Anthropology has been pressed into service by some critics in dealing with the whole question of archetypal patterns and the relation of literature to myth and ritual, Interest in myth has gone further in America than it has in England, but the interest has become fairly widespread even on this side of the Atlantic. The mythopoeic faculty of a poet like Yeats and the very different mythological imagination of Dylan Thomas have encouraged this interest. And Eliot's use of Jessie Weston's *From Ritual to Romance* and Frazer's *Golden Bough* in his *Waste Land* showed that the anti-romantic revolution had its own interest in myth and in anthropology.

3

Literary criticism can be concerned with any of a number of things. It can take up the philosophical question of the nature and value of literature; it can be normative in intention, concerned with assessing value and discriminating between the good and the bad; it can be descriptive or interpretative in a great variety of ways; it can be appreciative, seeking to communicate the critic's enjoyment of the work under discussion; it can be genetic, seeking to explain the origins and growth of a literary work in psychological or other terms. Some of the subtlest modern criticism is descriptive and interpretative; the most popular kinds are (for different reasons) the appreciative and the genetic, the most single-minded and dedicated is the normative. Arnold, seeing poetry about to replace fundamentalist religion in British civilization, insisted that 'the best poetry is what we want; the best poetry will be found to have a power of forming, sustaining, and delighting us, as nothing else can'. F. R. Leavis, also seeing imaginative literature as central to a culture, echoed Arnold's plea for *the best* and devoted himself to the task of critical discrimination. In his periodical *Scrutiny*, which ceased publication in December 1953 after a life of twenty-two years, Dr Leavis and his disciples waged a fierce campaign for critical standards, by both precept and example. *Scrutiny* was committed to a critical policy of unrelaxed vigilance, of a ruthless sifting of the little wheat of good and serious literature from the abundant chaff of triviality, shoddiness, pretentiousness, fashionableness, vulgarity and academicism. Its aim was partly to revalue the English literary tradition, demonstrating by close criticism the qualities of the relatively few writers considered to have real worth and importance, and partly to expose the laxity of modern criticism, both academic and journalistic, by exhibiting its shallowness and confusions. *Scrutiny* was also concerned with the cultural scene in general and its relation to the quality of contemporary art and criticism. But its great and dominating concern was with standards. 'The general dissolution of standards is a commonplace', the first editorial announced. 'Those who are aware of the situation will be concerned to cultivate awareness and will be actively concerned for standards.' Such concern could be demonstrated as much by exposing the bad as by demonstrating the good.

In a series of brilliant essays on English poetry and fiction, most of which later appeared in his *Revaluation, The Great Tradition*, and other books, Dr Leavis developed his own revaluation of the English literary tradition. So far as poetry was concerned, that was in general agreement with the views precipitated by the anti-romantic revolution discussed in the section on poetry; in fiction, with George Eliot and D. H. Lawrence emerging as heroes of the very highest stature, the

Leavis position tended to be more original. Dr Leavis opposed *a priori* theorizing about literature; criticism for him was a practical activity and properly consisted in the careful demonstration of the qualities of a work by a subtle blend of quotation, running commentary, and devices for communicating admiration or contempt. He had learned from Eliot's earlier critical essays and from the early Richards; but his tone and his sense of dedication were his own.

In general it might be said (though Dr Leavis would object to such a generalization) that for *Scrutiny* and its editor a great work of literature was one in which a genuine moral vision of experience was communicated through a fully particularized, fully realized imaginative rendering of life. Every detail in a novel had to be freshly imagined and had to spring from the true depths of the writer's moral being; a writer must be truly 'inward' with his subject and his work must reflect that inwardness. At bottom, Dr Leavis's criticism has always been moral, and he has consistently demonstrated a puritanical hatred of mere entertainment in literature. Further, for him the good was the enemy of the best: anything less than a fully realized work of art, reflecting the mature interests of the writer as an adult living responsibly in his own time, was a betrayal—or at least it was a betrayal of the critic's function to accept anything less. The great enemy was not only the various kinds of popular vulgarization that the modern world encouraged; it was also the genteel academic tradition, the urbane cultivation of letters by gentlemanly antiquaries for whom books were agreeable companions rather than explorers into experience. The dilettante, who made a virtue of his triviality of mind, the academic, who believed that all books written in the past were equally worth study, and the merely witty, who enjoyed (say) Aldous Huxley's early novels, were scourged equally. Literature was important; criticism was a serious and difficult activity; indulgence to the enemy was treason against civilization.

For Dr Leavis, then, the proper exercise of the critic's function was the most important thing in civilization. In practice, this often meant spending an enormous amount of time trying to see that people did not praise new work that was second-rate; the exposure of 'modishness' and fashionable literary cliques was part of the true critic's prime duty. The result of all this has been some brilliant criticism and a great deal of unnecessary polemic. In discussing works he admires, Dr Leavis is at his very best; in denouncing kinds of literary entertainment for not being what they never set out to be he is at his most tedious. He is often shrill and very often repetitive. But he is a prophet and a reformer, and that is the price that prophets and reformers must pay. Some of his younger disciples, who have learned his tone but have not his original insights, and apply his formulas with a mechanical regularity that is most wearisome, are sometimes wrongly taken to represent the master's method. On these occasions one feels that Dr Leavis requires to be saved from his disciples.

The neo-classicism of Hulme and Eliot and the new interest in the place of wit in poetry which it fostered; I. A. Richards's use of psychology and semantics both in his general critical theory and (more significantly) in his analytic practical criticism, and William Empson's development of Richards's ideas in his studies of ambiguity and complexity in literary expression; psychological and sociological criticism devoted to a study of sources and origins; the psychological-cum-anthropological interest in myth and symbol and in archetypal patterns; the neo-Arnoldian fight against the Philistines coupled with the Leavite rigour and insistence on standards—all this combined to produce the so-called 'New Criticism' in America. The 'New Criticism' has some brilliant practitioners—the names of Robert Penn Warren, John Crowe Ransom, Richard Blackmur, Cleanth Brooks, among others, are well known to British readers by now—though it has developed its own scholasticism, its own technical jargon (to which American criticism is much more prone than British) and its own tendency to talk as though not a great poem but the critic's subtle analysis of it represented the fine flower of civilization. It has also championed with particular insistence the view that criticism concerns itself with the analysis of individual works, not with writers as a whole or with movements or periods. What is fascinating to the British reader is to note that the American 'New Criticism' was originally born out of influences that came from England, but that, soon developing a full and healthy life of its own, it has recently come back to Britain as a purely American movement and as such is having considerable influence among a new generation.

One other point must be made about the modern critical scene: if the significant pioneer movements have been those described above, it should not be forgotten that the great bulk of run-of-the-mill criticism has flowed in more conventional channels. Dr Leavis's objection to the note of amateur chat in criticism is an objection to a deep-rooted characteristic of English critical discourse. In the literary weeklies, on the BBC's Third Programme, in many books and articles written by dons or literary journalists, urbane conversations about letters continue to be carried on with relaxed intelligence, considerable wit, and no very clear-cut critical principles. The work of Sir Maurice Bowra, combining an enormous range of literary and linguistic knowledge with a relatively superficial 'common sense' criticism, E. M. W. Tillyard's thoughtful and conscientious discussions of Shakespeare, Milton, and the English epic, C. S. Lewis's witty and erudite historical criticism in *The Allegory of Love* and elsewhere—these represent kinds of modern academic criticism which have in large measure remained unaffected by the new kind of analytic rigour, though aware of it and sometimes taking account of it. Though the names just cited may seem evidence to the contrary, it can scarcely be doubted that the older type of scholar critic represented by, say, Sir Herbert Grierson (who combined textual editing with philosophical criticism and the history of ideas) has for some time been giving way to a more specialized kind of scholarship, but this inevitable increase in specialization is in some degree offset by a new kind of intellectual liveliness among the younger academic teachers of English.

The most significant scholarly movement among men of letters in the modern period has been the growth of scientific bibliography. The pioneers here were A. W. Pollard, W. W. Greg and R. B. McKerrow, and the foundation of the Bibliographical Society in 1892 was the real starting point of the movement. Greg and McKerrow fought vigorously, in the first decade of this century, to get English scholars to adopt new standards of accuracy in bibliographical and textual matters. McKerrow's edition of Nashe was a landmark in the movement, while Greg's crushing reviews of scholars and editors who fell short of his high standard had enormous influence. Both men learned from Pollard, but went on to develop the new science of bibliography in new directions. The result of all this was a revolution in the study of Shakespeare's text and the establishment of bibliography as a specialized study involving considerable technical knowledge and a very high degree of accuracy. The new Cambridge edition of Shakespeare begun by Quiller-Couch and Dover Wilson and continued by Dover Wilson with other collaborators showed some of the results of the new bibliography: Dover Wilson, combining bibliographical knowledge with a certain imaginative boldness in reconstructing the history of a text from the moment it left the author's desk for the printing house to the appearance of the extant editions, used the new techniques with a freedom that sometimes shocked the more conservative. But by the middle of this century no serious editor of an Elizabethan, seventeenth-century or eighteenth-century text could ignore the claims of bibliography, and an apparatus for the establishment of the text of earlier authors existed more complicated and more accurate than anything that had existed before.

Side by side, then, with the Hulme-Eliot tradition in criticism there ran a new tradition in scholarship. Further, if the pioneer critical movement of our time was essentially anti-romantic, this does not mean that no significant criticism from the romantic standpoint has appeared in the present age. It is true that the terms 'classical' and 'romantic' are too loose to be useful, but if we mean by romantic criticism that which emphasises the transcendental nature of the truths communicated by great poetry or that which emphasises the element of self-expression in literature, then two at least of the important critics of our time can be called romantic—John Middleton Murry and Herbert Read. Among Read's critical essays the collection entitled *The True Voice of Feeling* reveals most clearly the romantic element in his criticism: linking together organic form, transcendentalism', 'sincerity', and 'the true voice of feeling', he postulates in these essays a kind of primal naturalness as the only true criterion of great art. Middleton Murry's numerous critical writings show him approaching the task of evaluating a writer by a process of *Einfühlung* which leads him to an intense personal identification with the writer and his work. This method has its dangers, but at its best it can project the inwardness of a writer's work with remarkable power and persuasiveness. Nothing could be further removed from the procedure favoured by the Hulme-Eliot tradition, and the fact that this method still persists is sufficient proof, if proof were needed, that whatever the anti-romantic revolution may have achieved it has not achieved the *Gleichschaltung* of English criticism.

4

In the field of history and biography, it might have been expected that the increase of specialized scholarship, which took place here as elsewhere, would have severely diminished the output of general 'literary' works designed for the intelligent layman. But this has not happened. This may be partly due to the influence of G. M. Trevelyan who, early in the century, turned deliberately against the German notion of the historian as a purely objective discoverer and recorder of facts in favour of a more imaginative and personal handling of historical material. Trevelyan fought for history as an art, and though at times it seemed that the younger professional historians were firmly committed to the opposing view that history was an exact science and that to make it popular or literary was to corrupt it, time has brought him ultimate victory. The public helped; for it is an interesting feature of British culture in the last twenty years or so that, in spite of the vulgarization and commercialization of so much of literature, in spite of the increasing gap between the ordinary reader and the expert with its attendant evils, there has been a remarkable revival of interest in biographical and historical writing among people who normally would be expected to read only light fiction and magazines. The Second World War awoke in many a new interest in the past of their country, and there was a heavy demand for works of history and biography. And the taste remained after the war was over, strengthened by Winston Churchill's own vivid history of the crisis through which the nation had just passed. Churchill's Gibbonian prose, put at the service of a highly personal and patriotic sense of the drama of history, his force and wit and his own deep implication in the story he was telling, produced a new kind of history, with a powerful appeal to a great variety of readers. But this was an exceptional case. Arthur Bryant on the Restoration period, A. L. Rowse on the Elizabethan age, C. V. Wedgwood on the seventeenth century, are historians of imagination and personality; in Rowse's case the personality appears to some to be excessive. These represent in some degree the re-popularization of history in the present age. It is worth noting, too, how many works of history have appeared in cheap series, such as Penguin Books, which have covered the history of England in eight volumes, or in the 'Teach Yourself History' library edited by Rowse. Arnold Toynbee's ambitious attempt to survey and interpret all human civilization in his *Study of History* can hardly be called a popular work—though it has been surprisingly widely read, particularly in its abbreviated one-volume form —but it is in some degree symbolic of the wide and continued interest in man's past which is characteristic of the mid-twentieth century.

If the repopularization of history has not led to a renewed interest in Macaulay, it is not because Macaulay's style is still regarded as wholly improper for a historian (as it was for so long) but rather that what is now called 'the Whig interpretation of history', of which Macaulay was a brilliant exponent, has come to be highly suspect. Like all historical over-simplifications, the Whig view of the progress of England from the 'Glorious Revolution' of 1688 to the commercial and imperial glories of Victoria's reign was bound to be challenged sooner or later; it had had a good run, and it was not surprising that it came under attack just at the time when the progress it had interpreted seemed to have come to an end. The late Victorian, looking back on English history from the Queen's Jubilee, could be pardoned for seeing the past of his country as a patterned progress leading up to and justified by the present moment. This was less easy and less justifiable in the confused and unhappy period between the two world wars, particularly the depression years of the early 1930's, when Professor Butterfield's influential little book, *The Whig Interpretation of History*, first appeared. But it was not only the decline of Britain as a world power that made the revaluation of the Whig tradition inevitable; there was also a religious influence at work, often taking the form of a re-estimate of the Anglo-Catholic tradition in English history, with an accompanying vindication of such characters as Charles II and James II. Butterfield's own view of history was strongly influenced by his Christian beliefs. In Scotland, Agnes Mure Mackenzie's series of volumes on Scottish history, written from a strongly Anglo-Catholic viewpoint, attacked the Covenanting interpretation of Scottish history (the Scottish version of the Whig tradition) and presented a picture of Scotland with the balance more heavily weighted at its mediaeval and Catholic past. A third factor in such critical revaluations has been the modern interest in tradition and continuity. This is seen, in a rather different way, in the later work of C. S. Lewis, who regards European history up to the nineteenth century as part of the history of 'Old Western Man', with no significant break at the Renaissance; the break for him has come with modern industrial and technological civilization, and for him therefore the main function of literary as of historical study is to make contact with that great tradition which for the first time since ancient classical times has been broken, with the breach widening daily.

Biography has proved even more popular than history in the present age. The sceptical wit of Lytton Strachey seemed at the time when it first appeared not only the complete answer to the Macaulay approach to the past but also to mean the permanent reservation of biographical if not also of historical studies for self-conscious and sophisticated highbrows. But the Strachey mode, while it had its imitators, lasted less long than was anticipated, though Strachey's brilliant demonstration that history was an *art* left a permanent impression. New psychological knowledge provided new ways of interpreting and making interesting figures of the past. Popular and semi-popular 'psychological' biographies have for some time been in great demand. So also, however, have more serious and scholarly biographical works. The growth of scholarship has, of course, helped; often letters are available which were not available earlier and new texts of a'l sorts have been made public. Serious modern biography has come in almost equal quantity and quality from three sides—that of the professional historian, that of the professional literary scholar or critic, and that of the free-lance writer (often female). The first has given us Miss Wedgwood's *William the Silent*, the second Lord David Cecil's two volumes on Lord Melbourne, and the third Mrs Cecil Woodham-Smith's life of Florence Nightingale, and biographies by James Pope-Hennessy. An extremely accomplished but perhaps more superficial biographer is Sir Harold Nicolson, who has devoted himself to the art over a long period of time. That biography *is* an art, and not merely a matter of grubbing up the facts or even of constructing a series of plausible psychological explanations, is a belief held in Britain today by a wide number of practitioners. One of the most obvious differences between biography and history as practised in Britain and in America is that America often produces the most painstaking scholars and the most thorough and exhaustive accounts of the relevant facts, while the English writer (often making use of American research) is more concerned to produce a well-composed and attractively written work. The best modern English biographers, however (like the four cited above), are both original scholars and competent literary artists.

5

If history and biography have become in some degree popular arts without losing their scholarly responsibility, the same cannot be said for philosophy, where the professional has now become almost if not wholly unintelligible to the

ordinary public. The late Victorian tradition of ethical idealism conveyed in sometimes difficult but never really obscure
prose has given way among serious philosophers to a technical interest in logic and semantics, in the limitations and
possibilities of expression in language and the kinds of meaning which may be involved in the word 'truth'. Though logical positivism is not, in the middle of the twentieth century,
the great challenging force it was in the 1930s, it still represents, if only symbolically, the kind of interest and the kind
of inquiry pursued by modern philosophers. The reduction of
ethics to a highly technical argument on the way in which
words are and can be used has done an enormous amount to
clear the air of philosophic fog; but the lay reader of philosophy has always been rather fond of philosophical fog and is
unlikely to read with any great interest the last work on
symbolic logic. Much recent philosophy has been concerned
not only with logic but with methodology, with ways of
establishing techniques for discussing reality; the layman
(where he is interested in philosophy at all) is waiting for the
picture of reality which the use of the technique, once established, will ultimately provide. Meanwhile, the works of
many philosophers are closer to mathematics than to literature. For a picture of reality the modern reader turns not to
the philosopher but to the scientist.

That the modern scientist should be able to write books of
some literary merit which appeal to the non-scientific reader
is at first sight a particularly puzzling paradox; for has not
modern science since Einstein become steadily more difficult, more specialized, more for highly trained experts, and
less capable of discussion in any literery way? The account
of the universe given by the modern physicist is much more
complicated than that provided by the Newtonian tradition,
and even in the matter of television and radio, those (like the
present writer) who thirty years ago could build their own
wireless set from a blue-print supplied by a magazine have

now been left far behind by the development of electronics and other mysteries and are only too glad to leave everything to the experts. Yet there has been a tradition in England that the scientist should periodically report to the people on the kind of universe his researches have led him to picture. Eddington and Jeans made such reports in the 1920s and 1930s in books that were widely read, and in the '50s Fred Hoyle has become the popular expounder of the view of the cosmos suggested by modern scientific knowledge. And the Penguin *Science News*, begun after the Second World War, continues to appear regularly and to be read by a very wide public. The problem of putting the complexities of modern scientific thought into language intelligible to the layman, even the unusually intelligent layman, is very difficult indeed, and if the results are not literature in the full sense they do at least reveal a skilful handling of words.

CHAPTER V

DRAMA

I

THE present century has seen some determined efforts to restore the drama to literature. This is not to say that there has been a return to the 'closet drama' of the Romantic Victorian poets or that the dramatist has turned his back on the theatre; far from it. But the 'well-made' play as the neatly constructed action dealing with stereotyped emotional situations in a quasi-realistic setting presented on a stage where the appeal to the eye and the 'personality' of the actor were more important than the pattern of meaning woven by the words spoken —this sort of play, which the twentieth century inherited from the nineteenth and which is still the staple of popular theatrical entertainment, has been challenged repeatedly in different ways and from different quarters. Wilde aerated Victorian social melodrama and farce by wit, but the tradition of wit which he bequeathed to the modern comedy of manners was too tenuous, and rapidly became too involved with sentimentality, to have achieved anything comparable in literary interest or complexity to Restoration comedy. Noel Coward's plays of the 1920s show Wildean wit reduced to modish sophistication and sentimentality, often cleverly enough, but ephemeral in tone and appeal. The iconoclastic mood of the 1920s, with its problem plays and 'frank' discussions of social and moral problems with a fashionable smartness that is very different from true wit, has not worn well; further, the plays it produced were not substantially different from the old well-made theatrical entertainments. Nor did the ingenious and in their way highly artful plays of Somerset Maugham or the compassionate social fables of Galsworthy seriously threaten the established theatrical pattern: Henry Arthur Jones and Arthur Pinero had also in their time combined high comedy, brisk dialogue revealing 'character', and advanced moral views. (One recalls that Jones's play, *The Case of the Rebellious Susan* (1894), was prefaced by an admonitory letter to Mrs Grundy.) Nor again did the influence of Ibsen and of the version of Ibsenism presented to the British public by Bernard Shaw produce as big a revolution in the theatre as is sometimes believed. The significant attempts to reclaim drama for literature, while insisting that it must be truly *drama*, came from other quarters.

Before we proceed to discuss these attempts, something must be said of Shaw's position as a dramatist, even though he really belongs to the period preceding that dealt with in this volume. Shaw's study of Ibsen, *The Quintessence of Ibsenism*, which appeared in 1891, presented the Norwegian dramatist as the exponent of a reforming naturalism with the emphasis on the prose 'social plays' such as *A Doll's House* and *Ghosts* and playing down the more poetic and symbolic plays. That the significance of Ibsen was thus narrowed and Shavianised is of less importance for the English theatre than the fact that in presenting him in this way Shaw was led to an attack on the theatre of his own time not only as being cowed by the censor into fatuous conventionality but also, and more significantly, for not realizing that 'it is the drama which makes the theatre, and not the theatre the drama'. His solution was to follow what he deemed to be Ibsen's method and write didactic plays intended to shock his audience into awareness of contemporary idiocies and abuses. 'I must warn my readers that my attacks are directed against themselves, not against my stage figures.' In his desire to shock rather than to lull, to provoke rather than to amuse, Shaw put into his characters' mouths discussions in which his characteristic wit and love of paradox were given full play. He had a special gift for standing the popular view on its head, which both outraged and titillated his audience. Yet structurally and, indeed, thematically Shaw followed the lines of the old well-made play. His years as a dramatic critic had given him an intimate knowledge of all the tricks of the trade, and he used them without scruple. Shaw held that Ibsen's originality had been the introduction of naturalism and of the discussion into drama, and his own plays are naturalistic in the sense of dealing largely with contemporary situations and they are full of witty and entertaining discussions. He set himself fiercely against the romantic Victorian stereotypes of human behaviour. Yet he was thoroughly 'theatrical' and he was also, in his own way, romantic and even sentimental (as, for example, the character of Eugene Marchbanks in *Candida* fully reveals). Further, though he brought a new kind of intelligence to the drama, he did not create—or attempt to create—a new dramatic idiom or even an idiom in which the total dramatic meaning could be fully expressed. His long and detailed stage directions in which not only the actions of his characters but their states of mind, emotions, tones of voice and intentions are fully described as though in a novel, confirm what is suggested by his criticisms of Shakespeare—that Shaw had no conception of the drama as a literary art-form in which the total pattern of meaning is achieved cumulatively and completely by the language put into the mouths of the characters as they talk to and interact with each other. Detailed psychological stage directions put the burden of conveying meaning on to the actor and producer and help to perpetuate that very dominance of the drama by the theatre that Shaw began by deploring. The dramatist's independence was not to be asserted in that way.

This is not to deny Shaw's importance, but it *is* to deny his importance as a great dramatic innovator. The 'new drama' fostered by J. T. Grein's Independent Theatre and so warmly cheered on by William Archer, the Ibsenite translator of Ibsen, was not as new *as drama* as it considered itself to be. Shaw's comedy of ideas was full of life and full of fun, but the life and the fun came from the sparkle of Shaw's mind, not from a fully realized dramatic projection of a complex vision of life. Of Shaw's later plays, which alone come properly within the scope of this volume, *Back to Methusaleh*—which he regarded as his masterpiece—is pretentious and dull, showing a most undramatic desire to reduce all human life to disembodied speculation, but *Saint Joan* remains justly popular. *Saint Joan* is not a tragedy, nor was it meant to be. Shaw called it a 'chronicle play', and in fact it is mostly a comedy, the comic effect being achieved by the device of interpreting the events of Joan's life with a brisk modernity, a refusal to be awed by historical or religious formulae and a determination to interpret everything as his own common sense suggests. This is not as crude or obvious a procedure as it may seem; it does mean that the author must seize on the reality of his subject vividly and independently, and the best moments in *Saint Joan* come when Shaw is doing that. It gives the play humour and vitality and conviction. But the humour and the vitality belong to the dramatist s world only, not to the world of his characters; Shaw had no historical imagination, and his way of making history live was to make all its characters into his own contemporaries, just as his way of putting the audience into sympathy with both sides of the conflict in which Joan was caught up was to make them debate questions of religion and politics in twentieth-century terms. Towards the end of *Saint Joan*, when the comic element fades and Shaw tries to make the heroine's last moments truly moving, he falls back on standard romantic notions of his own day ('if only I could still hear the wind in the trees, the larks in the sunshine, the young lambs crying through the healthy frost') which make nonsense of Joan's character and show Shaw invoking, as Raymond Williams has not unjustly observed, 'the nature-poetics of the late Victorians and Georgians'. It might be argued that a man who believed with incorrigible optimism in a Life Force working out all things for the best, a man who could write, as Shaw did, that 'I am prepared to back human society against any idea, positive or negative, that can be brought into the field against it', was bound to be incapable of tragedy. But this does not mean that he was not a brilliant, stimulating and entertaining writer who could make most effective use of the theatre.

It was J. M. Synge, drawing on the speech and imagination of Irish country people, who first tried to restore a new kind of artistic vitality to modern English drama. 'On the stage', he wrote in 1907 in his preface to *The Playboy of the Western World*, 'one must have reality, and one must have joy; and that is why the intellectual modern drama has failed, and people have grown sick of the false joy of the musical comedy, that has been given them in place of the rich joy found only in what is superb and wild in reality. In a good play every speech should be as fully flavoured as a nut or apple, and such speeches cannot be written by anyone who works among people who have shut their lips on poetry.' Though the terms in which Synge expressed himself on this matter may seem naïvely 'folksy' to some modern readers, he had hold of the root of the matter. All great drama tends towards poetry, because in the final analysis only speech with an element of poetry in it is rich and suggestive enough to enable the interacting speeches of characters to build up, without any explanatory interventions by the author writing in his own person, a significant complex of meaning. Explaining that he got much help from listening unobserved to the talk of servant girls in an old Wicklow house, Synge went on: 'This matter, I think, is of importance, for in countries where the imagination of the people, and the language they use, is rich and living, it is possible for a writer to be rich and copious in his words, and at the same time to give the reality, which is the root of all poetry, in a comprehensive and natural form.' Synge's own plays are not always successful in achieving both the richness of language and the reality in its comprehensive and natural form, though the *Playboy* succeeds triumphantly as a comedy which is also a profound 'criticism of life', while *Riders to the Sea* is a remarkable dramatic presentation of an elegiac situation redeemed from false pathos by the elemental dignity achieved by the language, and *Deirdre of the Sorrows*, in spite of its monotony of tone, is a fruitful experiment in a new kind of stylized, almost ritualistic, tragedy.

2

The mixture of drawing-room comedy and morality play has, however, continued to provide the ordinary fare of the British theatre-goer. After Wilde and Shaw some degree of wit and some degree of serious concern with the problems of modern social life have become *de rigueur* except, of course, for pure knock-about farce. Intelligent and skilful dramatists who artfully tailor their stories to the requirements of the theatre have not been lacking, from Somerset Maugham to Terence Rattigan; the tone can vary from sardonic irony to moral concern, the technique from straightforward use of realistically set scenes proceding in chronological order to the use of 'flash-backs', single symbolic settings or even a bare stage; the formula for middlebrow theatrical entertainment remains, however, surprisingly uniform. J. B. Priestley, whose humane interpretations of English middle-class life have an attraction of their own, has been fertile in 'experimental' theatrical devices; he is an agreeable, often amusing dramatist as he is novelist, but in neither capacity is he—nor does he claim to be—a significant pioneer or a great and original creative artist. The significant new things in modern English —and Anglo-Irish—drama have come not from the novelists but from the poets. Indeed, the revival of poetic drama has proved to be one of the most remarkable chapters in twentieth-century English literary history. W. B. Yeats and T. S. Eliot are the great names here, but there are others to be mentioned too, including Auden and Isherwood and Christopher Fry.

Of Yeats's twenty-six plays, half were written between 1892 and 1914 and the other half between 1919 and 1939. The earlier plays, which do not come within the purview of this volume, are often written in that incantatory dream idiom which we find also in his early poetry but which he learned to abandon in favour of a more complex and more disciplined language. Yeats's work for the Abbey Theatre and his involvement in the Irish literary movement gave him both a knowledge of theatrical technique and a body of mythological and other ideas to work with, but he never allowed himself to be overborne either by the men of the theatre or by the claims of the national movement. He sought more and more for a kind of poetic drama in which the whole burden of meaning is carried by the spoken word; he wanted the actors to keep 'still enough to give poetical writing its full effect upon the stage' and once went so far as to suggest that he might rehearse a dramatic company in barrels 'that they might forget gesture and have their minds free to think of speech for a while'. (The barrels, he added, 'might be on castors, so that I could shove them about with a pole when the action required it'.) He grew increasingly interested in the possibilities of a highly stylized, even ritualized, drama, something in the nature of the Japanese Nō plays, by which he was influenced. Stylization of action on the stage was to provide a conventional and symbolic context for the words, which constituted the play; the theatre was important, for Yeats wanted his plays to be acted and took the greatest pains to see that they were acted in the way he intended, but it was important as providing conditions of acting that would implement the patterns of meaning created by the poet's words, not for the exploitation of actors' personalities.

In Yeats's later plays the mingling of quiet, ritualistic patterns with moments of deliberate realism, of symbolic poetic statement with colloquial speech, of the ceremonial and the personal, results in a strangely complex dramatic pattern which is often more disturbingly suggestive than fully intelligible. Sometimes we feel that the distillation of meaning has gone somewhat too far and in attempting to achieve a quintessential patterning of experience Yeats has produced a dramatic ritual strangely impressive yet based on a religion we do not know. The alternation of formal lyrics and colloquial (but carefully cadenced) prose is sometimes highly successful, as in the arresting play *The Resurrection* which opens and closes with a song to accompany the unfolding and the folding of the curtain. *Deirdre* and *On Baile's Strand*, two of the earlier plays of his Deirdre cycle, are among his finest achievements, the rhythms and images of the poetic dialogue achieving a remarkable concentration of meaning instead of the dissipation to which conventional romantic treatment of such stories is likely to lead. The last play of this cycle, and the last play Yeats wrote, *The Death of Cuchulain*, with its quietly mocking prologue and deftly controlled overtones of ballad and folk song, is a powerful and haunting piece, and the final song tremulous with meanings that grip and disturb the reader:

> *Are those things that men adore and loathe*
> *Their sole reality?*
> *What stood in the Post Office*
> *With Pearse and Connolly?*
> *What comes out of the mountain*
> *Where men first shed their blood?*
> *Who thought Cuchulain till it seemed*
> *He stood where they had stood?*

Yeats's plays are not often performed on the stage and it is therefore difficult for most critics to form a confident estimate of their theatrical success. But of their originality, their dramatic brilliance and their poetic stature there can be no doubt. And even if they have had no direct influence on subsequent English drama, the fact that Yeats, a great poet and a man of the theatre, approached drama from a wholly new perspective has encouraged others to seek their own ways of bringing the poet back to the theatre.

3

T. S. Eliot's first complete verse drama, *Murder in the Cathedral*, shows him turning to Christian ritual in order to provide significant dramatic conventions or at least in order to give significance to the dramatic conventions which he employs. Choric speech chanted by a group of characters, echoing and iteration of phrases in order to build up a mood and an atmosphere, *recitative* spoken by different characters in a carefully ordered sequence, the set prose delivered by the hero to provide a moral focus for the play—these are difficult devices to employ with conviction in modern drama, but Eliot is successful with them because the ecclesiastical setting and the liturgical context enable him to subsume them in an extended and symbolic version of a Christian church service, so that the chanting seems natural and appropriate and the hero's central speech takes its place without forcing as a sermon delivered in the cathedral. There are of course colloquial elements in the speeches of the characters—Eliot was always much concerned with the counterpointing of the colloquial and the ritualistic—but they are skilfully manipulated to convey an ebb and flow of an emotional rhythm that runs right through the play and to suggest the various kinds of conflict between the sacramental and the casual aspects of a Christian's life.

Eliot never again found so happy a method of giving meaning and appropriateness to the more poetic and 'artificial' of the devices employed in his verse dramas, nor did he again find a plot which provided so adequate an objective correlative to the ideas and emotions contained in the play. In *The Family Reunion* he deals with the problem and guilt and expiation of a man haunted by the Furies and driven at last to seek release in some unexplained quest or mission. This grave theme, Christian with Sophoclean overtones, is treated in a context of contemporary social life—one might almost say, of contemporary social triviality. The skill with which Eliot modulates the colloquial into the ritualistic and back again is remarkable; the accents of conversation mingle or alternate with more formal kinds of utterance, choric or incantatory or stylized in one way or another, and the result is to provide a whole symbolic hinterland of meaning behind this overt action of the play. Nevertheless, the attempt to deal with a religious-mythological theme in terms of the problems posed by family relationships in a modern country house is not altogether successful. Levels of meaning, instead of reinforcing and subtilizing each other, sometimes get confused, and the symbolic reality that lies behind some social gesture is often too vague to be able to take its place in the general pattern of meaning with any significance. This is true even of the hero's final departure on some unexplained expiatory mission, saying 'My address, mother, will be care of the bank in London until you hear from me'.

Eliot's attempt to write religious drama in a context of drawing room comedy was continued in *The Cocktail Party* and *The Confidential Clerk*. In both these plays the technical achievement represented by the handling of the language is of the highest order. The verse, which to the ear is fluid, beautifully balanced colloquial prose but which on careful examination is seen to have, far below, a skeleton of the most delicately modulated formal verse rhythms, is a major contribution to dramatic technique. But in *The Cocktail Party* the theme of salvation, conveyed in terms at once psychiatric and mystical in a context of pseudo-Wildean wit and deliberate social triviality, rings hollow. The attempt to make the play at once sophisticated in a brittle, knowing way, and gravely serious, is not altogether successful. The unidentified gin-drinking guest of Act I, who turns out to be the psychiatrist-priest in Act II, is no more convincing than the transmutation of the interfering gossip Julia into one of the 'guardians'. In order to turn characters in an amusing drawing-room farce into serious symbols of a religious and moral order Eliot has to switch on the ritual tone too suddenly and too crudely to allow any subtlety of counterpointed meanings to result. The conclusion of Act II, with Reilly and his two helpers speaking 'the words for those who go upon a journey' and other incantations after a 'nurse-secretary' has brought in a decanter with three glasses is acutely embarrassing to many readers and spectators. We feel we are being bullied to accept the transformation of the everyday colloquial into the solemn ritualistic. It is sometimes charged against those who criticize *The Cocktail Party* in these terms that they are really rationalizing an inherent dislike of the theme (which seems to be that the only alternative to achieving salvation by allowing yourself to be eaten alive by ants is a resigned acceptance of routine), and it is true that the theme has aroused dislike in many. But a case can be made on purely technical grounds against the mingling of the farcical and the religious in Eliot's two latest plays. Though on the superficial level they are successful comedies—and have drawn large audiences—on any deeper level they seem to be defective. The comedy is not 'comic relief'. Eliot is not interspersing serious action with lighter situations; he is trying to make the same characters who appear at one point in irresponsibly farcical situations into grave and moving symbols of human fate. Such a task is not perhaps inherently impossible, but some at least are doubtful whether it has been achieved in Eliot's later plays.

Murder in the Cathedral represents still his finest dramatic achievement.

This is not to belittle the technical brilliance of *The Cocktail Party* and *The Confidential Clerk* or to deny the skill and beauty of many moments of dialogue and many individual speeches. But it is to suggest that Eliot in his later plays achieved a popular theatrical success at the cost of trying to build the deeper meanings on a foundation of sophisticated drawing-room wit, and that the cost has proved excessive. The wit and the colloquial elements in his earlier poetry—much of which is really dramatic in tone and form—might have shown him a better way of achieving this sort of combination.

Eliot's verse plays have bred a whole school of religious verse drama, none of it, however, as interesting or original as Eliot's own. Anne Ridler's *Shadow Factory*, Norman Nicholson's *Old Man of the Mountains* and Ronald Duncan's *This Way to the Tomb* all show the influence of Eliot's dramatic verse-line, sometimes with remarkable obviousness. These plays are technically interesting but they do not break any new ground or suggest any great individual vitality. They suggest that the neo-Christian poet is looking for a style that makes contact with the Christian tradition by its ritual overtones and at the same time takes account of the twentieth-century poetic revolution by use of the colloquial and the everyday. It is doubtful if this can be achieved by imitating the later Eliot.

4

The two plays which Auden wrote alone and the three which he wrote in collaboration with Christopher Isherwood are probably now more interesting as period pieces than as important dramatic works in their own right. Yet they are of considerable intrinsic interest, and while none is wholly successful as a verse drama (or as a prose-and-verse drama)

some show an impressive and even an exciting use of dramatic devices. Auden's 'charade' *Paid on Both Sides* and his verse
plot *The Dance of Death* show a characteristic mixture of social
concern and preposterous farce, of Freud, Marx and music-
hall, and the result is sometimes amusing, sometimes puzzling and occasionally stimulating. At the time of its first performance *The Dance of Death* seemed a challenging new development, and perhaps it is difficult to recapture now the feeling of exhilaration and admiring astonishment aroused in the
1930s by Auden's engaging irresponsibilities. The introduction of an Announcer, sitting on steps in front of the stage
'like the umpire at a tennis tournament', a jazz orchestra
down stage, and characters who speak from the auditorium,
showed Auden's deliberate intention to involve (or confuse)
art with life, to make the performance if not the reading of
the play an occasion when the audience becomes involved,
as individuals and as citizens rather than as spectators of a
drama. But side by side with this attempt to break down the
objectivity of art went a stylization in verse and dancing that
had the opposite effect. There is a considerable amount of
amusing verse (in the form of parodies of popular songs and
such) in the play, and much of it will still raise a smile if not
a laugh, but on the whole the mixture of clever flippancy and
serious social concern won't do. The Announcer explains at
the beginning what the play is about. 'We present to you this
evening a picture of the decline of a class, of how its members
dream of a new life, but secretly desire the old, for there is
death inside them. We show you that death as a dancer.'
This suggests a highly ritualized treatment of a grave theme.
One has only to quote the conclusion to show how Auden
succumbs to the temptation to clown:

> A. *Some brandy quick*
> *He's sick.*

> Announcer: *He's dead.*

(Noise without)

> *Quick under the table, it's the tecs and their narks,*
> *O no, salute—it's Mr Karl Marx.*

Chorus (Singing to Mendelssohn's 'Wedding March'):

> *O Mr Marx you've gathered*
> *All the material facts*
> *You know the economic*
> *Reasons for our acts.*

(Enter Karl Marx with two young communists.)

K.M. *The instruments of production have been too much for him. He is liquidated.*

(Exeunt to a Dead March.)

It has been worth pausing at this play, trivial though it is, partly because it illustrates a strain in Auden that he was never to abandon altogether and partly because it is of some historical interest as being the first production of the Group Theatre, which went on to produce the Auden-Isherwood plays. The first of these was *The Dog Beneath the Skin*. Here again we note the strain of exuberant farce in the treatment of a fundamentally serious theme, but here the general comic spirit is better sustained and the brilliance of the fun is unquestionable. The form of the play is more a parody of musical comedy than anything else, and the parody is often so perfect that it is impossible to distinguish from the real thing —which is surely not what the authors wanted. The plot concerns the search for a missing baronet, who, when found, upsets the conventional by turning seeker himself and leading the search further. That the search is symbolic of something like the striving for the good society is clear enough; but it is the brilliant passages of comic irony or parody or sheer musical-comedy *brio* that remain in the memory—not the choric statements of more positive themes. And the action itself does not build as it moves a coherent body of positive meaning.

The Ascent of F6 and *On the Frontier* are more ambitious and more fundamentally serious. The former is a carefully organized symbolic play of considerable power, with both political and psychological implications. The hero's ascent of the mountain is never related, either implicitly or explicitly, to any single objective which it is meant to symbolize; the attempt is rather to treat the whole situation—the ascent, the hero's relation to his mother and to his brother, the kind of knowledge achieved and of salvation attained—as part of a complex myth whose meanings combine and reverberate in all sorts of ways. Sometimes, however, we feel that instead of joining forces to build up a total complex of meaning, the different elements in the play criticize or even deny each other, and when we find, as we occasionally do, the same tone of colloquial cliché in passages of urgent and serious statement as in those of ironical comment, we cannot help wondering whether the authors had the ability to create a dramatic style flexible enough to present adequately a complex mythological plot. Nevertheless, *The Ascent of F6* is the most impressive of the Auden-Isherwood plays, and it has moving and powerful moments.

On the Frontier, described as a 'melodrama', is on a simpler political theme, and for that reason it is more successful, in its limited way, than the more ambitious and complex *Ascent of F6*. It is an affirmation of human values against political power and war done through type-characters involved in a characteristic 'modern' political situation. The atmosphere is clearly that of the late 1930s. Its interest and success as a morality play are too much bound up with its period—in spite of a wider treatment of the theme of love in a simple allegorical way.

In these plays Isherwood wrote the prose and Auden the verse. The prose is brisk and witty, and at the same time uncannily 'right' in catching the tone of popular discourse of the time. The verse is the usual Auden combination of irony, farce and affirmation, done in a variety of metres with considerable virtuosity. On the whole, the plot is carried on in prose dialogue and verse is used for choric comment, interpretative interludes and the more stylized and 'expressionist' pieces of dialogue.

Stephen Spender's *Trial of a Judge* is another politico-moral verse play set in the context of the politics of the late 1930s. (The theme, that of the liberal intellectual caught between the violent extremes of left-wing and right-wing politics, is almost identical with that of Rex Warner's novel, *The Professor*.) Spender attempts none of the verbal fireworks or shifts of tone that we find in Auden. The norm of his dramatic verse is a fairly simple rhetorical rhythmic statement, moving with considerable speed and gaining its effects by extension rather than depth. *Trial of a Judge* has considerable surface liveliness and emotional appeal; it makes its point about the untenable position of the liberal believer in impartial truth and justice during a period of sharp social and political conflict with force and dignity; but it remains too superficial a treatment of its theme to have claims for consideration as a poetic drama of any permanent value.

5

It was not only the poets who attempted to restore drama to literature. As early as 1904 the establishment of the Court Theatre to present serious plays in a series of short runs was a sign that reform was in the air. And though the Court Theatre produced mostly Shaw's plays, it also provided an opportunity for Harley Granville-Barker who acted and produced Shakespeare there and produced also Shaw, Galsworthy, some Greek drama, and plays by Granville-Barker himself. Actor, producer, critic and playwright, Granville-Barker seemed destined to bring a new glory to the English stage, but his own plays, of which so much was expected, disappointed.

They were moral and psychological explorations of modern problems, not fully realized works of the literary and dramatic imagination, and they made it clear (or at least it is clear in retrospect) that a true dramatic revival demanded more than a combination of thoughtfulness, psychological realism, and adroit stagecraft. But the repertory movement which sprang up in Britain as a result of a growing interest in the drama of ideas and in the 'new theatre' did succeed in keeping lively audiences available for original plays which would have little chance on the West End stage. The trouble is that—Shaw apart—there were only 'literary' plays (in the bad sense), ephemeral problem plays and journalistic stunts to put on at the repertory theatres before the poets started moving in. It was something, however, to have the idea of a serious drama in the air.

Ireland, of course, proved to be the salvation of English drama. It sent us Shaw and Synge and Yeats. It also sent Sean O'Casey, the one important prose dramatist of the Irish revival (for Shaw had nothing to do with the Irish revival) who transcended the local Irish situation as the Irish national playwrights from Lady Gregory to Lennox Robinson cannot be said to have done. O'Casey used Irish material like the others, but he used it, in his best plays, with a sense of tragic irony, a violent species of humour and a rich and highly flavoured language that gave his work real dramatic stature. His second play, *Juno and the Paycock*, remains his best, for here he successfully welds tragic melodrama (based in part on the real violence of the civil war), humour of character and irony of circumstance into an original and impressive unity. *The Plough and the Stars* might be called a symbolic documentary play, tragic in tone, presenting the pattern of Ireland's tragedy. In his later plays O'Casey's own passion and prejudices come between him and the dramatic work he is trying to create, and when in addition he turns to expressionist techniques suggested by German dramatists and by the

American Eugene O'Neill the result is generally unsuccessful. Further, the verbal vitality and the vivid humour which enabled him in his earlier plays to give tragic stature to the realities of Dublin slum life without denying its comic elements, and the dramatic tact which enabled him to subsume the Irish 'troubles' into a pattern of tragic violence, failed him, or at least diminished, in his later plays. The tricks of a conventionally 'colourful' language combine with inorganically used dramatic devices to lower the vitality of his work. His dramatic art functioned best when he dealt with the life he knew best, and his early plays of Dublin working-class life remain powerful and impressive, the best non-poetic English drama of the 1920s.

6

With Christopher Fry, drama looks to poetry again, but to a very different kind of poetry from that of either Yeats or Eliot. His airy, exuberant, copious and fanciful language, which show the author so obviously enjoying his own virtuosity, is something quite new in modern English drama, and the enthusiasm with which it has been received indicates that the time was ripe for the introduction of this kind of poetic ebullience into the theatre. Fry began by writing 'religious festival plays' which show the influence of Eliot and, later, of Charles Williams. But it was his comedies *A Phoenix too Frequent* and *The Lady's Not for Burning* that first made his reputation, and justly so, for they show an exciting verbal inventiveness and a merriness of imagination that are his most engaging characteristics. He remains, in a sense, a religious dramatist, full of a sense of the mysteries of life, with a compassionate and wondering observation of his fellow-men. *A Phoenix too Frequent* is about an Ephesian matron who is determined to starve herself on her husband's tomb but who changes her mind under the influence of the handsome young corporal of the guard (the plot is from Petronius). It is a theme exactly suited to Fry's wondering humour and his tremendous verbal high spirits, and so also is the theme of *The Lady's Not for Burning* which is reminiscent of the plot (but only the plot) of Synge's *Playboy*. *Venus Observed*, which is about an ageing duke wondering which of his former mistresses to marry and then falling in love with a young girl only to have her taken from him by his son, goes somewhat deeper into the meaning and motives of the characters (who are merely vehicles for the author's verbal fireworks and the exchange of whirling ideas in the earlier plays) but has the same irrepressible vitality. *The Dark is Light Enough* is an altogether more serious play, dealing with a situation not unlike that in Auden and Isherwood's *On the Frontier* though wholly different in tone. The language is a little more disciplined than in his early comedies, but it still gives the impression of inspired impromptu, with its breathless speed, provocative images, and humorous undertones.

All this suggests that Christopher Fry is a poetic dramatist of originality and daring who has restored to English drama something of the verbal sprightliness and the relish of the exploratory and suggestive use of language that we get in the Elizabethans. But one has serious reservations. Fry's poetic imagery is too indiscriminate, too loose, too much the same in different dramatic circumstances, to be the full and profound expression of completely realized drama. When we read:

> *Surely she knows*
> *If she is true to herself, the moon is nothing*
> *But a circumambulating aphrodisiac*
> *Divinely subsidised to provoke the world*
> *Into a rising birthrate—a veneer*
> *Of sheerest Venus on the planks of Time,*

or:

> *This evening is a ridiculous wisp of down*
> *Blowing in the air as disconsolately as dust,*

or:

> *For me*
> *The world is all with Charon, all, all*
> *Even the metal and the plume of the rose garden*
> *And the forest where the sea fumes overhead*
> *In vegetable tides, and particularly*
> *The entrance to the warm baths in Arcite Street*
> *Where we first met;—all!—the sun itself*
> *Trails an evening hand in the sultry river*
> *Far away down by Acheron. I am lonely,*
> *Virilius. Where is the punctual eye*
> *And where is the cautious voice which made*
> *Balance-sheets sound like Homer and Homer sound*
> *Like balance sheets?*

or:

> *The world is an arrow*
> *Or larksong, shot from the earth's bow, and falling*
> *In a stillborn sunrise—*

we can see something of the inorganic nature of his poetic matter. It is lively and eloquent and often arresting; but it might belong anywhere. One feels that a brilliant but lax imagination, going hand in hand with a sense of the humour and wonder of man and nature, is letting itself go. The same lack of emotional particularization and full realization is found in the development of his plots, which flow negligently on until he remembers to wind them up. It is all very attractive, and sometimes a deeper note is touched, half mystery, half wistfulness, which appeals in another way. But it is not mature art, and we can only wonder whether it will develop until it becomes so.

BIBLIOGRAPHY

BIBLIOGRAPHY

A BIBLIOGRAPHY of the literature of one's own time is bound to be incomplete, and it is also bound to be in some degree personal. To pick out the writers worth recording before time has done its winnowing work is difficult for any single individual, and there are bound to be both inclusions and omissions in the following lists which some readers will think unjustified. Some of the bibliographies are complete, some virtually complete, some highly selective, depending on the importance, nature and variety of an individual author's work. It is only the part of honesty to confess that a compiler of a list of this kind is compelled to rely in some instances on the opinions of other people, for who can be expected to have read every one of the multifarious books that have streamed from the Press during the last fifty years? This must be my apology for any apparent arbitrariness as well as for any genuine errors that may be discovered in the following pages.

On the whole, where I have dealt with a writer in the introductory survey I have not added any comments to the bibliography. Such comments as I have added to individual bibliographies are meant as sign-posts merely. In some cases, —for example, with a routine professional novelist more characteristic of his time than important as an individual example of creative genius—I may have made no comment. Sometimes the titles of the books themselves are sufficient indication of the nature of their contents.

The period covered here is, roughly, that between 1914 and the mid-1950s. While in general I have not included writers whose major works were written and whose reputations were established before the first war, I have occasionally done so if the writer remained active well into my period or if he represented a movement which belongs significantly to the present age. Wells, Shaw, Granville-Barker are writers that some may have expected to see represented here, but as full bibliographies are given in the previous volume in this series (*The Victorians and After*) I have not included them, though I have included Galsworthy, not only because he was still active in the 1920s and 1930s but also because the kind of thing he was doing was still something to be argued about. Wells's scientific humanism was essentially late Victorian, and so too was Shaw's iconoclastic wit, but Galsworthy's humane worrying about society remained important for a decade at least after the first war. I have included Barrie because he was left out of the previous volume, though he, too, really belongs to the earlier period. Chesterton and Belloc I finally decided not to include, both because they are in the earlier volume and because they represent a kind of literature that really belongs to the world before the first war. Readers may notice other inconsistencies, but I think I can safely say that none of the significant writers, whose careers span the late Victorian and the modern period, is omitted unless he is fully treated in *The Victorians and After*.

It will be noted that the earliest of the poets I have included is Yeats, and that I have set him apart in a class by himself. Yeats spans several periods, and his development is almost a history of modern poetry. And, of course, he is the greatest of the modern poets. He thus occupies a special place in the bibliography, appearing in a category of his own at the head of the poets.

The main problem in selection has been to decide which of the reasonably competent middlebrow entertainers among modern novelists to include. One must include some, otherwise the picture of modern fiction that is presented would be distorted: to include all, however, would be to leave room for little else. I am afraid I have simply been arbitrary about this and included a selection based on the accidents of my own knowledge and preferences.

There is no authoritative survey of the literature of the period—indeed, how could there be?—but G. S. Fraser's *The Modern Writer and His World* (1953) may be found helpful as an introduction to the subject. The nearest approach to a history of modern English literature is the American work, *Forces in Modern British Literature 1885-1946*, by William York Tindall (New York, 1947), a witty and provocative account. Indeed, the Americans have been altogether bolder than we in attempting to come to terms with our modern literature. Another most useful American work, though going only as far as 1935, is *Contemporary British Literature, a Critical Survey and 232 Author-Bibliographies*, by Fred B. Millett, 3rd edition, New York, 1935. Better known in this country is Edmund Wilson's *Axel's Castle* (1931). In poetry, the two Faber anthologies (*The Faber Book of Modern Verse*, 1936; *The Faber Book of Twentieth-Century Verse*) are most useful collections, as are the anthologies in the Penguin series. Among the numerous American anthologies of modern English poetry, Louis Untermeyer's *Modern British Poetry* (mid-century edition, New York, 1950) has biographical and critical notes; Kenneth Rexroth's *The New British Poets* (Norfolk, Connecticut) is an excellent selection from those poets who became known during or soon after the Second World War, and it has a most stimulating and well-informed introduction; Oscar Williams's *Little Treasury of Modern Poetry* (British and American) (1946, 1950) has a generous selection; and *Modern Poetry* (British and American), edited by Kimon Friar and John Malcolm Brinnin (New York, 1951), is an admirable anthology containing some brilliant critical notes and essays.

Of critical studies on modern English poetry, one of the most germinal is F. R. Leavis's *New Bearings in English Poetry*, 1932. A clear and concise survey is *The Trend of Modern Poetry*, by Geoffrey Bullough (1933, 1949). The present writer's *Poetry and the Modern World* (1940) is an account and interpretation of English poetry from the Georgians to Auden. Among American works, *Modern Poetry and the Tradition*, by Cleanth Brooks (1939) surveys the field from the point of view of the 'new criticism' and William Van O'Connor's *Sense and Sensibility in Modern Poetry* (1948) is an even more orthodox 'new critical' account.

The most important critical work on the novel has been done in studies of individual novelists, which are listed under the appropriate names. H. E. Bates's *The Modern Short Story* (1941) is a useful discussion. Bonamy Dobrée's *Modern Prose Style* is an important discussion of its subject. A penetrating and provocative study of modern drama is Raymond Williams's *Drama from Ibsen to Eliot* (1952). Other critical works are noted in individual bibliographies.

Bibliographies of the following will be found in the previous volume The Victorians and After.

POETRY

(A) YEATS

YEATS, William Butler (1865-1939)

POETRY:

Mosada, A Dramatic Poem, 1886.
The Wanderings of Oisin and Other Poems, 1889.
Poems, 1895.
The Wind Among the Reeds, 1899.
In the Seven Woods, 1903.
The Collected Works in Verse and Prose, 1908.
The Green Helmet and Other Poems, 1910.
Poems Written in Discouragement, 1913.
Responsibilities: Poems and a Play, 1914.
The Wild Swans at Coole, Other Verses and a Play in Verse, 1917.
Michael Robartes and the Dancer, 1920.
Seven Poems and a Fragment, 1922.
The Cat and the Moon and Certain Poems, 1924.
October Blast, 1927.
The Tower, 1928.
The Winding Stair, 1929.
Words for Music, Perhaps and Other Poems, 1932.
The Collected Poems of W. B. Yeats, 1933.
The Winding Stair and Other Poems, 1933.
The King of the Great Clock Tower, Commentaries and Poems, 1934.
New Poems, 1938.
Last Poems and Plays, 1940.
Collected Poems of W. B. Yeats (2nd ed., with later poems added), 1950.

PLAYS:

The Countess Kathleen and Various Legends and Lyrics, 1891.
The Land of Heart's Desire, 1894.
The Shadowy Waters, 1900.
Where There is Nothing (supplement to The United Irishman, vol. VIII), 1902.
The Hour-Glass, a Morality, 1903.
The Hour-Glass, Cathleen ni Houlihan, The Pot of Broth, 1904.
The King's Threshold, a Play in Verse, 1904.
The King's Threshold and On Baile's Strand, 1904.
Deirdre, 1907.
The Golden Helmet, 1908.
The Unicorn from the Stars and Other Plays (with Lady Gregory), 1908.

Plays for an Irish Theatre, 1911.
Two Plays for Dancers, 1919.
Four Plays for Dancers, 1921.
The Player Queen, 1922.
Plays in Prose and Verse (with Lady Gregory), 1922.
Plays and Controversies, 1923.
Wheels and Butterflies, 1934.
The Words Upon the Window Pane . . . with Notes upon the Play and
    its Subject, 1934.
The Collected Plays of W. B. Yeats, 1934.
The King of the Great Clock Tower, 1934.
A Full Moon in March, 1935.
The Herne's Egg, 1938.
Last Poems and Plays, 1940.
Collected Plays of W. B. Yeats (2nd ed., with later plays added), 1952.

ESSAYS, SHORT STORIES AND AUTOBIOGRAPHICAL
    WRITINGS:
Fairy and Folk Tales of the Irish Peasantry, 1888.
Representative Irish Tales, 1890.
John Sherman and Dhoya (by Ganconagh, *pseud.*), 1891.
Irish Fairy Tales, 1892.
The Celtic Twilight, 1893.
The Secret Rose, 1897.
The Tables of the Law, The Adoration of the Magi, 1897.
Literary Ideals in Ireland (with others), 1899.
Ideas of Good and Evil, 1903.
Stories of Red Hanrahan, 1904.
Discoveries, 1907.
Poetry and Ireland (with Lionel Johnson), 1908.
Synge and the Ireland of His Time, 1911.
The Cutting of an Agate, 1912.
Reveries Over Childhood and Youth, 1915.
Per Amica Silentia Lunae, 1918.
Four Years, 1921.
The Trembling of the Veil, 1922.
Essays, 1924.
The Bounty of Sweden, a Meditation, and a Lecture delivered before the
    Royal Swedish Academy, 1925.
A Vision, an Explanation of Life founded upon the Writings of Giraldus
    and upon Certain Doctrines attributed to Kusta ben Luka, 1925.
Autobiographies, 1926.
Estrangement, being some Fifty Thoughts from a Diary kept in 1909,
    1926.
The Death of Synge and Other Passages from an Old Diary, 1928.
A Packet for Ezra Pound, 1929.

St Patrick's Breastplate, 1929.
Stories of Michael Robartes and his Friends, 1931.
Letters to the New Island, 1934.
Dramatis Personae, 1896-1902, Estrangement, The Bounty of Sweden, 1936.
A Vision (new ed.), 1937.
Essays, 1931-1936, 1937.
The Autobiography of W. B. Yeats (the various autobiographical writings in a single volume), 1938 (New York), 1955 (London).
On the Boiler, 1939.
If I were Four and Twenty, 1940.
Pages from a Diary Written in 1930, 1945.

LETTERS:

Letters on Poetry from W. B. Yeats to Dorothy Wellesley, 1940.
Letters to Miss Florence Farr from G. B. Shaw and W. B. Yeats, 1941.
The Letters of W. B. Yeats, ed. Allan Wade, 1954.

BOOKS EDITED OR INTRODUCED:

The Works of William Blake (with Edwin Ellis), 1893.
The Poems of William Blake, 1893.
A Book of Irish Verse Selected from Modern Writers, 1895.
A Book of Images, by W. T. Horton (Introduction by Yeats), 1898.
Beltaine (the organ of the Irish Literary Theatre). An occasional publication edited by, and with articles by, Yeats. Three numbers were published in 1899 and 1900, after which the name was changed to Samhain.
Poems of Spenser (Selected with Introduction by Yeats), 1906.
The Arrow (ed. by Yeats and with articles by him), 1906-1907.
Certain Nō Plays of Japan (Introduction by Yeats), 1916.
Axel (Preface by Yeats), 1925.
Bishop Berkeley: His Life, Writings and Philosophy (Introduction by Yeats), 1931.
An Indian Monk, His Life and Adventures (Introduction by Yeats), 1932.
The Holy Mountain (Introduction by Yeats), 1934.
Aphorisms of Yoga (Introduction by Yeats), 1938.

TRANSLATIONS:

Sophocles's King Oedipus, a Version for the Modern Stage, 1928.
The Ten Principal Upanishads, put into English by Shree Purohit Swami and W. B. Yeats, 1937.

BIBLIOGRAPHY:

A Bibliography of the writings of W. B. Yeats, by Allan Wade, 1951 (rev. ed. 1957).

BIOGRAPHY AND CRITICISM:

Joseph Hone, W. B. Yeats (a biography), 1939.
Louis MacNeice, The Poetry of W. B. Yeats, 1941.
Richard Ellmann, Yeats, the Man and the Masks, 1948.
Norman Jeffares, W. B. Yeats, Man and Poet, 1949.
T. R. Henn, The Lonely Tower: Studies in the Poetry of W. B. Yeats, 1950.
The Permanence of Yeats: Selected Criticism, ed. James Hall and Martin Steinmann, 1950.
G. S. Fraser, W. B. Yeats (W.W.), 1954.

The Tower and *The Winding Stair* are Yeats's two most important volumes of poetry, though there are important poems in every volume from at least *In the Seven Woods* on. The 1937 edition of *A Vision* gives the fullest account of Yeats's philosophy of history and of personality, while his autobiographical writings and letters give a lively picture of his intellectual background and development. Ellmann's book is perhaps the most straightforward account of Yeats's development as a poet. There is also some detailed examination of Yeats's poetry and its development in F. R. Leavis's *New Bearings in English Poetry* and D. Daiches's *Poetry and the Modern World*, Chapters 7 and 8.

(B) GEORGIANS AND OTHERS

Æ pseud. (George William Russell) (1867-1935)

POETRY:

Homeward Songs by the Way, 1894.
The Earth Breath and Other Poems, 1897.
The Divine Vision and Other Poems, 1903.
The Nuts of Knowledge, Lyrical Poems Old and New, 1903.
By Still Waters, Lyrical Poems Old and New, 1906.
Collected Poems, 1913.
Gods of War, with Other Poems, 1915.
Salutation, a Poem on the Irish Rebellion of 1916, 1917.
Michael, 1919.
Voices of the Stones, 1925.
Collected Poems (2nd ed.), 1926.
Midsummer Eve, 1928.
Dark Weeping, 1929.
Enchantment and Other Poems, 1930.
Vale and Other Poems, 1931.
The House of the Titans and Other Poems, 1934.

PLAY:

Deirdre, a Drama in Three Acts, 1907.

SHORT STORIES:

The Mask of Apollo and Other Stories, 1904.
The Avatars, a Futurist Fantasy, 1933.

ESSAYS:

To the Fellows of the Theosophical Society, March 20th, 1894, 1894.
An Artist of Gaelic Ireland, 1902.
Some Irish Essays, 1906.
The Hero in Man, 1909.
The Renewal of Youth, 1911.
Imaginations and Reveries, 1915.
The Candle of Vision, 1918.
The Interpreters, 1922.
Song and its Fountains, 1932.

Like Yeats, but in a very different way, Æ combined an interest in theosophy, mysticism and oriental thought with an Irish political nationalism. He wrote many political pamphlets and essays (not listed here), from 'The Future of Ireland', 1897, to 'Thoughts for British Co-operators, being a Further Demand for a Public Enquiry into the Attacks on Co-operative Societies in Ireland', 1921. His poetry has nothing of the strength and complexity of the mature Yeats, but he often succeeds in expressing with quiet grace a mood of pantheistic peace or transcendent vision.

MEW, Charlotte Mary (1869-1928)

The Farmer's Bride, 1915.
The Rambling Sailor, 1929.
Collected Poems (with a Memoir by Alida Monro), 1953.

Her small output includes some sombre and powerful poems written in a highly individual idiom.

MOORE, Thomas Sturge (1870-1944)

POETRY AND DRAMA:
The Vinedresser and other Poems, 1899.
Aphrodite against Artemis, a tragedy, 1901.
Absalom, a chronicle play in three acts, 1903.
The Centaur's Booty, 1903.
Danaë, 1903.
The Rout of the Amazons, 1903.
The Gazelles and Other Poems, 1904.
Pan's Prophecy, 1904.
Theseus, Medea and Lyrics, 1904.
To Leda, and other Odes, 1904.
The Little School, 1905.
Mariamne, 1911.
A Sicilian Idyll and Judith, 1911.
The Sea is Kind, 1914.
The Powers of the Air, 1920.
Danaë, Aforetime, Blind Thamyris, 1920.
Tragic Mothers, 1920.
Judas, 1923.
Roderigo of Bivar, 1925.
Nine Poems, 1930.

Mystery and Tragedy, Two Dramatic Poems, 1930.
Poems (collected edition), 4 vols., 1931-33.
Selected Poems, 1934.

ESSAYS AND CRITICAL WRITINGS:

Altdorfer, 1900.
Dürer, 1904.
Correggio, 1906.
Art and Life, 1910.
Hark to These Three Talk about Style, 1915.
Some Soldier Poets, 1919.
Armour for Aphrodite, 1929.

Influenced by Flaubert, Arnold, Rossetti and Swinburne, and also by the French symbolists (he translated or adapted poems by Laforgue, Rimbaud, Baudelaire and Valéry), Sturge Moore developed his own version of the aestheticism of the 'nineties. He had a lively and original imagination combined with a sterner intellectual quality and a severer sense of form than were common among the 'nineties poets. He explained his own theory of art in his *Armour for Aphrodite*.

DAVIES, William Henry (1871-1940)

POETRY:

The Soul's Destroyer and other Poems, 1905.
New Poems, 1907.
Nature Poems and others, 1908.
Farewell to Poesy and other pieces, 1910.
Songs of Joy, 1911.
Foliage, 1913.
The Bird of Paradise and other Poems, 1914.
Child Lovers and other Poems, 1916.
Collected Poems, 1916.
Forty New Poems, 1918.
Raptures, 1918.
The Song of Life and other Poems, 1920.
The Captive Lion and other Poems, 1921.
The Hour of Magic and other Poems, 1922.
Collected Poems, second series, 1923.
Secrets, a Book of Poems, 1924.
A Poet's Alphabet, 1925.
The Song of Love, 1926.

A Poet's Calendar, 1927.
Collected Poems, 1928.
Moss and Feather, 1928.
Forty-nine Poems, 1928.
Ambition and other Poems, 1929.
In Winter, 1931.
Poems 1930-31, 1932.
The Lovers' Song-Book, 1933.
The Poems of W. H. Davies, 1934.
Love Poems, 1935.
The Birth of Song, 1936.
The Loneliest Mountain and other Poems, 1939.
Poems 1940, 1940.
Collected Poems (Introduction by O. Sitwell), 1943.
The Essential W. H. Davies, selected with an Introduction by B. Waters, 1951.

MISCELLANEOUS WRITINGS:

The Autobiography of a Super-tramp, 1908.
Beggars, 1909.
A Weak Woman, a Novel, 1911.
The True Traveller, 1912.
Nature, 1914.
A Poet's Pilgrimage, 1918.
True Travellers, a Tramps Opera in three acts, 1923.
Later Days, 1925.
The Adventures of Johnny Walker, Tramp, 1926.
Dancing Mad, a Novel, 1927.
My Birds, 1933.
My Garden, 1933.

———

BIOGRAPHY AND CRITICISM:
Thomas Moult, W. H. Davies, 1934.

Davies's autobiographical prose (notably in *The Autobiography of a Super-tramp*) has an appealing simplicity, but the more self-conscious simplicity of his poetry is often insipid and dull. A self-educated Wordsworthian, Davies made his own contribution to the Georgian cult of the bucolic; occasionally his quiet descriptive poems achieve a certain calm intensity, but often his deliberate innocence in observation or contemplation fails to produce poetry of any vitality.

DE LA MARE, Walter (1873-1956)

POETRY:

Songs of Childhood, 1902.
Poems, 1906.
The Listeners, 1912.
A Child's Day, 1912.
Peacock Pie, 1913.
The Sunken Garden, 1917.
Motley and other Poems, 1918.
Flora (drawings by Pamela Bianco), 1919.
Poems, 1901-1918, 1920.
The Veil, 1921.
Down-adown-Derry, 1922.
Thus Her Tale, 1923.
A Ballad of Christmas, 1924.
Alone, 1927.
Stuff and Nonsense, 1927.
The Captive and other Poems, 1928.
Self to Self, 1928.
A Snowdrop, 1929.
News, 1930.
Poems for Children, 1930.
To Lucy, 1931.
Old Rhymes and New, 1932.
The Fleeting and other Poems, 1933.
Poems, 1919-1934, 1935.
This Year, Next Year, 1937.
Memory, and other Poems, 1938.
Bells and Grass, 1941.
Collected Poems, 1942.
Love, 1943.
Collected Rhymes and Verses, 1944.
The Burning Glass, 1945.
Inward Companion, 1950.
Winged Chariot, 1951.

FICTION AND MISCELLANEOUS WRITINGS:

Henry Brocken, 1904.
The Three Mulla-Mulgars, 1910.
The Return, 1910.
Crossings, a Fairy Play, 1921.
Memoirs of a Midget, 1921.
Lispet, Lispett and Vaine, 1923.
The Riddle and other Stories, 1923.

Ding Dong Bell (verse epitaphs in a prose setting), 1924.
Two Tales, 1925.
Broomsticks and other Tales, 1925.
Miss Jemima, 1925.
The Connoisseur and other Stories, 1926.
Lucy, 1927.
Old Joe, 1927.
Told Again, 1927.
Readings, 1928.
At First Sight, 1928.
Stories from the Bible, 1929.
Desert islands and Robinson Crusoe, 1930.
On the Edge, Short Stories, 1930.
The Lord Fish, 1933.
A Froward Child, 1934.
Early One Morning, 1935.
Poetry in Prose, 1936.
Pleasures and Speculations, 1940.
The Magic Jacket and other Stories, 1943.
The Scarecrow and other Stories, 1945.
The Dutch Cheese and other Stories, 1946.
Private View, 1953.

SELECTIONS:

Story and Rhyme, a selection (by the author) from the writings of Walter
   de la Mare, 1921.
Stories, Essays and Poems, selected by M. M. Bozman, 1938.
Best Stories of Walter de la Mare, 1942.
Walter de la Mare: a Selection from his Writings with an Introduction
   by Kenneth Hopkins, 1956.

––––––––

BIOGRAPHY AND CRITICISM:

R. L. Mégroz, Walter de la Mare, a Biographical and Critical Study,
   1923.
Forrest Reid, Walter de la Mare, a Critical Study, 1929.
J. Atkins, Walter de la Mare, 1947.
Tribute to Walter de la Mare on his 75th Birthday (by various writers),
   1948.
Henry Charles Duffin, Walter de la Mare, a Study of his Poetry, 1949.
Kenneth Hopkins, Walter de la Mare (W.W.), 1953.
There is also an excellent brief critical discussion of de la Mare in F. R.
   Leavis's *New Bearings in English Poetry*, 1932 (2nd edition, 1950).

F. R. Leavis has called de la Mare 'the belated last poet of the Romantic tradition', and while this is in some degree just it is not the damning description it might seem to some modern ears to suggest. De la Mare has a delicately persuasive way with the fairy world, and his escape from modern civilization does not lead him (in his best poems) to self-indulgent dreaming but often to a magical brooding over the sense of loss and mystery that lies at the heart of experience. He can evoke the mind of a child with remarkable cunning (some of his best poems are, nominally at least, for children). He can handle terror as well as beauty, futility as well as magic. Few poets have dealt with such a 'romantic' subject-matter with less sentimentality. Of his prose works (which include short stories, novels, tales for children and critical essays), *Memoirs of a Midget* (a novel) has a strange and quiet power, *The Return* (short stories) deals more in mystery and terror, *The Lord Fish* is an appealing collection of stories for children, and *Early One Morning* is an oddly original book about childhood. A selection from de la Mare's poems has been translated into Scots ('Lallans') by Edith Anne Robertson, 1955.

GIBSON, Wilfrid Wilson, b. 1878

POETRY:

Urlyn the Harper and other Song, 1902.
Mountain Lovers, 1902.
The Queen's Vigil and other Song, 1902.
The Golden Helm and other Verse, 1903.
The Nets of Love, 1905.
On the Threshold, 1907.
The Stonefolds, 1907.
The Web of Life, 1908.
Akra the Slave, 1910.
Daily Bread, 1910.
Fires, 1912.
Thoroughfares, 1914.
Borderlands, 1914.
Battle, 1915.
Friends, 1916.
Livelihood, 1917.
Poems (1904-1917), 1917.
Whin, 1918.

Twenty-three Selected Poems, 1919.
Home, 1920.
Neighbours, 1920.
Krindlesyke, 1922
I heard a Sailor, 1925.
Collected Poems 1905-1925, 1926.
Sixty-three Poems, 1926.
The Early Whistler, 1927.
The Gold Room and other Poems, 1928.
Hazards, 1930.
Highland Dawn, 1932.
Islands, 1932.
Fuel, 1934.

PLAYS:

Womenkind, a Play in one act, 1912.
Kestrel Edge and other Plays, 1924.
Between Fairs, a Comedy, 1928.

Gibson began (as the titles of his first volumes indicate) with a highly decorated and very derivative kind of verse, suggesting Tennyson and Rossetti, but he soon developed into the determined poet of the ordinary world, writing, often in dramatic form, about the lives and passions of working people. *Daily Bread* and *Thoroughfares* contain his most successful poems in this vein, but too often the attempt to distil significance out of ordinary things seems rather mechanical.

MASEFIELD, John, b. 1878

POETRY:

Salt-Water Ballads, 1902.
Ballads, 1903.
Ballads and Poems, 1910.
The Everlasting Mercy, 1911.
The Widow in the Bye Street, 1912.
The Story of a Round-House and other Poems, 1912.
Dauber, a Poem, 1913.
The Daffodil Fields, 1913.
Philip the King and other Poems, 1914.
Good Friday and other Poems, 1916.
Sonnets and Poems, 1916.
Lollingdon Downs and other Poems, 1917.

The Cold Cotswolds, 1917.
A Poem and Two Plays, 1918.
Rosas, 1919.
Reynard the Fox, 1919.
Enslaved and other Poems, 1920.
Right Royal, 1920.
King Cole, 1921.
The Dream, 1922.
King Cole and other Poems, 1923.
The Collected Poems of John Masefield, 1923 (new and enlarged eds.,
    1932 and 1938).
Sonnets of Good Cheer, 1926.
Midsummer Night and other Tales in Verse, 1928.
South and East, 1929.
The Wanderer of Liverpool, 1930.
Minnie Maylow's Story and other Tales and Scenes, 1931.
A Tale of Troy, 1932.
A Letter from Pontus and other Verse, 1936.
Gautama the Enlightened and other Verse, 1941.
Natalie and Pavilastukay, Two Tales in Verse, 1942.
Land Workers, 1942.
Wonderings, 1943.
Poems, 1946.
On the Hill, 1949.

PLAYS:

The Tragedy of Nan and other Plays, 1909.
The Tragedy of Pompey the Great, 1910 (revised ed., 1914).
The Faithful, a Tragedy in Three Acts, 1915.
The Locked Chest, The Sweeps of Ninety-Eight, Two Plays in Prose,
    1916.
Melloney Hotspure, 1922.
Berenice, by Jean Racine (a verse translation), 1922.
Esther, by Jean Racine (a verse adaptation), 1922.
A King's Daughter, a Tragedy in Verse, 1923.
The Trial of Jesus, 1925.
Tristan and Isolt, a Play in Verse, 1927.
The Coming of Christ, 1928.
Easter, a Play for Singers, 1929.
End and Beginning, 1933.
A Play of St George, 1948.

FICTION:

A Mainsail Haul, 1905 (revised and enlarged ed., 1910).
Captain Margaret, a Romance, 1908.

BIBLIOGRAPHY

A Tarpaulin Muster, 1907.
Multitude and Solitude, 1909.
A Book of Discoveries, 1910.
Lost Endeavour, 1910.
Jim Davis, 1911.
Sard Harker, 1924.
Odtaa, 1926.
The Midnight Folk, 1927.
The Hawbucks, 1929.
The Bird of Dawning, 1933.
The Taking of the Gry, 1934.
A Box of Delights, or When the Wolves were Running, 1935
Victorious Troy, or The Hurrying Angel, 1935.
Eggs and Baker, or The Days of Trial, 1936.
The Square Peg, or The Gun Fella, 1937.
Dead Ned, the Autobiography of a Corpse, 1938.
Live and Kicking Ned. A Continuation of the Tale of Dead Ned, 1939.
Basilissa, 1940.
Conquer, 1941.
Badon Parchments, 1947.

MISCELLANEOUS WRITINGS:

Sea Life in Nelson's Time, 1905.
On the Spanish Main, 1906.
My Faith in Woman Suffrage, 1910.
William Shakespeare, 1911.
John M. Synge, 1915.
Gallipoli, 1916.
The Old Front Line, or The Beginning of the Battle of the Somme, 1917.
St George and the Dragon, 1919 (lectures delivered in America, published there in 1918 as The War and the Future).
John Ruskin, 1920.
A Foundation Day Address (at Bembridge School), 1921.
Shakespeare and the Spiritual Life, 1924.
With the Living Voice, an Address, 1924.
Chaucer, 1931.
Poetry, 1931.
The Conway from her Foundations to the Present Day, 1933.
Some Memories of W. B. Yeats, 1940.
In the Mill (autobiographical), 1941.
The Nine Days Wonder (Operation 'Dynamo'), 1941.
New Chum (autobiographical), 1944.
I Want! I Want! 1944.
A Macbeth Production, 1945.
Thanks before Going, 1946. (Enlarged edition, 1947.)
A Book of Prose Selections, 1950.

St Katherine of Ledbury, 1951.
So Long to Learn (autobiographical), 1952.

COLLECTED WORKS:

Wanderer Edition, 10 volumes, 1935-1938.

BIBLIOGRAPHY:

A Bibliography of John Masefield, by C. H. Simmons, 1930.

BIOGRAPHY AND CRITICISM:

I. A. Williams, John Masefield, 1921.
W. H. Hamilton, John Masefield, a Critical Study, 1922.
Cecil Biggane, John Masefield, a Study, 1924.
G. O. Thomas, John Masefield, 1932.
L. A. G. Strong, John Masefield (W.W.), 1952.

Salt-Water Ballads aroused considerable attention on its first appearance, its self-conscious realism in language and subject seeming to proclaim a poetic revolution. But early Yeats as well as Kipling influenced the young Masefield and the result was curiously conventional, for all the proclamation of a new vigour and toughness. *Ballads and Poems* similarly attempted to combine vigorous realism with a faded romance, and a lyric of some power and originality occasionally resulted. But his long narrative poems, where Crabbe and Chaucer are influences, are Masefield's most interesting and original work (though the extent to which the bounds of poetry were enlarged by the inclusion of an occasional swear-word was over-estimated by his early readers). *The Everlasting Mercy*, a tale of a poacher who goes berserk and finally reforms, told in octosyllabic couplets, has some vivid moments, and is less spoilt than *The Widow in the Bye Street* and *The Daffodil Fields* by a conventionally histrionic plot reminiscent of Victorian melodrama. The best of his narrative poems are *Dauber* (a sea story of the sensitive man among the Philistines) and the pseudo-Chaucerian *Reynard the Fox*, a skilful and lively account of a hunt in cantering couplets. Masefield's verse plays are stodgy affairs. His prose is often craftsmanlike and vigorous. His best novel is

Lost Endeavour. The Nine Days Wonder is a spirited account of the evacuation from Dunkirk. His *Shakespeare* is often perceptive and stimulating. There is an element of mysticism as well as of colloquial roughness in Masefield, and much of his work shows him seeking an effective way of combining the two.

MONRO, Harold (1879-1932)

POETRY:

Poems, 1906.
Judas, 1908.
Before Dawn, 1911.
Children of Love, 1914.
Trees, 1915.
Strange Meeting, 1917.
Real Property, 1922.
The Earth for Sale, 1928.
The Winter Solstice, 1928.
Elm Angel, 1930.
Collected Poems (ed. Alida Monro, with biographical sketch by F. S. Flint and critical note by T. S. Eliot), 1933.

MISCELLANEOUS WRITINGS:

The Evolution of the Soul, 1907.
The Chronicle of a Pilgrimage, 1910.
Some Contemporary Poets, 1920.

PLAY:

One Day Awake (A Morality), 1922.

A Georgian with a difference, Monro is best remembered for founding and running the Poetry Bookshop and for his generous encouragement of younger poets. His own poetry is limited in range and seems to seek but never quite attain the fresher idiom which the poetry of the period demanded. His original combination of whimsical imagination with Flemish portraits of domestic interiors occasionally produced verse of distinction and charm. He brilliantly edited the magazine *Poetry and Drama*, 1912-1913.

PALMER, Herbert Edward, b. 1880

POETRY:

Two Fishers, 1918.
Two Foemen, 1920.
Two Minstrels, 1921.
The Unknown Warrior, 1924.
Songs of Salvation, Sin and Satire, 1925.
The Armed Muse, 1930.
Jonah Comes to Nineveh, 1930.
Cinder Thursday, 1931.
Collected Poems, 1933.
Summit and Chasm, 1934.
The Vampire, 1936.
The Gallows-Cross, 1940.
Season and Festival, 1943.
A Sword in the Desert, 1946.
The Old Knight, 1949.

PLAYS:

The Judgment of François Villon, 1927.
The Dragon of Tingalam, 1945.

AUTOBIOGRAPHY:

The Mistletoe Child: Autobiography of Childhood, 1935.

CRITICAL WRITINGS:

The Teaching of English, 1930.
What the Public Wants, 1932.
Post-Victorian Poetry, 1938.

A spirited poet, whose verse has a gusto and vigour of its own, though the mood is not always fully realized in the texture and movement of the poem.

FREEMAN, John (1880-1929)

POETRY:

Twenty Poems, 1909.
Fifty Poems, 1911.
Stone Trees and other Poems, 1916.

Presage of Victory, 1916.
Memories of Childhood, 1918.
Memories of Childhood and other Poems, 1919.
Poems New and Old, 1920.
Music, 1921.
The Red Path, and The Wounded Bird, 1921.
The Grove and other Poems, 1924.
Prince Absalom, 1925.
Solomon and Balkis, 1926.
Collected Poems, 1928.
Last Poems, 1930.

CRITICAL WRITINGS:

The Moderns. 1916.
A Portrait of George Moore in a Study of his Work, 1922.
Punch and Holy Water, 1923.
English Portraits and Essays, 1924.
Herman Melville, 1926.

There is a firm craftsmanship about many of Freeman's poems that shows Georgian poetry at its best. He is most successful when most precise and limited in theme. His criticism is individual and discerning.

ABERCROMBIE, Lascelles (1881-1938)

POETRY:

Interludes and Poems, 1908.
Mary and the Bramble, 1910.
Emblems of Love, 1911.
Twelve Idylls and other Poems, 1928.
Collected Poems, 1930. This includes most of the plays.

PLAYS:

The Sale of St Thomas, 1911.
Deborah, 1913.
Four Short Plays, 1928.
Phoenix, 1923.
The Sale of St. Thomas (complete version), 1930.

CRITICAL AND MISCELLANEOUS WRITINGS:

Thomas Hardy, 1912.
Speculative Dialogues, 1913.
The Epic, 1914.
Poetry and Contemporary Speech, 1914.
An Essay towards a Theory of Art, 1922.
Communication versus Expression in Art, 1923.
Principles of English Prosody, 1923.
The Theory of Poetry, 1924.
The Idea of Great Poetry, 1925.
Romanticism, 1926.
Drowsie Frighted Steeds, 1928.
Progress in Literature, 1929.
A Plea for the Liberty of Interpreting, 1930.
Colloquial Language in Literature, 1931.
Poetry, its Music and Meaning, 1932.
Principles of Literary Criticism, 1932.
The Art of Wordsworth (1935, published 1952).

With considerable intellectual vigour and a powerful imagination, and with a capacity for handling strong and original imagery, Abercrombie should have been a better poet than he was. He never quite integrated his various qualities or found a style altogether unhampered by irrelevant Victorian poetic traditions, in spite of his admiration for and in some degree imitation of seventeenth-century poetry. Some of his verse plays show both intellectual and imaginative vigour in close-packed verse; *The Sale of Saint Thomas* is impressive. His criticism is thoughtful and perceptive, but neatly worked out rather than sharply original.

DRINKWATER, John (1882-1937)

POETRY:

Poems of Men and Hours, 1911.
Poems of Love and Earth, 1912.
Cromwell, and other Poems, 1913.
Swords and Ploughshares, 1915.
Olton Pools, 1916.
Poems, 1908-1914, 1917.
Tides, 1917.
Loyalties, 1918.
Poems, 1908-1919, 1919.

Seeds of Time, 1921.
Preludes, 1922.
Selected Poems, 1922.
Collected Poems, 1923.
New Poems, 1925.
Summer Harvest, Poems 1924-1933, 1933,
and others.

PLAYS:

Cophetua, 1911.
Rebellion, 1914.
The Storm, 1915.
Abraham Lincoln, 1918.
Collected Plays, 1925.
Bird in Hand, 1927.
A Man's House, 1934.

CRITICAL AND MISCELLANEOUS WRITINGS:

William Morris, 1912.
Swinburne, 1913.
Victorian Poetry, 1923.
Cromwell, 1927.
Inheritance (autobiographical), 1931.
Discovery (autobiographical), 1932.

A conscientious Georgian, Drinkwater wrote with intelligence
and craftsmanship, but under low pressure and without any striking individuality of style or imagination. His verse exhibits most of
the qualities of English poetry immediately before the Eliot revolution, traditional in imagery and verse-form and competent without being in any way exciting.

STEPHENS, James (1882-1950)

POETRY:

Insurrections, 1909.
The Lonely God, and other Poems, 1909.
The Hill of Vision, 1912.
Five New Poems, 1913.
The Adventures of Seumas Beg, 1915.
Songs from the Clay, 1915.
Green Branches, 1916.
Reincarnations, 1918.

A Poetry Recital, 1925.
Collected Poems, 1926.
The Outcast, 1929.
Theme and Variations, 1930.
Strict Joy, 1931.
King and the Moon, 1938.

FICTION:

The Charwoman's Daughter, 1912.
The Crock of Gold, 1912.
Here are Ladies, 1913.
The Demi-gods, 1914.
Hunger (by 'James Esse'), 1918.
Irish Fairy Tales, 1920.
Deirdre, 1923.
In the Land of Youth, 1924.

MISCELLANEOUS WRITINGS:

The Insurrection in Dublin, 1916.
Little Things, 1924.
Two Essays, 1928.
Optimist, 1929.

PLAY:

Julia Elizabeth, a Comedy in one Act, 1929.

Very much a product of the Irish Literary Revival, Stephens used Irish material with deftness and originality. His verse combines the playful and the mystical, and his style is marked by a disciplined simplicity that is often most impressive. His exuberant inventiveness combined with narrative skill made him a fine story teller (as in *The Crock of Gold*), but his prose can be realistic as well as humorous and fantastic.

SQUIRE, Sir John Collings, b. 1884

POETRY:

The Three Hills and other Poems, 1913.
The Survival of the Fittest and other Poems, 1916.
The Lily of Malud and other Poems, 1917.
Poems, first series, 1918.
The Birds and other Poems, 1919.

Poems, second series, 1921.
Poems in One Volume, 1926.
A Face in Candlelight and other Poems, 1932.

PARODIES:

Imaginary Speeches and other Parodies, 1912.
Steps to Parnassus, 1913.
Tricks of the Trade, 1917.
Collected Parodies, 1921.

SHORT STORIES:

The Grub Street Nights Entertainments, 1924.
Outside Eden, 1933.

CRITICAL WRITINGS:

Books in General (by 'Solomon Eagle'), 1918.
Books in General (by 'Solomon Eagle'), second series, 1920.
Life and Letters, 1920.
Books in General (by 'Solomon Eagle'), third series, 1921.
Essays at Large (by 'Solomon Eagle'), 1922.
Essays on Poetry, 1923.
Sunday Mornings, 1930.
Shakespeare as a Dramatist, 1935.

Squire also collaborated in writing a number of plays, including *Berkeley Square* (with John L. Balderston), 1928. His poetry is for the most part flat Georgian, but some of his parodies are brilliant. His criticism is 'common sense' and easy going.

WICKHAM, Anna (1884-1947)

POETRY:

The Contemplative Quarry, 1915.
The Man with a Hammer, 1916.
The Little Old House, 1921.

A poet of remarkable strength and individuality. 'The tumult of my fretted mind Gives me expression of a kind', she wrote in a poem called 'Self-Analysis', and it is the effective combination of irony and passion in her shorter poems of self-analysis that constitutes her best and most characteristic work.

YOUNG, Andrew John, b. 1885

POETRY:

The White Blackbird, 1935.
Collected Poems, 1936.
Speak to the Earth, 1939.
A Prospect of Flowers, 1945.
A Retrospect of Flowers, 1950.
Collected Poems, 1950.
Into Hades, 1952.
A Prospect of Britain, 1956.

A contemplative nature poet who, while traditional in form, is highly original in the nature of his sensibility and the precision of his observation. His religious play *Nicodemus* (1937) is included in his *Collected Poems*, 1950.

WOLFE, Humbert (1885-1940)

POETRY:

London Sonnets, 1920.
Shylock Reasons with Mr Chesterton and other Poems, 1920.
Kensington Gardens, 1924.
Lampoons, 1925.
The Unknown Goddess, 1925.
Humoresque, 1926.
News of the Devil, 1926.
Cursory Rhymes, 1927.
Requiem, 1927.
Veni Creator! 1927.
The Silver Cat and other Poems, 1928.
This Blind Rose, 1928.
Troy, 1928.
Early Poems, 1930.
The Uncelestial City, 1930.
Snow, 1931.
ABC of the Theatre, 1932.
X at Oberammergau, 1935.
Don J. Ewan, 1937.

MISCELLANEOUS WRITINGS:

Circular Saws, 1923.
Dialogues and Monologues, 1928.

Notes on English Verse Satire, 1929.
Signpost to Poetry, 1931.
Romantic and Unromantic Poetry, 1933.

TRANSLATIONS:

Anthologia Graeca: Others Abide, 1927.
Anthologia Graeca: Homage to Meleager, 1929.
Edmond Fleg, The Wall of Weeping, 1929.
Portrait of Heine, 1931.
Ronsard, Sonnets pour Hélène, 1934.

A poet of considerable craftsmanship and delicacy of touch, whose shorter and lighter poems are sometimes very successful. He tends to waver between the sentimental and the ironic, and is generally better with irony. Some of his verse satire is highly effective, though lacking complexity of reference and texture.

WILLIAMS, Charles (1886-1945)

POETRY:

The Silver Stair, 1912.
Poems of Conformity, 1917.
Divorce, 1920.
Windows of Night, 1925.
Heroes and Kings, 1930.
Taliessin through Logres, 1938.
The Region of the Summer Stars, 1944.

PLAYS:

Three Plays, 1931.
Thomas Cranmer of Canterbury, 1936.
Judgement at Chelmsford, 1939.
The House of the Octopus, 1945.
The Seed of Adam and other Plays, ed. Anne Ridler, 1948.

FICTION:

War in Heaven, 1930.
Many Dimensions, 1931.
The Place of the Lion, 1931.
The Greater Trumps, 1932.
Shadows of Ecstasy, 1933.
Descent into Hell, 1937.
All Hallows' Eve, 1945.

CRITICAL AND BIOGRAPHICAL WRITINGS:

Poetry at Present, 1930.
The English Poetic Mind, 1932.
Reason and Beauty in the Poetic Mind, 1933.
Bacon, 1933.
James I, 1934.
Rochester, 1935.
Queen Elizabeth I, 1936.
Henry VII, 1937.
The Figure of Beatrice, 1943.

RELIGIOUS AND THEOLOGICAL WRITINGS:

The Descent of the Dove, 1939.
Witchcraft, 1941.
Religion and Love in Dante: the Theology of Romantic Love, 1941.
The Forgiveness of Sins, 1942.

BOOKS EDITED OR INTRODUCED:

A Book of Victorian Narrative Verse, 1927.
The Poems of G. M. Hopkins, ed. Robert Bridges, 2nd ed. with appendix of additional poems and critical introduction by Charles Williams, 1930.
The New Book of English Verse (ed. with Lord David Cecil and others), 1935.
The English Poems of John Milton, with introd. and notes, 1940.
The New Christian Year, 1941.
The Letters of Evelyn Underhill, 1943.

––––––

BIOGRAPHY AND CRITICISM:

John Heath-Stubbs, Charles Williams (W.W.), 1955.

Williams was a Christian apologist with a remarkable power of presenting his views symbolically and imaginatively. His novels are 'supernatural thrillers', moral and theological mystery stories in which strange symbolic events are set against a background of modern daily life. His poetry lies outside the mainstream of modern English poetry, and his early poems are not wholly successful in their attempts to achieve a traditional high style. But the last two volumes of poetry listed here—sequences of poems on the

Arthurian legend—are an original symbolic treatment of traditional material which, surprisingly enough, yields new and impressive meanings. Williams had a naturally mythopoeic mind, and
made a gallant effort to revive symbolic and emblematic forms of
discourse in a context of sophisticated modern awareness. His
reputation has grown steadily since his death in 1945.

SASSOON, Siegfried, b. 1886

POETRY:

Poems, 1906.
Orpheus in Dilocrym, 1908.
Sonnets, 1909.
Hyacinth, 1912.
Discoveries, 1915.
The Redeemer, 1916.
The Old Huntsman and other Poems, 1917.
Counter-Attack and other Poems, 1918.
The War Poems of Siegfried Sassoon, 1919.
Selected Poems, 1925.
Satirical Poems, 1926.
The Heart's Journey, 1927.
Poems of Pinchbeck Lyre, 1931.
Vigils, 1934.
Rhymed Ruminations, 1941.
Collected Poems, 1949.
Sequences, 1956.

SEMI-AUTOBIOGRAPHICAL FICTION:

Memoirs of a Fox-Hunting Man, 1928.
Memoirs of an Infantry Officer, 1930.
Sherston's Progress, 1936.
The Old Century and Seven More Years, 1938.

CRITICAL BIOGRAPHY:

George Meredith, 1948.

Sassoon began as a faded romantic, but the First World War
developed in him a bitter satiric note, and some of his war poems
have a spontaneous violence that is most effective. In his later
poetry he shows a meditative lyricism expressing itself, often without any great original force, in traditional techniques. He also

wrote some clever parodies. His prose is distinctive, and *Memoirs of a Fox-Hunting Man* is an impressive rendering of the tone and rhythm of a kind of English life that has by now almost completely passed away—that of the cultivated squirearchy in the large country-house.

CORNFORD, Frances Crofts, b. 1886

POETRY:

Poems, 1910.
Spring Morning, 1915,
Autumn Midnight, 1923,
Different Days, 1928.
Mountains and Molehills, 1935.
Travelling Home, 1948.
Collected Poems, 1954.

(C) ELIOT AND OTHERS

MUIR, Edwin, b. 1887

POETRY:

First Poems, 1925.
Chorus of the Newly Dead, 1926.
Six Poems, 1932.
Variations on a Time Theme, 1934.
Journeys and Places, 1937.
The Narrow Place, 1943.
The Voyage and other Poems, 1946.
The Labyrinth, 1949.
Collected Poems 1921-1951, ed. J. C. Hall, 1952.
Prometheus, 1954.
One Foot in Eden, 1956.

CRITICAL AND BIOGRAPHICAL WRITINGS:

Latitudes, 1924.
Transition, 1926.
The Structure of the Novel, 1928.
John Knox, 1929.
Scott and Scotland, 1936.
The Present Age, from 1914, 1939.
Essays on Literature and Society, 1949.

FICTION:

The Marionette, 1927.
The Three Brothers, 1931.
Poor Tom, 1932.

AUTOBIOGRAPHY:

The Story and the Fable, 1940.
An Autobiography (a revised and expanded ed. of the above), 1954.

TOPOGRAPHICAL AND POLITICAL WRITINGS:

Scottish Journey, 1935.
Social Credit and the Labour Party, 1937.
The Scots and their Country, 1946.

BIOGRAPHY AND CRITICISM:

J. C. Hall, Edwin Muir (W.W.), 1956.

SITWELL, Dame Edith, b. 1887

POETRY:

The Mother, 1915.
Twentieth-Century Harlequinade and other Poems, 1916 (with O. Sitwell).
Clown's Houses, 1918.
The Wooden Pegasus. 1920.
Façade, 1922.
Bucolic Comedies, 1923.
The Sleeping Beauty, 1924.
Troy Park, 1925.
Poor Young People and other Poems, 1925 (with O. and S. Sitwell).
Elegy on Dead Fashion, 1926.
Rustic Elegies, 1927.
Popular Song, 1929.
Gold Coast Customs, 1929.
Collected Poems, 1930.
Epithalamium, 1931.
In Spring. 1931.
Five Variations on a Theme, 1933.
Selected Poems, 1936.
Poems New and Old, 1940.
Green Song and other Poems, 1944.
The Song of the Cold, 1945.
The Shadow of Cain, 1947.
The Canticle of the Rose, 1949.
Façade and other Poems, 1920-1935, 1950.
Gardeners and Astronomers, 1953.

FICTION:

I Live Under a Black Sun, 1937. (Based on the life of Swift.)

CRITICAL AND MISCELLANEOUS WRITINGS:

Children's Tales—from the Russian Ballet, 1920.
Poetry and Criticism, 1925.
Alexander Pope, 1930.
Bath, 1932.
The English Eccentrics, 1933.

Aspects of Modern Poetry, 1934.
Victoria of England, 1934.
Three Eras of Modern Poetry (in *Trio* by Osbert, Edith and Sacheverell
    Sitwell, 1938).
English Women, 1942.
A Poet's Notebook, 1943.
Fanfare for Elizabeth, 1946.
A Notebook on William Shakespeare, 1948.

ANTHOLOGIES:

Wheels, 1916-21.
The Pleasures of Poetry, 3 vols., 1930-32.
Edith Sitwell's Anthology, 1940.
Look: the Sun, 1941. (Anthology for children.)
Planet and Glow-worm, a Book for the Sleepless, 1944.
The American Genius, 1951.
A Book of Flowers, 1952.

———

BIOGRAPHY AND CRITICISM:

John Lehmann, Edith Sitwell (W.W.), 1952.

ELIOT, Thomas Stearns, b. 1888

POETRY:

Prufrock and other Observations, 1917.
Poems, 1919.
Ara Vos Prec, 1920.
The Waste Land, 1922.
Poems 1909-25, 1925.
Journey of the Magi, 1927.
A Song for Simeon, 1928.
Animula, 1929.
Ash Wednesday, 1930.
Marina, 1930.
Triumphal March, 1931.
Collected Poems, 1909-35, 1936.
Old Possum's Book of Practical Cats, 1939.
East Coker, 1940.
Burnt Norton, 1941 (first ptd. in Coll. Poems, 1936).
The Dry Salvages, 1941.
Little Gidding, 1942.

Four Quartets (the four above poems), 1943.
The Complete Poems and Plays, New York, 1952.
The Cultivation of Christmas Trees, 1954.

PLAYS:

Sweeney Agonistes, 1932.
The Rock, 1934.
Murder in the Cathedral, 1935.
The Family Reunion, 1939.
The Cocktail Party, 1950.
The Confidential Clerk, 1954.

CRITICAL AND MISCELLANEOUS WRITINGS

Ezra Pound, his Metric and Poetry, New York, 1917. (Pub. anon.)
The Sacred Wood: Essays on Poetry and Criticism, 1920.
Homage to John Dryden, 1924.
For Lancelot Andrewes: Essays on Style and Order, 1928.
Dante, 1929.
Thoughts after Lambeth, 1931.
John Dryden, New York, 1932.
Selected Essays, 1932. (Enlarged ed., 1951.)
The Use of Poetry and the Use of Criticism, 1933.
After Strange Gods: a Primer of Modern Heresy, 1934.
Elizabethan Essays, 1934.
Essays Ancient and Modern, 1936.
The Idea of a Christian Society, 1939.
The Music of Poetry, 1942.
The Classics and the Man of Letters, 1942.
Reunion by Destruction (on Church Union), 1943.
What is a Classic? 1945.
Milton, 1947.
Notes towards the Definition of Culture, 1948.
Poetry and Drama, 1951.
American Literature and the American Language, St Louis, 1953.
The Three Voices of Poetry, 1953.
Essays on Poets and Poetry, 1957.

TRANSLATION:

Anabasis—a Poem by St J. Perse with a Translation by T. S. Eliot, 1930.

———

BIBLIOGRAPHY:

A Bibliography of T. S. Eliot, by Donald Gallup, 1952.

BIOGRAPHY AND CRITICISM:

F. O. Matthiessen, The Achievement of T. S. Eliot, 1935. (Revised ed., 1947.)
B. Rajan (ed.), T. S. Eliot: A Study of his Writings by Various Hands, 1947.
L. Unger (ed.), T. S. Eliot, a Selected Critique, New York, 1948.
R. March and Tambimuttu (ed.), T. S. Eliot, a Symposium, 1948.
H. Gardner, The Art of T. S. Eliot, 1949.
E. Drew, T. S. Eliot, the Design of his Poetry, 1950.
G. Williamson, A Reader's Guide to T. S. Eliot, 1953.
M. C. Bradbrook, T. S. Eliot (W.W.), 1950, revised 1951.

There are important studies of Eliot in F. R. Leavis's *New Bearings in English Poetry*, Edmund Wilson's *Axel's Castle*, Wyndham Lewis's *Men Without Art*, and Bonamy Dobrée's *The Lamp and the Lute*.

WELLESLEY, Dorothy Violet (1889-1956)

POETRY:

Poems, 1920.
Genesis, 1926.
Jupiter and the Nun, 1932.
Matrix, 1928.
Deserted House, 1930.
Poems of Ten Years 1924-1934, 1934.
Selections from the Poems of Dorothy Wellesley, introd. by W. B. Yeats, 1936.
Lost Planet and other Poems, 1942.
Desert Wells, 1946.
Selected Poems, 1949.
Far Have I Travelled, 1952.
Early Light: Collected Poems, 1956.

A poet much admired by W. B. Yeats for her elemental imagery, masculine rhythm and precision of style.

WALEY, Arthur David, b. 1889

170 Chinese Poems, 1919.
Japanese Poetry, 1919.
The Nō Plays of Japan, 1919.
Introduction to the Study of Chinese Painting, 1923.
The Tale of Genji (6 vols.), 1925ff.

The Pillow-Book of Sei Shanagon, 1928.
The Way and Its Power, 1935.
The Book of Songs, 1937.
The Analects of Confucius, 1939.
Three Ways of Thought in Ancient China, 1939.
Monkey, 1942.
Chinese Poems, 1946.
The Life and Times of Po Chü-i, 1948.
The Poetry and Career of Li Po, A.D. 701-762, 1951.

Waley's translations from Chinese poetry have had considerable influence on the practice of poetry in both England and America.

TURNER, Walter James Redfern (1889-1946)

POETRY:

The Hunter and other Poems, 1916.
The Dark Fire, 1918.
The Dark Wind, 1920.
In Time like Glass, 1921.
Paris and Helen, 1921.
Landscape of Cytherea, 1923.
Smaragda's Lover, 1924.
The Seven Days of the Sun, 1925.
Marigold, 1926.
The Aesthetes, 1927.
New Poems, 1928.
A Trip to New York, 1929.
Miss America, Altiora in the Sierra Nevada, 1930.
Pursuit of Psyche, 1931.
Jack and Jill, 1934.
Songs and Incantations, 1936.
Selected Poems, 1916-1936, 1937.
Fossils of a Future Time, 1948.

PLAY:

The Man who ate the Popomack, 1922.

FICTION:

Blow for Balloons, 1935.
Henry Airbubble, 1936.

CRITICAL AND MISCELLANEOUS WRITINGS:

Music and Life, 1921.
Variations on the Theme of Music, 1924.

Orpheus, or The Music of the Future, 1926.
Beethoven, the Search for Reality, 1927.
Musical Meanderings, 1928.
Music, a Short History, 1932.
Facing the Music: Reflections of a Music Critic, 1933.
Wagner, 1933.
Berlioz, the Man and his Work, 1934.
Mozart, 1938.

An undisciplined, but strikingly original and sometimes fantastic imagination is at work both in Turner's poetry and in his prose. The boldness of his imagery combined with the simple strength of his rhythms often yield impressive results, and sometimes his combination of imaginative boldness with a tone of sardonic comment produces something quite individual. But his poetry is uneven. His satiric humour and fantasy are best revealed in *The Man who ate the Popomack* and *Blow for Balloons*.

ROSENBERG, Isaac (1890-1918)

POETRY:

Night and Day, 1912.
Youth, 1915.
Moses, a Play, 1916.
Poems, selected and ed. by Gordon Bottomley, introductory memoir by Lawrence Binyon, 1922.
The Collected Works of Isaac Rosenberg, ed. by Gordon Bottomley and Denys Harding, with foreword by Siegfried Sassoon 1937, 1949.

A poet of great imaginative power who was breaking new ground in imagery, rhythms and the handling of dramatic effects in verse at the time of his death in the First World War. His originality, integrity and feeling for poetic texture make his poetry some of the most interesting in the period; his premature death in war was a major loss to English poetry.

SITWELL, Sir Osbert, Bt., b. 1892

POETRY:

Twentieth-Century Harlequinade and other Poems, 1916 (with E. Sitwell).

Argonaut and Juggernaut, 1919.
The Winstonburg Line, 1920.
Out of the Flame, 1923.
Winter the Huntsman, 1924.
Poor Young People and other Poems, 1925 (with E. and S. Sitwell).
England Reclaimed: A Book of Eclogues, 1927.
Miss Mew, 1929.
Three-Quarter Length Portrait of Michael Arlen, 1931.
The Collected Satires and Poems, 1931.
A Three-Quarter-Length Portrait of Viscountess Wimborne, 1931.
Mrs Kimber, 1937.
Selected Poems: Old and New, 1943.
Four Songs of the Italian Earth, 1948.
Demos the Emperor: A Secular Oratorio, 1949.
Wrack at Tidesend, 1952.

FICTION:

Triple Fugue, 1924.
Before the Bombardment, 1926.
The Man Who Lost Himself, 1929.
Dumb Animal, and other Stories, 1930.
Miracle on Sinai, 1933.
Those Were the Days, 1938.
A Place of One's Own, 1941.
Open the Door! 1941.
The True Story of Dick Whittington, 1945.
Death of a God, 1949.

CRITICAL AND MISCELLANEOUS WRITINGS:

Who killed Cock Robin? Reflections on Modern Poetry. 1921.
Discursions on Travel, Life and Art, 1925.
C. R. W. Nevison, 1925.
Sober Truth, a Collection of 19th-Century Episodes (with Margaret
    Barton), 1930.
Victoriana (compiled and ed. with Margaret Barton), 1931.
Dickens, 1932.
Winters of Content: More Discursions on Travel, Art and Life, 1932.
Brighton, 1935.
Penny Foolish, 1935.
Dickens and the Modern Novel, etc. (In *Trio*, by Osbert, Edith and
    Sacheverell Sitwell, 1938).
Escape with Me! An Orientai Sketch Book, 1939.
Two Generations. A Double Biography, 1940.
A Letter to My Son, 1944.
Sing High! Sing Low! 1944.
The Novels of George Meredith, 1947. (Lecture)

AUTOBIOGRAPHY:

Left Hand! Right Hand! 1944.
The Scarlet Tree, 1945.
Great Morning, 1947.
Laughter in the Next Room, 1948.
Noble Essences, 1950.

BIOGRAPHY AND CRITICISM:

Roger Fulford, Osbert Sitwell (W.W.), 1951.

Osbert Sitwell's early poetry is satirical, and he has some bitter war poems and lively satires on types of English character. He has also written poems of a baroque beauty more reminiscent of his sister's. *Before the Bombardment* is the best of his novels, a skilful satirical portrait of Scarborough on the eve of the First World War seen as reflecting the last phase of a Victorian society. His five-volume autobiography is also, very consciously, the portrait of an age, done with an aristocratic nostalgia: 'I belonged by birth education, nature, outlook, and period to the pre-war era, a proud citizen of the great free world of 1914, in which comity prevailed.' It is a remarkable achievement.

SACKVILLE-WEST, Hon. Victoria, b. 1892

POETRY:

Poems of East and West, 1917.
Orchard and Vineyard, 1921.
The Land, 1926.
King's Daughter, 1929.
Invitation to Cast out Care, 1931.
Sissinghurst, 1931.
Collected Poems, 1933.
Selected Poems, 1941.
Nursery Rhymes, 1947.

FICTION:

Heritage, 1910.
The Dragon in Shallow Waters, 1921.
The Heir, 1922.
Challenge, 1923.
Grey Wethers, 1923.

Seducers in Ecuador, 1924.
The Edwardians, 1930.
All Passion Spent, 1931.
Family History, 1932.
The Death of Noble Godavary and Gottfried Künstler, 1932.
Thirty Clocks Strike the Hour and other Stories, 1932.
The Dark Island, 1934.

MISCELLANEOUS WRITINGS:

Knole and the Sackvilles, 1922.
Aphra Behn, 1927.
Passenger to Teheran, 1926.
Twelve Days, 1928.
Andrew Marvell, 1929.
Saint Joan of Arc, 1936.
Pepita, 1937.
Some Flowers, 1937.
Solitude, 1938.
Country Notes, 1939.
Country Notes in Wartime, 1940.
English Country Houses, 1941.
The Garden, 1946.
In Your Garden, 1951.

A versatile and talented writer with a deep feeling for and knowledge of the English countryside and its history. She has what might be called an aristocratic sensibility, displayed in her contemplation of English character in her novels.

SHANKS, Edward Buxton (1892-1953)

POETRY:

Songs, 1915.
Poems, 1916.
The Queen of China and other Poems, 1919.
The Island of Youth and other Poems, 1921.
Fête Galante, 1923.
The Shadowgraph and other Poems, 1925.
Collected Poems, 1909-1925, 1926.
Poems 1912-1932, 1933.
My England, 1938.
The Night Watch for England and other Poems, 1942.
Images from the Progress of the Seasons, 1947.
The Dogs of War, 1948.

FICTION:

The Old Indispensables, 1919.
The People of the Ruins, 1920.
The Richest Man, 1923.
Queer Street, 1932.
The Enchanted Village, 1933.
Tom Tiddler's Ground, 1934.

CRITICAL AND MISCELLANEOUS WRITINGS:

First Essays on Literature, 1923.
Bernard Shaw, 1924.
Second Essays on Literature, 1927.
Bo and his Circle, 1931.
Edgar Allan Poe, 1937.
Rudyard Kipling, 1940.
The Universal War and the Universal State, 1946.

Essentially a Georgian poet, but more various and enterprising than most.

CHURCH, Richard, b. 1893

POETRY:

Flood of Life, 1917.
Hurricane, 1919.
Philip, 1923.
Portrait of the Abbot, 1926.
The Dream, 1927.
Theme and Variations, 1928.
Mood without Measure, 1928.
The Glance Backward, 1930.
News from the Mountain, 1932.
Twelve Noon, 1936.
The Solitary Man, 1941.
20th Century Psalter, 1943.
The Lamp, 1946.
Collected Poems, 1948.
Poems for Speaking, 1949.
Selected Lyrical Poems, 1951.
The Prodigal, 1953.

FICTION:

Oliver's Daughter, 1930.
High Summer, 1931.

The Prodigal Father, 1933.
Apple of Concord, 1935.
The Porch, 1937.
The Stronghold, 1939.
Calling for a Spade, 1939.
The Room Within, 1940.
Rufus, 1941.
Green Tide, 1944.
The Cave, 1950.
Dangerous Ages, 1955.
The Dangerous Years, 1956.

MISCELLANEOUS WRITINGS:

Mary Shelley, 1928.
Eight for Immortality, 1941.
Kent, 1948.
Portrait of Canterbury, 1953.

AUTOBIOGRAPHY:

Over the Bridge, 1955.

A sensitive poet of impressive integrity, whose unadventurous-
ness in technique is balanced by the genuine originality and true
inwardness of the texture of his verse. His autobiographical work,
Over the Bridge, is a minor classic of its kind.

OWEN, Wilfred (1893-1918)

Poems, with introd. by Siegfried Sassoon, 1920.
Poems, a new edition including many hitherto unpublished pieces and
notices of his life and work, ed. by Edmund Blunden, 1931.

A poet of great originality and technical skill, killed in the First
World War. His war poems show a remarkable combination of
irony and pity. The publication of the 1931 edition of his poems
brought him to the attention of the young poets of the day, whom
he influenced considerably. His death in war and that of Isaac
Rosenberg represented the same kind of loss to English poetry—
the loss of pioneering poetic spirits who were in the process of developing a new poetic idiom.

READ, Sir Herbert, b. 1893

POETRY:

Songs of Chaos, 1915.
Eclogues, 1919.
Naked Warriors, 1919.
Mutations of the Phoenix, 1923.
Collected Poems 1913-1925, 1926.
The End of a War, 1933.
Poems 1914-1934, 1935.
Thirty-five Poems, 1940.
A World Within a War, 1944.
Collected Poems, 1946 (2nd ed., 1953).
Moon's Farm, 1955.

FICTION:

The Green Child, 1935.

CRITICAL AND MISCELLANEOUS WRITINGS:

English Stained Glass, 1926.
Reason and Romanticism, 1926.
English Prose Style, 1928.
Phases of English Poetry, 1928.
The Sense of Glory, 1929.
Staffordshire Pottery Figures, 1929.
Wordsworth, 1930.
Julien Benda and the New Humanism, 1930.
Ambush, 1930.
The Meaning of Art, 1931.
The Place of Art in a University, 1931.
Form in Modern Poetry, 1932.
Art Now, 1933.
Art and Industry, 1934.
Essential Communism, 1935.
In Defence of Shelley, 1936.
Art and Society, 1937.
Poetry and Anarchism, 1938.
The Philosophy of Anarchism, 1940.
To Hell with Culture, 1940.
The Future of Industrial Design, 1943.
Education through Art, 1943.
The Politics of the Unpolitical, 1943.
Henry Moore, 1944.
The Education of Free Men, 1944.
A Coat of Many Colours, 1945.

The Grass Roots of Art, 1947.
Gauguin, 1948.
Klee, 1948.
Coleridge as Critic, 1949.
Education for Peace, 1950.
Contemporary British Art, 1951.
Art and the Evolution of Man, 1951.
Byron, 1951.
The Philosophy of Modern Art, 1952.
The True Voice of Feeling, 1953.
Icon and Idea, 1955.
The Art of Sculpture, 1956.

AUTOBIOGRAPHY:

In Retreat, 1925.
The Innocent Eye, 1933.
Annals of Innocence and Experience, 1940, which includes the above.

ANTHOLOGIES:

The London Book of English Prose (with B. Dobrée), 1931.
The English Vision, 1933.
The Knapsack, 1939.
The London Book of English Verse (with B. Dobrée), 1949.

———

BIOGRAPHY AND CRITICISM:

An Introduction to his Work by Various Writers, 1944.
Francis Berry, Herbert Read (W.W.), 1953.

An unusual combination of poet, literary critic and art critic, Read has been an interesting force in modern culture. In his best poems as well as in his autobiographical prose, he has cultivated 'the innocent eye' with clarity. His view of literary form, which distinguishes between inherent organic form and imposed abstract form, deriving in some measure from Coleridge and the romantic critics, led him to a revaluation of romantic poetry on quite different lines from the prevailing anti-romanticism of the period. It is this view of the importance of an inherent organic form which also led him to reject all imposed forms in human organization (hence his political 'anarchism'). In his art criticism, Read has done much to explain and make known modern idioms and movements and to assert the claims of art in education and in modern society generally.

216

GRAVES, Robert Ranke, b. 1895

POETRY:

Over the Brazier, 1916.
Fairies and Fusiliers, 1917.
Country Sentiment, 1920.
The Pier Glass, 1921.
The Feather Bed, 1923.
Whipperginny, 1923.
Mock Beggar Hall, 1924.
The Marmosite's Miscellany, 1925 (by John Doyle, *pseud.*).
Welchman's Hose, 1925.
Poems (1914-26), 1927.
Poems (1926-1930), 1931.
Poems (1930-1933), 1933.
Collected Poems, 1938.
Collected Poems, 1948.
Poems and Satires, 1951.
Poems, 1953.

FICTION:

I, Claudius, 1934.
Claudius the God, 1934.
Antigua Penny Puce, 1936.
Count Belisarius, 1938.
Sergeant Lamb of the Ninth, 1940.
Proceed, Sergeant Lamb, 1941.
Wife to Mr Milton, 1943.
The Golden Fleece, 1944.
King Jesus, 1946.
Seven Days in New Crete, 1949.
The Isles of Unwisdom, 1950.
Homer's Daughter, 1955.

CRITICAL AND MISCELLANEOUS WRITINGS:

On English Poetry, 1922.
The Meaning of Dreams, 1924.
Poetic Unreason and other Studies, 1925.
Another Future of Poetry, 1926.
Lars Porsena, or The Future of Swearing, 1927.
Lawrence and the Arabs, 1927.
A Survey of Modernist Poetry (with Laura Riding), 1927.
Mrs Fisher or The Future of Humour, 1928.
A Pamphlet against Anthologies (with Laura Riding), 1928.
The Real David Copperfield, 1933.

The English Ballad, 1937.
The Long Week-End (with Alan Hodge), 1940.
The White Goddess, 1947.
The Common Asphodel (Collected Essays on Poetry), 1949.
Occupation: Writer, 1951.
The Nazarene Gospel Restored (with Joshua Podro), 1953.
The Greek Myths, 1955.
The Crowning Privilege, 1955.

AUTOBIOGRAPHY:

Good-bye to all that, 1929.
But It Still Goes On, 1930.
T. E. Lawrence to his Biographer, 1937.

————

BIOGRAPHY AND CRITICISM:

M. Seymour-Smith, Robert Graves (W.W.), 1956.

One of the most original creative and provocative minds of his generation. His poetry often represents a surrender to an impersonal vision, which appears to take control with a combination of cunning thought and almost mystic clarity. There is also a quizzical intelligence at work in much of his verse. His interest in the sources of poetry (mytholʒoical and psychological) and in the origin and development of myth has produced some of his most interesting work. His originality sometimes runs to wilfulness. The Claudius novels are the work of a remarkable historical and psychological imagination; the story of the Emperor Claudius is told in the first person by the Emperor himself. Sometimes (as in *Wife to Mr Milton*) his own prejudices can distort a historical reconstruction; but the result is always lively and persuasive. His criticism is fresh, original, provocatively unorthodox, occasionally preposterous, nearly always vigorous and exciting. *The Long Week-End* is an admirable social history of the inter-war years. *The Nazarene Gospel Restored* is a bold reinterpretation of the origins of Christianity which was bitterly resented by the orthodox for its apparently arbitrary use of a very real scholarship.

BLUNDEN, Edmund, b. 1896

POETRY:

Poems, 1913 and 1914, 1914.

The Barn, 1916.
The Harbingers, 1916.
Pastorals, 1916.
The Waggoner and other Poems, 1920.
Old Homes, 1922.
The Shepherd and other Poems of Peace and War, 1922.
Dead Letters, 1923.
To Nature, 1923.
English Poems, 1925.
Far East, 1925.
Masks of Time, 1925.
Japanese Garland, 1928.
Retreat, 1928.
Winter Nights, 1928.
Near and Far, 1929.
The Poems of Edmund Blunden, 1914-1930, 1930.
A Summer's Fancy, 1930.
Constantia and Francis, 1931.
In Summer, 1931.
To Themis, 1931.
Halfway House, 1932.
Choice or Chance, 1934.
An Elegy and other Poems, 1937.
Poems, 1930-1940, 1940.
Shells by a Stream, 1944.
After the Bombing, 1948.

CRITICAL AND MISCELLANEOUS WRITINGS:

The Bonadventure, 1922. (Travel.)
On the Poems of Henry Vaughan, 1927.
Undertones of War, 1928.
Nature in English Literature, 1929.
Leigh Hunt, a Biography, 1930.
The Face of England, 1932.
Charles Lamb and his Contemporaries, 1934.
The Mind's Eye, 1934.
Keats's Publisher, 1936.
English Villages, 1941.
Thomas Hardy, 1942.
Cricket Country, 1944.
Shelley, a Life Story, 1946.
The Dede of Pittie (dramatic scenes), 1953.

A Georgian nature poet with a difference, combining (sometimes effectively and sometimes oddly) a precise observation with imaginative violence. *Undertones of War* is an outstanding book of reminiscences of the First World War.

PITTER, Ruth, b. 1897

First Poems, 1920.
First and Second Poems, 1927.
Persephone in Hades, 1931.
A Mad Lady's Garland, 1934.
A Trophy of Arms, 1936.
The Spirit Watches, 1939.
The Rude Potato, 1941.
The Bridge, 1945.
Pitter on Cats, 1946.
Urania, 1951. (The author's own choice of her poems.)
The Ermine, 1953.

A skilful and delicate artist, whose verse, though calm on the surface, shows an occasional streak of wildness.

SITWELL, Sacheverell, b. 1897

POETRY:

The Hundred and One Harlequins, 1922.
Poor Young People and other Poems, 1925 (with O. and E. Sitwell).
The Rio Grande (music by Constant Lambert), 1929.
Doctor Donne and Gargantua, 1930.
Canons of Giant Art, Twenty Torsos in Heroic Landscapes, 1933.
Dance of the Quick and the Dead, 1936.
Sacred and Profane Love, 1940.
Selected Poems, 1948,
and others.

CRITICAL AND MISCELLANEOUS WRITINGS:

Southern Baroque Art, 1924.
German Baroque Art, 1927.
The Gothick North, 1929.
Spanish Baroque Art, 1931.
Mozart, 1932.
Liszt, 1934.
Roumanian Journey, 1938.
Primitive Scenes and Festivals, 1942.
British Architects and Craftsmen, 1945.

The Netherlands, 1948.
Spain, 1950.
Truffle Hunt with Sacheverell Sitwell, 1953.
Portugal and Madeira, 1954.
Selected Works, 1955.

AUTOBIOGRAPHY:

All Summer in a Day, an Autobiographical Fantasia, 1926.

A poet whose work is nourished as much by art (painting and music as well as literature) as by life, with the result sometimes of a happy stylization or a curiously effective distilled quality. His studies of baroque art show a highly individual, imaginative approach.

CAMPBELL, Ignatius Roy Dunnachie (1902-1957)

POETRY:

The Flaming Terrapin, 1924.
The Wayzgoose, a South African Satire, 1928.
Adamastor, 1930.
The Gum Trees, 1930.
Poems, 1930.
Choosing a Mast, 1931.
The Georgiad, a Satirical Fantasy in Verse, 1931.
Mithraic Emblems, 1936.
Pomegranates, 1932.
Flowering Reeds, 1933.
Flowering Rifle, 1939.
Talking Bronco, 1946.
Collected Poems, 1949.
Poems of St John of the Cross, 1952. (Translations.)

CRITICAL AND MISCELLANEOUS WRITINGS:

Burns, 1932.
Taurine Provence, 1932.
Frederic Garcia Lorca, 1951.

AUTOBIOGRAPHY:

Broken Record, an Autobiography, 1934.
Light on a Dark Horse, 1955.

A Right-wing poet with an Augustan satiric gift and a rich and strong use of language that can impress by its fullness and cogency where it is not too highly-coloured and rhetorical. Roy Campbell has also translated from the Portuguese, the Norwegian and the Spanish, in addition to his verse rendering of St John of the Cross listed above.

ROBERTS, Michael (1902-1949)

POETRY:
Poems, 1936. (Rev. ed. 1956)

CRITICAL WRITINGS:
Critique of Poetry, 1934.
The Modern Mind, 1937.
T. E. Hulme, 1938.

ANTHOLOGIES:
New Signatures, 1932.
New Country, 1933.
The Faber Book of Modern Verse, 1935.

GRIGSON, Geoffrey, b. 1905

POETRY:
Several Observations, 1939.
Under the Cliff, and other Poems, 1943.
The Isles of Scilly, and other Poems, 1946.

CRITICAL AND MISCELLANEOUS WRITINGS:
Samuel Palmer, 1947.
Places of the Mind, 1949.
The Crest on the Silver, 1950.
Essays from the Air, 1951.
Gardenage, 1952.
Freedom of the Parish, 1954.
The Englishman's Flora, 1955.
English Drawings, 1955.

A craftsmanlike poet and a writer of precise critical and descriptive prose in rather neglected fields. He edited the important periodical anthology *New Verse* (1933-39).

(D) AUDEN AND OTHERS

DAY LEWIS, Cecil, b. 1904

POETRY:

Beechen Vigil, 1925.
Country Comets, 1928.
Transitional Poem, 1929.
From Feathers to Iron, 1931.
The Magnetic Mountain, 1933.
A Time to Dance and Other Poems, 1935.
Collected Poems 1929-1933, 1935.
Overtures to Death, 1938.
Poems in Wartime, 1940.
Word Over All, 1943.
Collected Poems, 1929-1936, 1948.
Poems 1943-1947, 1948.
An Italian Visit, 1953.
Collected Poems, 1954.

PLAY:

Noah and the Waters, 1936.

VERSE TRANSLATIONS:

The Georgics of Virgil, 1941.
Le Cimetière Marin by Paul Valéry, 1946.
The Aeneid of Virgil, 1952.

FICTION:

Dick Willoughby, 1933.
The Friendly Tree, 1936.
Starting Point, 1937.
Child of Misfortune, 1939.
The Otterbury Incident, 1948.

CRITICAL AND MISCELLANEOUS WRITINGS:

A Hope for Poetry, 1934.
Revolution in Writing, 1935.
Poetry for You, 1944.
The Colloquial Element in English Poetry, 1947.

Enjoying Poetry, 1947.
The Poetic Image, 1947.
The Poet's Task, 1951.
The Lyrical Poetry of Thomas Hardy, 1951.
The Grand Manner, 1952.
Notable Images of Virtue, 1954.

BIOGRAPHY AND CRITICISM:
Clifford Dyment, Cecil Day Lewis (W.W.), 1955.

Cecil Day Lewis has also written a number of detective stories under the pseudonym 'Nicholas Blake'.

WATKINS, Vernon Phillips, b. 1906

POETRY:
Ballad of the Marl Lwyd and other Poems, 1941.
The Lamp and the Veil, 1945.
The Lady with the Unicorn, 1948.
Selected Poems, U.S.A., 1948.
The Death Bell, 1954.
Poems and Ballads, 1954.

TRANSLATION:
Heine's The North Sea, U.S.A., 1951 and London, 1955.

A Welsh poet whose verse shows that spirit and eloquence associated with modern Welsh poets writing in English. There is an elemental quality in his imagery which can be highly effective.

BOTTRALL, Francis James Ronald, b. 1906

POETRY:
The Loosening and other Poems, 1931.
Festivals of Fire, 1934.
The Turning Path, 1939.
Selected Poems, 1946.
The Pallisades of Fear, 1949.
Adam Unparadised, 1954.

Bottrall is very much aware of the ironic complexities of modern civilization, and aims at a verse subtle and allusive enough to be able to contain an adult response to it—critical, yet not didactic, satirical, yet uncommitted. His poetry is always interesting and at its best provocative and exciting; but he has a tendency to drop into the mere exercise.

BETJEMAN, John, b. 1906

POETRY:

Mount Zion, or In Touch with the Infinite, 1931.
Continual Dew: a Little Book of Bourgeois Verse, 1937.
Old Lights for New Chancels: Verses both Typographical and Amatory, 1940.
New Bats in Old Belfries, 1945.
Selected Poems, 1948.
A Few Late Chrysanthemums, 1954.

CRITICAL AND MISCELLANEOUS WRITINGS:

Ghastly Good Taste, 1933.
Antiquarian Prejudices, 1939.
John Piper, 1944.
First and Last Loves, 1952.

Betjeman's most characteristic verse captures with witty accuracy the very tone and accent of tennis-playing suburbia. He is also a topographical poet, with a witty eye for places and their human and (especially) class associations. He has achieved, almost single-handed, a revival of interest in and admiration for Victorian architecture. He is at his best in dry topographical verses; when he tries to be profound or to launch satire directly (instead of through delicate indirection) he is not so satisfactory. A poet whom it is impossible to classify; he has invented a new kind of verse.

AUDEN, Wystan Hugh, b. 1907

POETRY:

Poems, 1930.
The Orators, 1932.

225

Look Stranger, 1936. (U.S. title: On this Island).
Selected Poems, 1940.
Another Time, 1940.
New Year Letter, 1941.
For the Time Being, 1944.
Nones, 1951.
The Shield of Achilles, 1955.

PLAYS:

The Dance of Death, 1933.
The Dog beneath the Skin (with Christopher Isherwood), 1935.
The Ascent of F6 (with Christopher Isherwood), 1936.
On the Frontier (with Christopher Isherwood), 1938.
Libretto of The Rake's Progress (with Chester Kallman; music by Igor
    Stravinsky), 1951.

CRITICAL AND MISCELLANEOUS PROSE:

Letters from Iceland (with Louis MacNeice), 1937.
Journey to a War (with Christopher Isherwood), 1939.
The Enchafèd Flood, 1950.

ANTHOLOGIES:

The Poet's Tongue (with John Garrett), 1935.
Oxford Book of Light Verse, 1938.
Tennyson (selections), 1946.
Poets of the English Language (with N. H. Pearson), 5 vols., 1952
    (U.S.A., 1950).
50 Selections from Kirkegaard, 1952.
Kierkegaard (selections and introd.), 1955.

TRANSLATION:

The Knights of the Round Table (fr. French play of Jean Cocteau), 1954.

———

BIOGRAPHY AND CRITICISM:

Richard Hoggart, W. H. Auden: An Introductory Essay, 1951.

MACNEICE, Louis, b. 1907

POETRY:

Blind Fireworks, 1929.
Poems, 1935.

Out of the Picture, 1937.
The Earth Compels, 1937.
Autumn Journal, 1939.
Plant and Phantom, 1941.
Springboard, 1944.
The Dark Tower, 1946.
Holes in the Sky, 1948.
Collected Poems, 1949.
Ten Burnt Offerings, 1952.
Autumn Sequel, 1954.

CRITICAL AND MISCELLANEOUS WRITINGS:

Letters from Iceland (with W. H. Auden), 1937.
I Crossed the Minch, 1938.
Modern Poetry, 1938.
W. B. Yeats, 1941.

TRANSLATIONS

The Agamemnon of Aeschylus, 1937.
Goethe's Faust, 1951.

RAINE, Kathleen Jessie, b. 1908

POETRY:

Stone and Flower, 1943.
Living in Time, 1946.
The Pythoness, 1949.
The Year One, 1952.
Collected Poems, 1956.

CRITICAL WRITINGS:

William Blake (W.W.), 1951.
Coleridge (W.W.), 1953.

TRANSLATION:

Lost Illusions, by Honoré de Balzac, 1951.

SPENDER, Stephen, b. 1909

POETRY:

Twenty Poems, 1930.
Poems, 1933.

Vienna, 1934.
Poems for Spain, 1939.
The Still Centre, 1939.
Ruins and Visions, 1941.
Poems of Dedication, 1946.
The Edge of Being, 1949.
Collected Poems, 1954.

PLAY:

The Trial of a Judge, 1938.

FICTION:

The Burning Catus, 1936.
The Backward Son, 1940.

CRITICAL AND MISCELLANEOUS WRITINGS:

The Destructive Element, 1935.
Forward from Liberalism, 1937.
European Witness, 1946.
Learning Laughter (travels in Israel), 1952.
The Creative Element, 1953.
Shelley (W.W.), 1952.
The Making of a Poem, 1955.

AUTOBIOGRAPHY:

World within World, 1951.

Spender is co-editor of the Anglo-American magazine *Encounter*.

RODGERS, William Robert, b. 1909

POETRY:

Awake, and other Poems, 1941.
Europa and the Bull, 1952.

Rodger's poetry has a strength and fluency that are not on the whole characteristic of modern verse. Its texture is open, its tone that of courteous eloquence.

228

DURRELL, Lawrence George, b. 1912

POETRY:

Pied Piper of Lovers, 1935.
Private Country, 1943.
Cities, Plains and People, 1946.
On Seeming to Presume, 1948.
A Landmark Gone, 1949.
The Tree of Idleness, 1955.
Selected Poems, 1956.

PLAY:

Sappho, 1950.

FICTION:

Panic Spring, 1937 (by Charles Norden, *pseud.*)
Cefalu, 1947.
The Black Book, Paris, 1938.
Prospero's Cell, 1945.
Reflections on a Marine Venus, 1953.
Justine, 1957.

MADGE, Charles, b. 1912

POETRY:

The Disappearing Castle, 1937.
The Father Found, 1941.

SOCIOLOGY:

Britain by Mass Observation (with others), 1938.

A Professor of Social Science whose poetry combines precision of observation with imaginative and sometimes abstract speculation.

(E) THE YOUNGER GENERATION

SCARFE, Francis Harold, b. 1911

POETRY:

Inscapes, 1940.
Poems and Ballads, 1941.
Underworlds, 1950.

FICTION:

Promises, 1950.
Single Blessedness, 1951.
Unfinished Woman, 1954.

CRITICAL WRITINGS:

Auden and After, 1942.
W. H. Auden, Monaco, 1949.
The Art of Paul Valéry, 1954.

A vein of reminiscence and brooding description runs through much of Scarfe's poetry, which is sometimes marred by an emotional facility, but at its best it is authentic and moving.

PRINCE, Frank Templeton, b. 1912

POETRY:

Poems, 1938.
Soldiers Bathing, 1954.

CRITICAL STUDY:

The Italian Element in Milton's Verse, 1954.

An observant poet with a variety of styles moving between epigram and a lax discursiveness.

RIDLER, Anne, b. 1912

POETRY:

Poems, 1939.
The Little Book of Modern Verse (ed.), 1941
The Nine Bright Shiners, 1943.
The Golden Bird and other Poems, 1951.

PLAYS:

The Shadow Factory, a Nativity Play, 1946.
Henry Bly and other Plays, 1950.

A devotional poet, much influenced by the later Eliot.

HENDRY, James Frank Williamson, b. 1912

POETRY:

The Bombed Happiness, 1942.
The Orchestral Mountain, 1943.

AUTOBIOGRAPHY:

Fernie Brae: a Scottish Childhood, 1947.

ANTHOLOGIES:

Three 'New Apocalypse' anthologies:
  The New Apocalypse, an anthology of Criticism, Poems and Stories,
    (with others), 1941.
  The White Horseman, Prose and Verse of the New Apocalypse (with
    H. Treece), 1941.
  The Crown and the Sickle (with H. Treece), 1944.
Scottish Short Stories, 1943.

FULLER, Roy Broadbent, b. 1912

POETRY:

Poems, 1939.
The Middle of a War, 1942.
A Lost Season, 1944.
Epitaphs and Orations, 1949.
Counterparts, 1954.

FICTION:

Savage Gold, 1946 (for children).
With My Little Eye, 1948 (for children).
The Second Curtain, 1953.
Fantasy and Fugue, 1954.
Image of a Society, 1956.

Fuller's characteristic poetry is open-worked and discursive.

TREECE, Henry, b. 1912

Invitation and Warning, 1942.
The Black Seasons, 1945.
Collected Poems, 1946.
The Haunted Garden, 1947.
The Exiles, 1952.
The Rebels, 1953.
Desperate Journey, 1954.
The Eagles Have Flown, 1954.
Ask for King Billy, 1955.
Carnival King, 1955.
The Dark Island (novel), 1952.
I Cannot go Hunting Tomorrow (short stories), 1946.

A leader of the 'New Apocalypse' movement whose poetry shows the influence of Dylan Thomas and of Surrealism. Treece edited two anthologies of the New Apocalypse movement, *The White Horseman* (with J. F. Hendry) and *The Crown and the Sickle* (with J. F. Hendry) and wrote *How I see Apocalypse* in 1946. He also wrote a study of Dylan Thomas in 1949 and edited an introduction to the work of Herbert Read in 1944.

BARKER, George Granville, b. 1913

POETRY:

Thirty Preliminary Poems, 1933.
Alanna Autumnal, 1933.
Poems, 1935.
Janus, 1935.

Calamiterror, 1937.
Lament and Triumph, 1940.
Eros in Dogma, 1944.
News of the World, 1950.
The Dead Seagull, 1950.
The True Confession of George Barker, 1950.
A Vision of Beasts and Gods, 1954.
Collected Poems, 1957.

THOMAS, Dylan (1914-1953)

POETRY:

Eighteen Poems, 1934.
Twenty-five Poems, 1936.
The Map of Love, 1939.
The World I Breathe (New Directions, U.S.A.; poems and stories), 1939.
New Poems (New Directions, U.S.A.), 1942.
Deaths and Entrances, 1946.
Selected Writings (New Directions, U.S.A.; poems and stories), 1946.
In Country Sleep (New Directions, U.S.A.), 1952.
Collected Poems, 1953.

FICTION AND MISCELLANEOUS WRITINGS:

Portrait of the Artist as a Young Dog, 1940.
The Doctor and the Devils, 1953. Film scenario (about the murderers
    Burke and Hare).
Under Milk Wood, 1954. Play for voices.
Quite Early One Morning, 1954. Broadcast talks.
A Prospect of the Sea, 1955.
Adventures in the Skin Trade, 1955.

———

BIBLIOGRAPHY:

J. Alexander Rolph, A Bibliography, 1956.

BIOGRAPHY AND CRITICISM:

Derek Stanford, Dylan Thomas, 1954.
Elder Olsen, The Poetry of Dylan Thomas, 1954.
J. M. Brinnin: Dylan Thomas in America, 1955.
Henry Treece, Dylan Thomas. Revised ed., 1956.
G. S. Fraser, Dylan Thomas (W.W.), 1957.

NICHOLSON, Norman Corntheaite, b. 1914

POETRY:

Five Rivers, 1944.
Rock Face, 1948.
The Pot Geranium, 1954.

VERSE PLAYS:

The Old Man of the Mountains, 1946.
Prophesy to the Wind, 1950.
A Match for the Devil, 1955.

CRITICAL AND MISCELLANEOUS WRITINGS:

Man and Literature, 1943.
Cumberland and Westmorland, 1949.
William Cowper, 1951.
The Lakers, 1955.

LEE, Laurie, b. 1914

POETRY:

The Bloom of Candles, 1947.
The Voyage of Magellan, 1948.
My Many-coated Man, 1955.
A Rose for Winter, 1955.

DYMENT, Clifford Henry, b. 1914

POETRY:

First Day, 1935.
Straight or Curly, 1937.
Selected Poems, 1943.
The Axe in the Wood, 1944.
Poems, 1935-48, 1949.
Experiences and Places, 1955.

CRITICAL WRITINGS:

Matthew Arnold: an Introduction and a Selection, 1948.
Thomas Hood: a Selection of his Serious Poems with an Introduction,
   1949.
C. Day Lewis, (W.W.), 1955.

DICKINSON, Patric, b. 1914

POETRY:

The Seven Days of Jericho, 1944.
Theseus and the Minotaur and Poems, 1946.
Stone in the Midst and Poems, 1949.
The Sailing Race and other Poems, 1952.
The Scale of Things: Poems, 1955.

FRASER, George Sutherland, b. 1915

POETRY:

The Fatal Landscape, 1942.
Home Town Elegy, 1944.
The Traveller Has Regrets, 1947.

CRITICAL WRITINGS:

The Modern Writer and his World, 1953.
W. B. Yeats (W.W.), 1954.

A Scottish poet who began by becoming involved in the 'New Apocalypse' movement, but soon discovered that his real sympathies lay elsewhere. His independence and integrity give him, if in a rather subdued way, a tone of his own. He himself has said of one of his best poems, 'Letter to Anne Ridler', that it gains 'by a lack of group assurance and a certain honest provincial awkwardness'.

LEWIS, Alun (1915-1944)

POETRY:

Raider's Dawn, 1942.
Ha! Ha! Amongst the Trumpets, 1945.
In the Green Tree, 1948.

FICTION:

The Last Inspection, 1943.

A promising poet of the Second World War, who was in the process of developing a surer style when he died in the Burma campaign.

GASCOYNE, David Emery, b. 1916

POETRY:

Roman Balcony and other Poems, 1932.
Poems 1937-1942, 1948.
A Vagrant and other Poems, 1950.
Night Thoughts, 1956 (for radio).

FICTION:

Opening Day, 1933.

CRITICAL WRITINGS:

A Short Survey of Surrealism, 1935.
Hölderlin's Madness, 1938.
Carlyle (W.W.), 1952.

A poet with some of the qualities of George Barker. Influenced by surrealism and the modern interest in the archetypal image, his poetry is often both sad and violent.

TILLER, Terence, b. 1916

POETRY:

Poems, 1941.
The Inward Animal 1943.
Unarm, Eros, 1947.

MOORE, Nicholas, b. 1918

POETRY:

A Book for Priscilla, 1941.
The Island and the Cattle, 1941.
A Wish in Season, 1941.

236

The Cabaret, the Dancer and the Gentleman, 1943.
The Glass Tower, 1944.
Recollections of the Gala: Selected Poems 1943-48, 1950.

A fluent and copious poet, with an odd twist of fantasy in his imagination. He was associated with the founding of the 'New Apocalypse' movement, and has since been influenced by modern American poetry.

HEATH-STUBBS, John Francis, b. 1918

POETRY:

Wounded Thammuz, 1942.
Beauty and the Beast, 1943.
The Divided Ways, 1946.
The Swarming of the Bees, 1950.
A Charm Against the Toothache, 1954.

CRITICAL WRITINGS:

The Darkling Plain, 1950 (Criticism: From Darley to Yeats.)
Charles Williams (W.W.), 1955.

ANTHOLOGIES:

Images of Tomorrow, an Anthology of Recent Poetry (ed.), 1953.
The Faber Book of Twentieth-Century Verse (ed., with David Wright), 1953.

A 'romantic' interest in myth (and in history as myth) and in elemental imagery is characteristic of Heath-Stubbs as of many of the poets of his generation.

COMFORT, Alexander, b. 1920

POETRY:

France and other Poems, 1942.
A Wreath for the Living, 1943.
Elegies, 1944.
The Song of Lazarus, 1945.
The Signal to Engage, 1947.
And All But He Departed, 1951.

FICTION:

The Almond Tree, 1943.
The Powerhouse, 1944.
On This Side Nothing, 1948.
A Giant's Strength, 1952.

CRITICAL WRITINGS:

Art and Social Responsibility, 1947.
The Novel and Our Time, 1948.
Barbarism and Sexual Freedom, 1948.
Authority and Delinquency in the Modern State, 1950.

KEYES, Sidney (1922-1943)

POETRY:

The Iron Laurel, 1942.
The Cruel Solstice, 1943.
Collected Poems, 1946.

One of the most original and promising of the young poets
killed in the Second World War.

KIRKUP, James, b. 1923

POETRY:

The Cosmic Shape, 1947.
The Drowned Sailor, 1948.
The Creation, 1950.
The Submerged Village, 1951.
A Correct Compassion, 1952.
A Spring Journey, 1954.

PLAYS:

Upon This Rock, 1955.
The Triumph of Harmony (a Masque), 1955.

AUTOBIOGRAPHY:

The Only Child, 1957.

A subdued and artful poetry, with a tone of combined reverie
and chat.

(F) THE SCOTTISH RENAISSANCE

The new movement in Scottish poetry can be studied in two anthologies: *Modern Scottish Poetry: an Anthology of the Scottish Renaissance 1920-1945*, edited by Maurice Lindsay, 1946, and *Scottish Verse 1851-1951*, edited by Douglas Young, 1952. The latter collection, going back into the heart of the 'kailyard' tradition, shows very vividly the development from it to the modern movement. Numerous periodicals, some of them very short-lived, reflect and illustrate the new trends, which are first seen in Hugh MacDiarmid's editing of anthologies of Scottish poetry entitled *Northern Numbers*. The serious student of modern Scottish literature will want to go through the files of such periodicals as *The Modern Scot, Scottish Life and Letters, Poetry Scotland, The Voice of Scotland, The Saltire Review* and *Lines*, as well as investigate the spate of books and pamphlets—much of it of ephemeral interest but all of it reflecting aspects of the modern Scottish cultural scene—published by William Maclellan, in his *Poetry Scotland* series and elsewhere. Maclellan of Glasgow was for a long time almost the official publisher to the Scottish national movement, and was more enthusiastic than discriminating. More recently, M. Macdonald of Edinburgh has taken over the publication of Scottish 'little magazines' (including *The Voice of Scotland* and *Lines*) and of books of verse by Lallans poets.

Not all Scottish poets are listed in this section, but only those who write in Lowland Scots ('Lallans') or who are in some other way consciously Scottish.

MACDIARMID, Hugh *pseud.* (Christopher Murray Grieve) b. 1892

POETRY:

Sangschaw, 1925.
Pennywheep, 1926.
A Drunk Man Looks at the Thistle, 1926.
To Circumjack Centrastus, 1930.

Selected Poems, 1930.
First Hymn to Lenin and Other Poems, 1931.
Second Hymn to Lenin, 1932.
Scots Unbound and Other Poems, 1932.
Stony Limits, and Other Poems, 1934.
Second Hymn to Lenin and Other Poems, 1935.
Selected Poems, ed. R. Crombie Saunders, 1944.
A Kist of Whistles, 1946.
Selected Poems, ed. Oliver Brown, 1954.
In Memoriam James Joyce, 1955.

CRITICAL AND MISCELLANEOUS WRITINGS:

Annals of the Five Senses, 1923.
Contemporary Scottish Studies, 1927.
Albyn, or Scotland and the Future, 1927.
At the Sign of the Thistle, 1934.
Scottish Scene (with Lewis Grassic Gibbon), 1934.
Lucky Poet (Autobiography), 1934.
The Islands of Scotland, 1949.
Cunninghame Graham, a Centenary Study, 1952.
Francis George Scott, an Essay on his 75th Birthday, 1955.

WORKS EDITED OR TRANSLATED:

The Handmaid of the Lord (a novel, translated from the Spanish of
    Ramon Maria de Tenreiro), 1929.
Living Scottish Poets, 1931.
The Birlinn of Clanranald (verse translation from the Gaelic of Alasdair
    MacMhaighsur Alasdair), 1934.
Golden Treasury of Scottish Poetry, 1946.
Collected Poems of William Soutar, 1948.
Selected Poems of Robert Burns, 1949.
Selected Poems of William Dunbar, 1952.

SOUTAR, William (1898-1943)

POETRY:

Conflict, 1931.
Seeds in the Wind, 1933.
The Solitary Way, 1934.
Brief Words, 1935.
Poems in Scots, 1935.
A Handful of Earth, 1936.
The Expectant Silence, 1944.
Collected Poems, 1948.

AUTOBIOGRAPHY:
Diaries of a Dying Man (ed. Alexander Scott), 1954.

Soutar had a most interesting mind and sensibility, as the diaries he kept during his years of lingering illness impressively show. His best poetry is in Scots.

GARIOCH, Robert *pseud.* (Robert Garioch Sutherland), b. 1909

POETRY:
Seventeen Poems for Sixpence (with Somhairle Maclean), 1940.
Chuckies on the Cairn, 1948.
The Masque of Edinburgh, 1954.

A poet who uses Scots with skill and integrity, resisting the tendency, succumbed to by so many of the Lallans poets, to bolster the emotional tone of his poetry by the picturesqueness of an antique romantic vocabulary. There is a fine dryness about the texture of his verse.

McCAIG, Norman, b. 1910

Far Cry, 1943.
The Inward Eye, 1946.
Riding Lights, 1955.

It is perhaps inconsistent to put Norman McCaig among the Scottish group when other Scottish poets who write in English, such as Edwin Muir, are put in the general category. But, although McCaig's language is English, his sensibility and often his subject matter are so clearly Scottish that one cannot help thinking of him first as a Scottish poet. His combination of visual perception and subtle speculation in his poetry—Louis MacNeice has called McCaig's poetry 'physical metaphysical'—is individual and impressive.

GRAHAM, William Sydney, b. 1917

POETRY:

Cage without Grievance, 1943.
Seven Journeys, 1944.
2nd Poems, 1945.
The White Threshold, 1949.
The Nightfishing, 1955.

Graham's poetry is listed here, out of its chronological order, because it belongs beside McCaig's: both poets write profoundly Scottish poems in English, and, in spite of a marked difference in style and sensibility, both combine description and a highly individual kind of speculation. *The Nightfishing* is Graham's best work to date.

YOUNG, Douglas, b. 1913

POETRY:

Auntran Blads, 1944.
A Braird o Thristles, 1947.
Selected Poems, 1950.

CRITICAL AND MISCELLANEOUS WRITINGS:

Plastic Scots and the Scottish Literary Tradition, 1948.
Chasing an Ancient Greek, 1950.

ANTHOLOGY:

Scottish Verse 1851-1951, 1952.

Scholar, linguist, translator, poet and politician, Douglas Young is a central figure in the modern Scottish movement. He has encouraged and welcomed all forms of Scottish national expression, he has translated modern Gaelic poetry into Scots, and has written technically skilful Lallans verse.

SMITH, Sydney Goodsir, b. 1915

POETRY:

Skail Wind, 1941.
The Wanderer and other Poems, 1943.

The Deevil's Waltz, 1946.
Selected Poems, 1947.
Under the Eildon Tree, 1948.
So Late Into the Night, 1952.
Figs and Thistles, 1953.
Cokkils, 1954.
Orpheus and Eurydice, 1955.
The Merrie Life and Dowie Death of Colickie Meg, the Carlin Wife of
 Ben Nevis, 1956.

FICTION:

Carotid Cornucopius, the first four fitts, 1947.

CRITICAL WRITINGS:

A Short Introduction to Scottish Literature, 1951.
Robert Fergusson, 1750-1774, Bicentenary Essays (ed.), 1952.

SCOTT, Tom, b. 1917

POETRY:

Seeven Poems o Maister Francis Villon made owre intil Scots, 1953.

SCOTT, Alexander, b. 1920

POETRY:

The Latest in Elegies, 1949.
Selected Poems, 1950.
Mouth Music, 1954.

PLAYS:

Untrue Thomas, 1952.
Shetland Yarn,1954.

EDITED BOOKS:

Selected Poems of William Jeffrey, 1951.
The Poems of Alexander Scott, c. 1530- c. 1584, 1952.
Diaries of a Dying Man by William Soutar, 1954.

Scott has done some effective translations in Lallans from the Gaelic and from the Anglo-Saxon. He edits the *Saltire Review*, founded in 1954, which prints new Scottish poetry and criticism.

See also under FICTION: Powys, Ford, Coppard, Joyce, Mottram, Mackenzie, Cary, Lawrence, Benson, Aldington. Under GENERAL PROSE: Empson, Strong, Gibbons, Plomer, Rex Warner.

FICTION

(A) THE OLDER GENERATION

GALSWORTHY, John (1867-1933)

NOVELS:

Jocelyn, 1898.
Villa Rubein, 1900.
The Island Pharisees, 1904.
The Man of Property, 1906.
The Country House, 1907.
Fraternity, 1909.
The Patrician, 1911.
The Dark Flower, 1913.
The Freelands, 1915.
Beyond, 1917.
A Saint's Progress, 1919.
In Chancery, 1920.
To Let, 1921.
The Forsyte Saga, 1922.
The White Monkey, 1924.
The Silver Spoon, 1926.
Swan Song, 1928.
A Modern Comedy, 1929,
Maid in Waiting, 1931.
Flowering Wilderness, 1932.
Over the River, 1933.

SHORT STORIES:

From the Four Winds, 1897.
A Man of Devon, 1901.
A Commentary, 1908.
A Motley, 1910.
Five Tales, 1918.
Tatterdamalion, 1920.
Captures, 1923.
Caravan, 1925 (collected stories).
Two Forsyte Interludes, 1927.
On Forsyte Change, 1930.
Soames and the Flag, 1930.
End of the Chapter, 1935.
Forsytes, Pendyces and Others, ed. Ada Galsworthy, 1935.
Selected Short Stories, ed. T. W. Moles, 1935.

PLAYS:

The Silver Box. Joy. Strife, 1909.
Justice, 1910.
The Little Dream, an allegory in six scenes, 1911.
The Pigeon, 1912.
The Eldest Son, 1912.
The Fugitive, 1913.
A Bit o' Love, 1915.
The Foundations, 1920.
The Skin Game, 1920.
Six Short Plays, 1921.
Windows, 1922.
A Family Man, 1922.
Loyalties, 1922.
The Forest, 1924.
The Little Man, 1924.
Old English, 1924.
The Show, 1925.
Escape, 1926.
Exiled, 1929.
The Plays of John Galsworthy, 1929.
The Roof, 1929.
The Winter Garden, 1935.

———

BIBLIOGRAPHY:

H. V. Marrot, A Bibliography, 1928.

BIOGRAPHY AND CRITICISM:

L. Schalit, John Galsworthy, A Survey, 1929.
N. Croman, John Galsworthy, 1933.
S. H. Davies, Galsworthy the Craftsman, 1933.
Hermon Ould, John Galsworthy, 1934.
H. V. Marrot, The Life and Letters of John Galsworthy, 1935.
A. Galsworthy, Over the Hills and Far Away, 1937.
R. H. Mottram, John Galsworthy (W.W.), 1953.
R. H. Mottram, For Some We Loved, 1956.

Galsworthy's first two volumes of short stories and his first two novels
were published under the pseudonym 'John Sinjohn'. The Manaton
Edition of his works was published in 30 volumes, 1923–6.

Galsworthy's Forsyte novels document an era with perceptive-
ness and intelligence, and his plays are the sometimes powerful
record of a troubled and compassionate mind confronting some

of the more intractable social and moral problems of his day. His art is nevertheless on the whole a surface one: he never quite succeeded in rendering the life he saw fully in the texture and movement of his novels or plays, and it is when he tries to be most profoundly symbolic (as in the portrait of Irene in *A Man of Property*) that he is least successful. His humanity and powers of social observation exceeded his creative and imaginative powers as a literary artist.

DOUGLAS, Norman (1868-1952)

NOVELS:

South Wind, 1917.
They Went, 1920.
In the Beginning, 1927.

SHORT STORIES:

Unprofessional Tales (by 'Normyx'), 1901.
Nerinda, 1929.

MISCELLANEOUS WRITINGS:

The Blue Grotto and its Literature, 1904.
The Forestal Conditions of Capri, 1904, and other materials for a description of Capri.
Siren Land, 1911.
Fountains in the Sand, 1912.
Old Calabria, 1915.
London Street Games, 1916.
Alone, 1921.
Together, 1923.
Experiments, 1925.
Birds and Beasts of the Greek Anthology, 1927.
The Angel of Manfredonia, 1929.
One Day, 1929.
How about Europe?, 1930 (Am. Ed., Goodbye to Western Culture)
Paneros, 1931.
Summer Islands, 1931.
Late Harvest, 1946.

AUTOBIOGRAPHY:

Looking Back, an Autobiographical Excursion, 1933.

BIBLIOGRAPHY:
Cecil Woolf, A Bibliography, 1954.

BIOGRAPHY AND CRITICISM:
R. M. Dawkins, Norman Douglas, 1933.
Ian Greenlees, Norman Douglas (W.W.), 1957.

A sardonic hedonist, whose *South Wind* is a minor classic oi ironic contemplation of the human scene in a wickedly chosen *milieu*. *Old Calabria* is a fascinating travel book.

MAYNE, Ethel Colburn (187?-1941)

NOVELS:

Jessie Vandeleur, 1902.
The Fourth Ship, 1908.
Gold Lace, 1913.
One of Our Grandmothers, 1916.

SHORT STORIES:

The Clearer Vision, 1898.
Things That No One Tells, 1910.
Come In, 1917.
Nine of Hearts, 1923.
Inner Circle, 1925.
Blindman, 1919.

RICHARDSON, Henry Handel *pseud.* (Mrs J. G. Robertson) (1870-1946)

NOVELS:

Maurice Guest, 1908.
The Getting of Wisdom, 1910.
Australia Felix, 1917.
The Way Home, 1925.
Ultima Thule, 1929.
The Fortunes of Richard Mahoney, 1930.
    (The above three novels are a trilogy entitled The Fortunes of Richard
    Mahoney.)
The End of a Childhood, 1934.

Edwin Muir's comment is worth repeating: '*Maurice Guest* seems to me superior to any other novel of the time. It shows perhaps too clearly the influence of the Russians, and of Dostoevsky in particular; but it has an impressive dramatic power, and a profound grasp of character. It contains half a dozen figures moulded on a scale slightly larger than the human, yet with intimate truth . . . *Maurice Guest* is probably the last great novel in the traditional style which has appeared in English, and it remains as astonishing today as when it was first produced.'

POWYS, John Cowper, b. 1872

NOVELS:

Wood and Stone, 1915.
Rodmoor, 1916.
Ducdame, 1925.
Wolf Solent, 1929.
A Glastonbury Romance, 1933.
Maiden Castle, 1936.
Morwyn, 1937.
Porius, 1951.
The Inmates, 1952.
The Brazen Head, 1956.

CRITICAL AND MISCELLANEOUS WRITINGS:

Visions and Recisions, 1915.
Suspended Judgements, 1916.
The Meaning of Culture, 1930.
A Philosophy of Solitude, 1933.
The Art of Happiness, 1935.
The Pleasures of Literature, 1938.
The Art of Growing Old, 1943.
Dostoievsky, 1946.
Rabelais, 1947.
In Spite Of, 1953.
Atlantis, 1954.

POETRY:

Wolfsbane Rhymes, 1916.
Mandragora, 1917.
Samphire, 1922.

Powys is a writer of extraordinarily imaginative powers, who combines magic and myth with realism to produce a strange kind of clairvoyance. His masterpiece is *A Glastonbury Romance*, one of the most remarkable and original novels of the century. One has the feeling that Powys has re-thought out for himself the whole meaning of life; his use of the Grail myth in a modern context, his highly individual style, both grand and colloquial, and the core of mysticism, together give us a quite new rendering of experience yet one that is related to many of the 'archetypal' notions of man.

FORD, Ford Madox [originally Hueffer] (1873-1939)

NOVELS:

The Fifth Queen, 1905.
The Benefactor, 1905.
Privy Seal, 1907.
An English Girl, 1907.
The Fifth Queen Crowned, 1908.
Mr Apollo, 1908.
The 'Half Moon', 1909.
The Portrait, 1910.
Ladies Whose Bright Eyes, 1911.
The Panel, 1912.
Mr Fleight, 1913.
The Young Lovell, 1913.
The Good Soldier, 1915.
The Marsden Case, 1923.
Some Do Not, 1924.
No More Parades, 1925.
A Man Could Stand Up, 1926.
The Last Post, 1928.
   (The above four novels constitute a sequence, which were published
   in a single volume in New York in 1950 under the title *Parade's End*.)
A Little Less than Gods, 1928.
When the Wicked Plan, 1932.
The Rash Act, 1933.

CRITICAL WRITINGS:

Ford Madox Brown, 1896.
Rossetti, 1902.
Hans Holbein the Younger, 1905.
Henry James, 1913.

Joseph Conrad, 1924.
The English Novel, 1929.
Mightier than the Sword, 1938.

AUTOBIOGRAPHY:

Ancient Lights, 1911.
Thus to Revisit, 1921.
No Enemy, 1929.
Return to Yesterday, 1931.
It was the Nightingale, 1933.

POETRY:

Songs from London, 1910.
Collected Poems, 1913.
On Heaven, 1918.
Poems Written on Active Service, 1918.
New Poems, 1927.

———

BIOGRAPHY AND CRITICISM:

Stella Bowen, Drawn from Life, 1940.
Douglas Goldring, The Last Pre-Raphaelite, 1948.
Kenneth Young, F. M. Ford (W.W.), 1956.

Ford's novel sequence, the Tietjens series, is a most remarkable performance, far too little appreciated in Britain today (but better known in America). Graham Greene has said that these novels 'seem to me almost the only adult novels dealing with the sexual life that have been written in England. They are our only reply to Flaubert'. The four novels were misread on first publication as 'war novels', because they are set in the war years and the characters are involved in the war; but in fact they are subtle studies of human relationships done with a part Flaubertian and part Jamesian artistry. Ford was one of the most deliberate and conscious artists among English novelists.

ONIONS, Oliver, b. 1873

NOVELS:

Little Devil Doubt, 1909.
Good Boy Seldom, 1911.

In Accordance with the Evidence (Vol. I of a trilogy), 1912.
The Debit Account (Vol. II of a trilogy), 1913.
The Story of Louie (Vol. III of a trilogy), 1913.
The New Moon, 1918.
A Case in Camera, 1920.
The Tower of Oblivion, 1921.
Peace in Our Time, 1923.
Ghosts In Daylight, 1924.
The Spite of Heaven, 1925.
Cut Flowers, 1927.
The Open Secret, 1930.
A Certain Man, 1931.
Catalan Circus, 1934.
Collected Ghost Stories, 1935.
The Hand of Cornelius Voyt, 1939.
The Story of Ragged Robin, 1945.
Poor Man's Tapestry, 1946.
Arras of Youth, 1949.
A Penny for the Harp, 1951.
Bells Ring Backward, 1953.

BARING, Maurice (1874-1945)

NOVELS:

A Triangle, 1923.
'C', 1924.
Cat's Cradle, 1925.
Tinker's Leave, 1927.
Comfortless Memory, 1928.
Coat without Seam, 1929.
Robert Peckham, 1930.
Friday's Business, 1932.

SHORT STORIES:

Orpheus in Mayfair, 1909.
The Glass Mender, 1910.
Half a Minute's Silence, 1925.

POETRY:

Sonnets and Short Poems, 1906.
Collected Poems, 1911.
Poems 1914-1917, 1918.
Poems, 1914-1919, 1921.
Collected Poems, 1925.
Selected Poems, 1930.

PLAYS:

Desiderio, 1906.
Diminutive Dramas, 1911.
Ten Diminutive Dramas, 1951.

CRITICAL AND MISCELLANEOUS WRITINGS:

An Outline of Russian Literature, 1915.
The Puppet-Show of Memory, 1922.
French Literature, 1927.
In My End is My Beginning, 1931.
Sarah Bernhardt, 1933.

MAUGHAM, William Somerset, b. 1874

NOVELS:

Liza of Lambeth, 1897.
The Making of a Saint, 1898.
The Hero, 1901.
Mrs Craddock, 1902.
The Merry-Go-Round, 1904.
The Bishop's Apron, 1906.
The Explorer, 1908.
The Magician, 1908.
Of Human Bondage, 1915.
The Moon and Sixpence, 1919.
The Painted Veil, 1925.
Cakes and Ale, 1930.
The Narrow Corner, 1932.
Theatre, 1937.
Christmas Holiday, 1939.
Up at the Villa, 1931.
The Hour Before the Dawn, 1942.
The Razor's Edge, 1944.
Then and Now, 1946.
Catalina, 1948.

SHORT STORIES:

Orientations, 1899.
Flirtation, 1906.
The Trembling of a Leaf, 1921.
The Casuarina Tree, 1926.
Ashenden, or The British Agent, 1928.
Sadie Thompson and other Stories of the South Seas, 1928.

Rain and other Stories of the South Sea Islands, 1931.
(The above two collections contain the stories in *The Trembling of a Leaf*.)
Six Stories Written in the First Person Singular, 1931.
Ah King, 1933.
Altogether, Collected Short Stories, 1934.
Cosmopolitans, 1936.
The Mixture as Before, 1940.
The Round Dozen, 1940.
Creatures of Circumstance, 1947.
Here and There, 1948.
Quartet, Stories by W. S. Maugham, Screen Plays by R. C. Sherriff, 1948.
Trio, Stories by W. S. Maugham, Screen Adaptations by W. S. Maugham, R. C. Sherriff and N. Langley, 1950.

PLAYS:

A Man of Honour, 1903.
Lady Frederick, 1912.
Jack Straw, 1912.
Mrs Dot, 1912.
Penelope, 1912.
The Explorer, 1912.
The Tenth Man, 1913.
Landed Gentry, 1913.
Smith, 1913.
The Land of Promise, 1913.
The Unknown, 1920.
The Circle, 1921.
Caesar's Wife, 1922.
East of Suez, 1922.
Our Betters, 1923.
Home and Beauty, 1923.
The Unattainable, 1923.
Loaves and Fishes, 1924.
The Letter, 1927.
The Constant Wife, 1927.
The Sacred Flame, 1928.
The Breadwinner, 1930.
For Services Rendered, 1932.
Sheppey, 1933.

MISCELLANEOUS WRITINGS:

The Land of the Blessed Virgin: Sketches and Impressions in Andalusia, 1905.
On a Chinese Screen, 1922.

The Gentlemen in the Parlour: A Record of a Journey from Rangoon to Haiphong, 1930.
Don Fernando, or Variations on some Spanish Themes, 1935.
The Summing Up, 1938.
Strictly Personal 1941.
A Writer's Notebook, 1949.

BIBLIOGRAPHY:

K. W. Jonas, A Bibliography, New Brunswick, N.J., 1950.
Raymond T. Stott, A Bibliography, 1956.

BIOGRAPHY AND CRITICISM:

R. H. Ward, W. Somerset Maugham, 1937.
R. A. Cordell, William Somerset Maugham, 1937.
R. Aldington, W. Somerset Maugham, An Appreciation, New York, 1939.
John Brophy, Somerset Maugham (W.W.), 1952.

Maugham is an accomplished professional writer who, without any original vision of humanity or any great distinction of style, has cultivated an uncommitted sardonic observation of the human scene. His novels and stories, often told with an almost nonchalant conversational air, are for the most part deftly constructed and shrewdly imagined; his plays, comedies or farces, which derive their humour from the amusing manipulation of somewhat ephemeral social and psychological situations, are perhaps rather more dated. Maugham's writings are offered as entertainment rather than as profound and original interpretations of the human situation, but his irony, his careful observation, and his conscientiousness as a craftsman, distinguish him from the mass of writers of popular fiction.

BUCHAN, John, Lord Tweedsmuir (1875-1940)

NOVELS:

John Burnet of Barns, 1898.
A Lodge in the Wilderness, 1906.
Prester John, 1910.
Salute to Adventurers, 1915.

The 39 Steps, 1915.
Greenmantle, 1916.
The Path of the King, 1921.
The Three Hostages, 1924.
The Blanket of the Dark, 1931.
The Gap in the Curtain, 1932.

BIOGRAPHY:

Sir Walter Raleigh, 1911.
Lord Minto, 1924.
Montrose, 1928.
Julius Caesar, 1932.
Sir Walter Scott, 1932.
Oliver Cromwell, 1934.
Augustus, 1937.

AUTOBIOGRAPHY:

Pilgrim's Way, 1940.

A first-class story-teller, whose adventure novels are fast moving and skilfully wrought. His biographical writing is fresh and firm: his lives of Montrose and of Scott are among his best.

HUDSON, Stephen *pseud.* (Sidney Schiff) (-1944)

NOVELS:

Concessions, 1913.
Richard Kurt, 1919.
Elinor Colhouse, 1921.
Prince Hempseed, 1922.
Tony, 1924.
Myrtle, 1925.
Richard, Myrtle and I, 1926.
A True Story, 1930.
The Other Side, 1937.

A novelist who is interested in the precise documentation of individual character. *A True Story* contains his best work. He completed Scott Moncrieff's translation of Proust's *Remembrance of Things Past.*

POWYS, Theodore Francis (1875-1953)

NOVELS:

Black Bryony, 1923.
Mark Only, 1924.
Mr Tasker's Gods, 1925.
Mockery Gap, 1925.
Innocent Birds, 1926.
Mr Weston's Good Wine, 1927.
Kindness in a Corner, 1930.
Unclay, 1931.

SHORT STORIES:

The Left Leg, 1923.
Feed My Swine, 1926.
The Rival Pastors, 1927.
The Dewpond, 1928.
The House with the Echo, 1928.
Fables, 1929.
Christ in the Cupboard, 1930.
The Key of the Field, 1930.
The White Paternoster, 1930.
Uncle Dottery, 1931.
When Thow Wast Naked, 1931.
The Two Thieves, 1932.
Captain Patch, 1935.
Goat Green, 1937.
Bottle's Path, 1946.
God's Eyes a-Twinkle, 1947,
and others.

Powys's allegorical stories of rural life, with their deceptively simple surface and brooding preoccupation with death and evil underneath, have an uncanny power of their own.

REID, Forrest (1876-1947)

NOVELS:

The Bracknels, 1911.
Following Darkness, 1912.
The Gentle Lover, 1913.
At the Door of the Gate, 1915.
A Garden by the Sea: stories and sketches, 1918.

Pender Among the Residents, 1922.
Apostate, 1926.
Demophon, 1927.
Uncle Stephen, 1931.
Brian Westby, 1934.
The Retreat, 1936.
Private Road, 1940.
Young Tom, 1944.
The Malk of Paradise, 1946.

DEEPING, Warwick (1877-1950)

NOVELS:

Bess of the Woods, 1906.
Bertrand of Brittany, 1908.
The Red Saint, 1909.
Marriage by Conquest, 1916.
Second Youth, 1919.
Apples of Gold, 1923.
Sorrel and Son, 1925.
Doomsday, 1927.
Kitty, 1927.

COPPARD, Alfred Edgar (1878-1957)

SHORT STORIES:

Adam and Eve and Pinch Me, 1921.
Clorinda Walks in Heaven, 1922.
The Black Dog, 1923.
Fishmonger's Fiddle, 1925.
The Field of Mustard, 1926.
Silver Circus, 1928.
Count Stefan, 1928.
The Gollan, 1929.
My Hundredth Tale, 1930.
Nixey's Harlequin, 1921.
Cheefoo, 1932.
Dunky Fitlow, 1933.
Ninepenny Flute, 1937.
Selected Tales, 1946.
Fearful Pleasures, 1946.
Dark Eyed Lady, 1947.
Lucy In Her Pink Jacket, 1954.

POETRY:

Hips and Haws, 1922.
Pelagea and other poems, 1926.
Yokohama Garland, 1926.
The Collected Poems of A. E. Coppard, 1928.
Easter Day, 1931.

A short-story writer of professional cunning.

FORSTER, Edward Morgan, b. 1879

NOVELS:

Where Angels Fear to Tread, 1905.
The Longest Journey, 1907.
A Room with a View, 1908.
Howard's End, 1910.
A Passage to India, 1924.

SHORT STORIES:

The Celestial Omnibus and Other Stories, 1914.
The Story of the Siren 1920.
The Eternal Moment and Other Stories, 1928.
Collected Short Stories, 1948.

CRITICAL AND MISCELLANEOUS WRITINGS:

Alexandria: a History and Guide, 1922. (rev. ed., 1938)
Pharos and Pharillon, 1923.
Anonymity: An Enquiry, 1925.
Aspects of the Novel, 1927.
A Letter to Madam Blanchard, 1931.
Original Letters from India (ed.), 1931.
Goldsworthy Lowes Dickinson, 1934. A biography.
Abinger Harvest—A Miscellany, 1936.
Reading As Usual, 1939.
What I Believe, 1939.
Nordic Twilight, 1940.
Virginia Woolf, 1942.
The Development of English Prose between 1918 and 1939, 1945.
Two Cheers for Democracy, 1951.
The Hill of Devi, 1953.
Marianne Thornton, 1956.

PAGEANT PLAY:

England's Pleasant Land, 1940.

OPERA LIBRETTO:

Billie Budd: An Opera adapted (with E. Crozier) for Benjamin Britten
from the story by Herman Melville, 1951.

———

BIOGRAPHY AND CRITICISM:

Rose Macaulay, The Writings of E. M. Forster, 1938.
Lionel Trilling, E. M. Forster, 1944.
Rex Warner: E. M. Forster (W.W.), 1950.

Forster's place as a minor classic among English novelists is
secure. His chief theme is the subtle exploration of the deficiencies,
in sensibility and in emotional understanding, of the English
middle-class character, and at his best he handles this with irony
and a delicate symbolic treatment of events and objects. *Howard's
End* shows his most mature development of this theme in an English social context, but when, in *A Passage to India*, he sets his
English characters among Indians a richer and profounder novel
results.

WODEHOUSE, Pelham Greville, b. 1881

NOVELS:

The Pothunters, 1902.
A Good Bet, 1904.
The Head of Kay's, 1905.
Love Among the Chickens, 1906.
The White Feather, 1907.
The Swoop, 1908.
Enter Psmith, 1909.
A Gentleman of Leisure, 1910.
Psmith in the City, 1910.
The Prince and Betty, 1911.
The Little Nugget, 1912.
Psmith, Journalist, 1915.
Something Fresh, 1915.
Uneasy Money, 1917.

Piccadilly Jim, 1918.
A Damsel in Distress, 1919.
Jill the Reckless, 1920.
The Coming of Bill, 1920.
The Indiscretions of Archie, 1921.
The Clicking of Cuthbert, 1922.
The Girl on the Boat, 1922.
Leave it to Psmith, 1923.
The Inimitable Jeeves, 1924.
Carry On, Jeeves, 1925.
Sam the Sudden, 1925.
The Heart of a Goof, 1926.
The Small Bachelor, 1927.
Money for Nothing, 1928.
Summer Lightning, 1929.
Very Good, Jeeves, 1930.
Doctor Sally, 1932.
Hot Water, 1932.
Heavy Weather, 1933.
Thank You, Jeeves, 1934.
Right Ho, Jeeves, 1934.
Blandings Castle, 1935.
The Luck of the Bodkins, 1935.
Young Men in Spats, 1936.
Laughing Gas, 1936.
Summer Moonshine, 1938.
The Code of the Woosters, 1938.
Uncle Fred in the Springtime, 1939.
Eggs, Beans and Crumpets, 1940.
Quick Service, 1940.
Full Moon, 1947.
Uncle Dynamite, 1948.
Mating Season, 1949.
Old Reliable, 1951.
Barmy in Wonderland, 1952.
Pigs Have Wings, 1952.
Ring for Jeeves, 1953.
The Return of Jeeves, 1954.
Jeeves and the Feudal Spirit, 1954.
Bertie Sees it Through, 1955.
Something Fishy, 1956.

SHORT STORIES:

A Prefect's Uncle, 1903.
Tales of St Austin's, 1903.
Meet Mr Mulliner, 1927.

Mr Mulliner Speaking, 1929.
Louder and Funnier, 1932.
Mulliner Nights, 1933.
Mulliner Omnibus, 1935.
Lord Emsworth and Others, 1937.
Nothing Serious, 1950.

AUTOBIOGRAPHY:

Performing Flea, 1953.

This remarkable list of titles is worth quoting at length (it is not complete and does not include eighteen musical comedies). Wodehouse is a unique English institution; his Edwardian humour (which has been admirably analysed in an essay by George Orwell) represents a peculiar stylization of a phase of the English class situation which has long passed away but which, having been given its own fictional conventions, has been granted a life long outliving that of the social facts it presupposes. The efficient-servant-versus-idle-gentleman contrast, on which the humour of the Jeeves stories is based, and the languid slang which was out of date even before it was employed, represent a considerable feat of creative humour. *Performing Flea* is an interesting autobiography and apologia.

MYERS, Leopold Hamilton (1881-1944)

NOVELS:

The Orissers, 1923.
The Clio, 1925.

The Near and the Far, 1927.   }   these, with 'Rajah Amar' added,
Prince Jali, 1930.   compose The Root and the Flower,
                                  1935.

Strange Glory, 1936.
The Pool of Vishnu, 1940.

The Root and the Flower, with *The Pool of Vishnu* to complete it, is one of the most distinguished philosophical novels of our time.

(B) THE AGE OF EXPERIMENT

WOOLF, Virginia (1882-1941)

NOVELS:

The Voyage Out, 1915.
Night and Day, 1919.
Jacob's Room, 1922.
Mrs Dalloway, 1925.
To the Lighthouse, 1927.
Orlando, 1928.
The Waves, 1931.
The Years, 1937.
Between the Acts, 1941.

SHORT STORIES:

The Mark on the Wall, 1919.
Kew Gardens, 1919.
Monday or Tuesday, 1921.
A Haunted House, 1943.

CRITICAL AND MISCELLANEOUS WRITINGS:

Mr Bennett and Mrs Brown, 1924.
The Common Reader, 1925.
A Room of One's Own, 1929.
On Being Ill, 1930.
Beau Brummell, New York, 1930.
Flush: A Biography, 1932.
A Letter to a Young Poet, 1932.
The Common Reader: Second Series, 1932.
Walter Sickert: A Conversation, 1934.
Three Guineas, 1938.
Reviewing, 1938.
Roger Fry, 1940.
The Death of the Moth, 1942.
The Moment and other Essays, 1947.
The Captain's Death-Bed, 1950.

BIBLIOGRAPHY:

B. J. Kirkpatrick, A Bibliography, 1957.

BIOGRAPHY AND CRITICISM:

W. Holtby, Virginia Woolf, 1935.
E. M. Forster, Virginia Woolf, 1942.
David Daiches, Virginia Woolf, 1942.
Joan Bennett, Virginia Woolf, 1945.
R. L. Chambers, The Novels of Virginia Woolf, 1947.
B. Blackstone, Virginia Woolf: A Commentary, 1948.
B. Blackstone, Virginia Woolf (W.W.), 1952.

JOYCE, James (1882-1941)

NOVELS:

A Portrait of the Artist as a Young Man, 1916.
Ulysses, 1922.
Finnegans Wake, 1939.

SHORT STORIES:

Dubliners, 1915.

PLAY:

Exiles, 1936.

POETRY:

Chamber Music, 1923.
Pomes Penyeach, 1927.

———

BIBLIOGRAPHY:

J. J. Slocum and H. Cahoon, 1953.

BIOGRAPHY AND CRITICISM:

Stuart Gilbert, James Joyce's *Ulysses*, 1930.
Frank Budgen, James Joyce and the Making of *Ulysses*, 1934.
Herbert Gorman, James Joyce (a biography), 1939.
Harry Levin, James Joyce, 1941.
J. Campbell and H. M. Robinson, A Skeleton Key to *Finnegans Wake*,
   1944.
Seon Givens (ed.), James Joyce: Two Decades of Criticism, New York,
   1948.
William Y. Tindall, James Joyce, 1950.

There is a study of Joyce in Edmund Wilson's *Axel's Castle* and there are three chapters on Joyce in David Daiches's *The Novel and the Modern World*.

RICHARDSON, Dorothy, b. 1882

NOVELS:

Pointed Roofs, 1915.
Backwater, 1916.
Honeycomb, 1917.
The Tunnel, 1919.
Interim, 1919.
Deadlock, 1921.
Revolving Lights, 1923.
The Trap, 1925.
Oberland, 1927.
Dawn's Left Hand, 1931.
Clear Horizon, 1935.
Dimple Hill, 1938.

These novels are part of a single sequence, entitled *Pilgrimage*, dealing with the sensibilities and emotional development of the heroine. Dorothy Richardson was a pioneer in the 'stream-of-consciousness' method of writing fiction, and her novels pursue this method with delicacy and single-mindedness.

EVANS, CARADOC (1883-1945)

NOVELS:

Nothing to Pay, 1930.
Wasps, 1933.
This Way to Heaven, 1934.
Morgan Bible, 1943.

SHORT STORIES:

My People, 1915.
Capel Sion, 1916.
My Neighbours, 1919.
Pilgrims in a Foreign Land, 1942.
The Earth Gives All and Takes All, 1946.
Mother's Marvel, 1949.

PLAY:

Taffy, 1923.

A satirist of Welsh life.

MOTTRAM, Ralph Hale, b. 1883

NOVELS:

The Spanish Farm, 1924.
Sixty-four, Ninty-four! 1925.
The Crime at Vanderlynden's, 1926.
(The above three novels form the Spanish Farm Trilogy.)
Our Mr Dormer, 1927.
Our English Miss, 1928.
The Boroughmonger, 1929.
Europa's Beast, 1930. (Am. Ed., A Rich Man's Daughter.)
Castle Island, 1931.
Home for the Holidays, 1932.
Dazzle, 1932.
The Lame Dog, 1933. (Am. Ed., At the Sign of the Lame Dog.)
Bumphrey's, 1934.
Flower Pot End, 1935.
Time to be Going, 1937.
Trader's Dream, 1939.
The Ghost and the Maiden, 1941.
Buxton the Liberator, 1946.
The Gentlemen of Leisure, 1948.
The Part that is Missing, 1952.
Over the Wall, 1955.

SHORT STORIES:

Ten Years Ago: Armistice and other memories, 1928.
The Headless Hound, 1931.
The Banquet, 1934.

MISCELLANEOUS WRITINGS:

A History of Financial Speculation, 1929.
Miniature Banking Histories, 1930.
John Crome of Norwich, 1931.
East Anglia, England's Eastern Province, 1933.
The Broads, 1952.
John Galsworthy (W.W.), 1953.

267

POETRY:

Poems Old and New, 1930.

The Spanish Farm Trilogy is important as a contribution to the fiction of the First World War and as a document of its times.

MACKENZIE, Sir Edward Montague Compton, b. 1883

NOVELS:

The Passionate Elopement, 1911.
Carnival, 1912.
Sinister Street Vol. I, 1913.
Sinister Street Vol. II, 1914.
Guy and Pauline, 1915.
Sylvia Scarlett, 1918.
Sylvia and Michael, 1919.
The Altar Steps, 1922.
Rogues and Vagabonds, 1927.
Extraordinary Women, 1928.
The Three Couriers, 1929.
Our Street, 1931.
West to North, 1940.
The East Wind of Love, 1937.
The South Wind of Love, 1937.
The West Wind of Love, 1940.
The North Wind of Love, Vol I, 1944, Vol. II, 1945.
    (The above four novels form 'The Four Winds of Love'.)
Monarch of the Glen, 1941.
Whiskey Galore, 1947.
Ben Nevis Goes East, 1954.
Thin Ice, 1956.

PLAYS:

The Gentleman in Grey, 1906.
Carnival, 1912.
Columbine, 1920.
The Lost Cause, 1931.

CRITICAL AND MISCELLANEOUS WRITINGS:

Gallipoli Memories, 1929.
First Athenian Memories, 1931.
Greek Memories, 1932.

Prince Charlie, 1932.
Literature in my Time, 1933.
Reaped and Bound, 1933.
Prince Charlie and his Ladies, 1934.
Marathon and Salamis, 1934.
Catholicism and Scotland, 1936.
Pericles, 1937.

POETRY:

Poems, 1907.
Kensington Rhymes, 1912.

Sinister Street remains Compton Mackenzie's most serious work, with its brilliant surface colour and psychological awareness. Since then, he has tended increasingly to fall into poses and cultivate attitudes. His best later work has been his light-hearted comic novels, where he displays a fine sense of farcical situation.

WALPOLE, Sir Hugh (1884-1941)

NOVELS:

The Wooden Horse, 1909.
Maradick at Forty, 1910.
Mr Perrin and Mr Traill, 1911.
Fortitude, 1913.
The Dark Forest, 1916.
The Secret City, 1919.
The Cathedral, 1922.
Portrait of a Man with Red Hair, 1925.
The Silver Thorn, 1928.
The Fortress, 1932.
Vanessa, 1933.
The Inquisitor, 1933.
Head in Green Bronze, 1938.
Roman Fountain, 1940.
The Blind Man's House, 1941.
Katherine Christian, 1944.

BIOGRAPHY AND CRITICISM:

R. Hart-Davis, Hugh Walpole, 1952.

A talented and ambitious novelist who never succeeded, in spite of his genuine gifts, in achieving anything more than competent middlebrow fiction. A certain facility, an artistic carelessness, a lack of emotional discipline, prevented him from achieving the kind of fully realized literary art towards which at one time he seemed to be moving.

LEWIS, Percy Wyndham (1884-1957)

NOVELS:

Tarr, 1918.
The Childermass Vol. I, 1928.
The Apes of God, 1930.
Snooty Baronet, 1932.
The Revenge For Love, 1937.
The Vulgar Streak, 1941.
Self Condemned, 1954.
Monstre Gai, 1955.
Malign Fiesta, 1955.
    (The last two complete The Childermass.)

SHORT STORIES:

The Wild Body, 1927.
Rotting Hill, 1951.

CRITICAL AND MISCELLANEOUS WRITINGS:

The Caliph's Design: Architects! Where is Your Vortex?, 1919.
Harold Gilman, 1919.
The Art of Being Ruled, 1926.
Time and Western Man, 1927.
The Lion and the Fox: the role of hero in the plays of Shakespeare, 1927.
Paleface, 1929.
The Diabolical Principle and the Dithyrambic Spectator, 1931.
Hitler, 1931.
The Doom of Youth, 1932.
Men Without Art, 1934.
Left Wings Over Europe, 1936.
Count Your Dead: They Are Alive! 1937.
The Mysterious Mr Bull, 1938.
The Jews, Are They Human? 1939.
The Hitler Cult and How It Will End, 1939.
America I Presume, 1940.

America and Cosmic Man, 1948.
The Writer and the Absolute, 1952.
The Demon of Progress in the Arts, 1954.

AUTOBIOGRAPHY:

Blasting and Bombardiering, 1937.
Rude Assignment, 1950.

PLAY:

The Enemy of the Stars, 1932.

POETRY:

One Way Song, 1933,
and other works.

> He edited *Blast*, together with Ezra Pound, 1914-15. This 'review of the
> great English Vortex' gives a lively and even violent picture of Lewis's
> reaction to the culture of his time and of the short-lived 'Vorticist'
> movement which he championed.

BIOGRAPHY AND CRITICISM:

H. G. Porteous, Wyndham Lewis: A Discursive Exposition, 1932.
Geoffrey Grigson, A Master of Our Time: A Study of Wyndham Lewis,
  1951.
Hugh Kenner, Wyndham Lewis, 1954.
E. W. F. Tomlin, Wyndham Lewis (W.W.), 1955.

A remarkable original creative and critical mind, out of sympathy with all modern progress and *avant garde* movements emana-
ting from Bloomsbury and Bohemia; he satirizes the latter with
enormous comic gusto in his massive ironic novel, *The Apes of God*.
His most remarkable achievement is *The Childermass* and its se-
quels, *Monstre Gai* and *Malign Fiesta*, visionary novels of strange
power. *The Childermass* is set in a waste land outside heaven,
where the 'emigrant mass' of humanity awaits examination by the
Bailiff. The hallucinatory atmosphere, the grotesquerie, the
power and conviction of the narrative, the ritualistic and symbolic overtones of meaning, together make this novel sequence
something quite unique in modern literature. His critical and

philosophical works show the same independence of thought and Right-wing scorn of all 'softness' in modern life and letters. *Time and Western Man* is a key work in the interpretation of Lewis's thought as well as an important critical work in its own right. It is impossible to summarize Lewis's position; but it might be said that he stands for intellect and order and the importance of 'non-human' values against subjectivism, immersion in the flux of consciousness, surrender to the 'dark gods' within and to time and change.

SWINNERTON, Frank Arthur, b. 1884

NOVELS:

The Merry Heart, 1909.
The Young Idea, 1910.
The Casement, 1911.
The Happy Family, 1912.
On the Staircase, 1914.
The Chaste Wife, 1916.
Nocturne, 1917.
Shops and Houses, 1918.
September, 1919.
Coquette, 1921.
Three Lovers, 1922.
Young Felix, 1923.
The Elder Sister, 1925.
Summer Storm, 1926.
A Brood of Ducklings, 1928.
Sketch of a Sinner, 1929.
The Georgian House, 1932.
Elizabeth, 1934.
Harvest Comedy, 1937.
The Two Wives, 1939.
Thankless Child, 1942.
A Woman in Sunshine, 1944.
Faithful Company, 1948.
The Cats and Rosemary, 1950.
A Flower For Catherine, 1950.
The Doctor's Wife Comes to Stay, 1950.
Master Jim Probity, 1952.

AUTOBIOGRAPHY:
Swinnerton, An Autobiography, 1937.

CRITICAL AND MISCELLANEOUS WRITINGS:
George Gissing, 1912.
R. L. Stevenson, 1914.
Tokefield Papers, 1927.
The Georgian Literary Scene, 1935.
The Reviewing and Criticism of Books, 1939.
Arnold Bennett (W.W.), 1950.
Background with Chorus, 1956.

POWYS, Llewellyn (1884-1939)

NOVEL:
Apples be Ripe, 1930.

MISCELLANEOUS WRITINGS:
Thirteen Worthies, 1923.
Ebony and Ivory, 1923.
Black Laughter, 1924.
The Cradle of God, 1929.
The Pathetic Fallacy, a study of Christianity, 1930.
Impassioned Clay, 1931.
A Pagan's Pilgrimage, 1931.
Now that the Gods are Dead, 1932.
Earth memories, 1934.
Glory of Life, 1934.
Dorset Essays, 1936.
Somserset Essays, 1937.
Love and Death, 1939.

AUTOBIOGRAPHY:
Confessions of Two Brothers, 1916.
Skin for Skin, 1925.
The Verdict of Bridlegoose, 1926.

Edwin Muir's brief description is worth preserving: 'A pessimistic Pantheist, but a charming writer with an exquisite visual talent.'

273

HOLME, Constance (-1955)

NOVELS:

Crump Folk Going Home, 1913.
The Lonely Plough, 1914.
The Old Road from Spain, 1916.
Beautiful End, 1918.
The Splendid Fairing, 1919.
The Trumpet in the Dust, 1921.
The Things which Belong, 1925.
He-Who-Came, 1930.

SHORT STORIES:

The Wisdom of the Simple, 1937.

FIRBANK, Ronald (1886-1926)

NOVELS:

Odette D'Antrevernes, 1905.
A Study in Temperament, 1905.
Odette, a Fairy Tale for Weary People, 1916.
Valmouth, 1919.
The Princess Zoubaroff, 1920.
The Flower beneath the Foot, 1923.
Sorrow in Sunlight, 1924 (American title: Prancing Nigger).

A novelist of sophisticated fantasy, whose stories are full of absurdly brilliant inconsequential conversation and a desperate brightness. There is an odd mixture of decadence and innocence about his work.

McKENNA, Stephen (1888-1956)

NOVELS:

The Reluctant Lover, 1912.
Sheila Intervenes, 1913.
The Sixth Sense, 1915.
Sonia, 1917.
Nine-six Hours' Leave, 1917.

Midas and Son, 1919.
Lady Lility, 1920.
The Education of Eric Lane, 1921.
The Confessions of a Well-Meaning Woman, 1922.
Soliloquy, 1922.
Vindication, 1923.
Tales of Intrigue and Revenge, 1924.
An Affair of Honour, 1925.
The Oldest God, 1926.
Saviours of Society, 1926.
The Secretary of State, 1927.
The Unburied Dead, 1928.
The Datchley Inheritance, 1929.
The Cast-Iron Duke, 1930.
Beyond Hell, 1931.
Pandora's Box, 1932.
Namesakes, 1933.
Portrait of His Excellency, 1934.
Sole Death, 1935.
Lady Cynthia Clandon's Husband, 1936.
Last Confession, 1937.
Breasted Amazon, 1938.
A Life for a Life, 1939.
Mean, Sensual Man, 1943.
Pearl Wedding, 1951.

CARY, A. Joyce L. (1888-1957)

NOVELS:

Aissa Saved, 1932.
An American Visitor, 1933.
The African Witch, 1936.
Castle Corner, 1938.
Mister Johnson, 1939.
Charley is my Darling, 1940.
A House of Children, 1941.
Herself Surprised, 1941.
To Be a Pilgrim, 1942.
The Horse's Mouth, 1944.
The Moonlight, 1946.
A Fearful Joy, 1949.
Prisoner of Grace, 1952.
Except the Lord, 1953.
Not Honour More, 1955.

POETRY:

Marching Soldier, 1945.
The Drunken Sailor, 1947.

———

BIOGRAPHY AND CRITICISM:

Walter Allen: Joyce Cary (W.W.), 1953.

Cary's African novels (the first three listed above, together with *Mister Johnson*) are penetrating and original studies of problems of life and character involving African and Englishman, showing a remarkable imaginative understanding of the different kinds of personality involved in these problems. The three linked novels, *Herself Surprised*, *To be a Pilgrim*, and *The Horse's Mouth* have the same qualities but show also a buoyancy, a rich sense of life and colour and of the individuality of people and things, which account for his having been hailed as a 'positive' novelist in an age without faith.

JESSE, Fryniwyd Tennyson

NOVELS:

The Milky Way, 1913.
Beggars on Horseback, 1915.
Secret Bread, 1917.
The White Riband, or, A Young Female's Folly, 1921.
Tom Fool, 1926.
The Moonraker, 1927.
Many Latitudes, 1928.
The Lacquer Lady, 1929.
The Solange Stories, 1931.
A Pin to See the Peepshow, 1934.
The Alabaster Cup, 1950.

PLAYS:

Billeted, 1920 (with H. M. Harwood).
Anyhouse, 1925.
The Pelican, 1926 (with H. M. Harwood).
How to be Healthy though Married, 1930 (with H. M. Harwood).
A Pin to see the Peepshow, 1934 (with H. M. Harwood).

MISCELLANEOUS WRITINGS:

The Sword of Deborah, 1919.
Murder and its Motives, 1924.
The Trial of S. H. Dougal, 1928 (Notable British Trial Series).
London Front, 1940.
While London Burns, 1942.
The Saga of San Demetrio, 1946.
The Story of Burma, 1946.
Comments on Cain, 1948.

A talented journalist and a novelist of imagination and dramatic sense. She has edited a number of cases for the 'Notable British Trials' series in addition to that listed above.

LAWRENCE, David Herbert (1885-1930)

NOVELS:

The White Peacock, 1911.
The Trespasser, 1912.
Sons and Lovers, 1913.
The Rainbow, 1915.
Women in Love, 1920.
The Lost Girl, 1920.
Aaron's Rod, 1922.
Kangaroo, 1923.
The Boy in the Bush (with M. L. Skinner), 1924.
The Plumed Serpent, 1926.
Lady Chatterley's Lover, 1928.
The Virgin and the Gipsy, 1930.

SHORT STORIES:

The Prussian Officer and other Stories, 1914.
England, My England, 1922.
The Ladybird, 1923. (American ed.: The Captain's Doll.)
St Mawr: together with The Princess, 1925.
Sun, 1926.
Glad Ghosts, 1926.
Rawdon's Roof, 1928.
The Woman Who Rode Away, 1928.
Sun (unexpurgated edition), 1928.
The Escaped Cock (later called The Man Who Died), 1929.
Love Among the Haystacks, 1930.
The Lovely Lady and other Stories, 1933.

The Tales of D. H. Lawrence, 1934.
A Modern Lover, 1934.
A Prelude, 1949.

POETRY:

Love Poems and Others, 1913.
Amores, 1916.
Look! We Have Come Through, 1917.
New Poems, 1918.
Bay, 1919.
Tortoises, 1921.
Birds, Beasts and Flowers, 1923.
Collected Poems, 1928.
Pansies, 1929.
Nettles, 1930.
The Triumph of the Machine, 1930.
Last Poems, 1932.
Collected Poems, 1932
The Ship of Death and other Poems, 1933.
Selected Poems (selected by R. Aldington), 1934.
Fire and other Poems, 1940.

CRITICAL AND MISCELLANEOUS WRITINGS:

The Widowing of Mrs Holroyd, 1914.
Twilight in Italy, 1916.
Touch and Go, 1920.
Sea and Sardinia, 1921.
Movements in European History (by 'Lawrence H. Davison'), 1921.
Psychoanalysis and the Unconscious, 1921.
Fantasia of the Unconscious, 1922.
Studies in Classic American Literature, 1923.
Reflections on the Death of a Porcupine, 1925.
David, 1926.
Mornings in Mexico, 1927.
My Skirmish with Jolly Roger, 1929.
Pornography and Obscenity, 1929.
A Propos of Lady Chatterley's Lover, 1930.
Assorted Articles, 1930.
Apocalypse, 1931.
Etruscan Places, 1932.
The Plays of D. H. Lawrence, 1933.
We Need One Another, 1933.
A Collier's Friday Night, 1934.
The Spirit of Place (anthology compiled by R. Aldington), 1935.
Phoenix, 1936.
Selected Literary Criticism, ed. A. Beal, 1956.

BIBLIOGRAPHY

TRANSLATIONS:

Verga, Giovanni. Mastro-don Gesualdo, New York, 1923.
Verga, Giovanni. Little Novels of Sicily, New York, 1925.
Verga, Giovanni. Cavalleria Rusticana and Other Stories, London, 1928.
Lasca, Il. The Story of Doctor Manente: Being the Tenth and Last
  Story from the Suppers of A. F. Grazzini Called Il Lasca, Florence,
  1929.

LETTERS:

The Letters of D. H. Lawrence, ed. A. Huxley, 1932.
D. H. Lawrence's Letters to Bertrand Russell, ed. H. T. Moore, New
  York, 1948.
Letters, selected by R. Aldington, 1950

BIBLIOGRAPHY:

E. D. McDonald, A Bibliography, 1925. (Supplement, 1931.)

BIOGRAPHY AND CRITICISM:

A spate of books about Lawrence poured from the Press in the years following his death. Most of these were personal reminiscences, and they
  reflected the strong feelings (both pro and con) aroused among
  different kinds of people by Lawrence's personality. A selection of the
  more interesting of these is given:
Not I, But the Wind, by F. E. J. Lawrence, 1934. Personal reminiscences
  by his wife.
Son of Woman, by J. M. Murry, 1931.
The Savage Pilgrimage, by C. R. Carswell, 1932. A passionately sym-
  pathetic account by one who accepted most of Lawrence's ideas.
Reminiscences of D. H. Lawrence, by J. M. Murry, 1933.
D. H. Lawrence, a Personal Record, by E. T., 1936. (E.T. was the origi-
  nal of Miriam in Sons and Lovers.)
A Poet and Two Painters, by K. Merrild, 1938.
Portrait of a Genius, But . . ., by Richard Aldington, 1950. An account
  by a writer who knew him but who did not share his views.
D. H. Lawrence and Human Existence, by W. Tiverton, 1951.
D. H. Lawrence, by Kenneth Young (W.W.), 1952.
The Intelligent Heart, by Harry T. Moore, 1955. A detailed and sym-
  pathetic biography by a scholar who was not involved in the Lawrence
  circle and was thus able to tell the story objectively and calmly.
D. H. Lawrence: Novelist, by F. R. Leavis, 1955.
The Dark Sun, by G. Hough, 1956.

MANSFIELD, Katherine (1888-1923)

SHORT STORIES:

In a German Pension, 1911.
Prelude, 1918.
Bliss, 1920.
The Garden Party, 1922.
The Dove's Nest, 1923.
Something Childish, 1924.
The Aloe, 1930. (The original form of *Prelude*.)

POETRY:

Poems, 1923.

CRITICAL AND MISCELLANEOUS WRITINGS:

Journal, ed. by J. M. Murry, 1927.
Novels and Novelists, 1930.
The Scrapbook of Katherine Mansfield, ed. J. M. Murry, 1930.

————

BIOGRAPHY AND CRITICISM:

S. Berkman, Katherine Mansfield, A Critical Study, 1951.
A. Alpers, Katherine Mansfield, a Biography, 1954.
I. A. Gordon: Katherine Mansfield (W.W.), 1954.

MACAULAY, Rose, b. 1889

NOVELS:

The Valley Captives, 1911
The Lee Shore, 1912.
Views and Vagabonds, 1912.
The Making of a Bigot, 1914.
What Not, 1919.
Potterism, 1920.
Dangerous Ages, 1921.
Mystery at Geneva, 1922.
Told by an Idiot, 1923.
Orphan Island, 1924.
Crewe Train, 1926.
Keeping Up Appearances, 1928. (Am. Ed., Daisy and Daphne.)
Staying with Relations, 1930.

They Were Defeated, 1932.
Going Abroad, 1934.
I Would Be Private, 1937.
Fabled Shore, 1949.
The World My Wilderness, 1950.
The Towers of Trebizond, 1956.

CRITICAL AND MISCELLANEOUS WRITINGS:

A Casual Commentary, 1925.
Some Religious Elements in English Literature, 1931.
John Milton, 1933.
The Minor Pleasures of Life, 1934.
Personal Pleasures, 1935.
The Writings of E. M. Forster, 1938.
Life Among the English, 1942.
Pleasure of Ruins, 1953.

A novelist of wit and intelligence, who casts a mildly satirical eye on the human comedy.

DELAFIELD, E. M. *pseud.* (Elizabeth M. Dashwood) (1890-1943)

NOVELS:

Zella Sees Herself, 1917.
The Pelicans, 1918.
The War-Workers, 1918.
Consequences, 1919.
Tension, 1920.
The Heel of Achilles, 1921.
Humbug, 1921.
The Optimist, 1922.
A Reversion to Type, 1923.
Mrs Harter, 1924.
The Chip and the Block, 1925.
Jill, 1926.
The Way Things Are, 1927.
The Suburban Young Man, 1928.
What is Love? 1928. (Am. Ed., First Love.)
Diary of a Provincial Lady, 1930.
Turn Back the Leaves, 1930.
Challenge to Clarissa, 1931. (Am. Ed., House Party.)
The Provincial Lady Goes Further, 1932. (Am. Ed., The Provincial Lady in London.)

Thank Heaven Fasting, 1932. (Am. Ed., A Good Man's Love.)
Gay Life, 1933.
Faster! Faster! 1936.
As Others Hear Us, 1937.
Three Marriages, 1939.
Late and Soon, 1943.

PLAYS:

To See Ourselves, 1930.
The Glass Wall, 1933.
The Mulberry Bush, 1935.

The Way Things Are and *Diary of a Provincial Lady* show a lively yet cool observation at work. Her pose of studied objectivity yields its own kind of irony.

HERBERT, Sir Alan Patrick, b. 1890

NOVELS:

The Secret Battle, 1919.
House by the River, 1920.
The Old Flame, 1925.
Trials of Topsy, 1928.
Topsy, M.P., 1929.
The Water Gipsies, 1930.
Holy Deadlock, 1934.
Topsy Turvy, 1947.
Topsy Omnibus, 1949.

POETRY:

The Bomber Gipsy, and other Poems, 1918.
Full Enjoyment and other Verses, 1952.

LIBRETTI:

The Water Gipsies (from the novel), 1930.
Tantivy Towers, 1931.
Derby Day, 1931.
Big Ben, 1946.

MISCELLANEOUS WRITINGS:

Misleading Cases in the Common Law, 1927.
More Misleading Cases, 1930.

No Boats on the River, 1932.
Uncommon Law, 1935.
The Right to Marry, 1954.

A witty and engaging writer, whose championship of English waterways and campaign for altering the divorce laws are often happily illustrated in his fiction. His humour often has a sting to it; *Misleading Cases*, while uproariously funny, also illustrates some of the fatuities of the law.

GUNN, Neil Miller, b. 1891

NOVELS:

Morning Tide, 1931.
Sun Circle, 1933.
Butcher's Broom, 1934.
Highland River, 1937.
Wild Geese Overhead, 1939.
The Silver Darlings, 1941.
The Serpent, 1943.
The Green Isle and the Great Deep, 1944.
Drinking Well, 1946.
The Shadow, 1948.
The Lost Chart, 1949.
The Well at the World's End, 1951.
Bloodhunt, 1952.
The Other Landscape, 1954.

SHORT STORIES:

Hidden Doors, 1929.
Storm and Precipice, 1942.
Young Art and Old Hector, 1942.
The White Hour, 1950.

TRAVEL:

Off in a Boat, 1938.
Highland Pack, 1950.

A Scottish novelist with a strong sense of the organic rhythms of the old Highland life and of the workings of the Highland imagination. There is a deliberate Celtic streak in his writing, which is sometimes authentic and moving. *Morning Tide* remains one of his best novels.

BENSON, Stella (1892-1933)

NOVELS:

I Pose, 1915.
This is the End, 1917.
Living Alone, 1919.
The Poor Man, 1922.
Pipers and a Dancer, 1924.
Goodbye, Stranger, 1926.
Tobit Transplanted, 1931 (The Far-Away Bride, Am. Ed.).
Mundos, 1935.

SHORT STORIES:

The Awakening, 1925.
The Man Who Missed the 'Bus, 1928.
Hope Against Hope and other stories, 1931.
Christmas Formula and other stories, 1932.

TRAVEL:

The Little World, 1925.
Worlds Within Worlds, 1928.

POETRY:

Twenty, 1918.

A highly original novelist whose tragic view of life is artfully disposed behind a façade of remarkable comic wit.

ALDINGTON, Richard, b. 1892

NOVELS:

Death of a Hero, 1929.
Roads to Glory, 1930.
The Colonel's Daughter, 1931.
Last Straws, 1931.
Soft Answers, 1932.
All Men are Enemies, 1933.
Women Must Work, 1934.
Seven Against Reeves, 1938.
Rejected Guest, 1939.
The Romance of Casanova, 1947.

BIBLIOGRAPHY

CRITICAL AND MISCELLANEOUS WRITINGS:

Literary Studies, 1924.
French Studies, 1925.
Voltaire, 1926.
A Wreath For San Gemignano, 1945.
Great French Romances, 1946.
Wellington, 1946.
Portrait of a Genius, But . . ., 1950 (biography of D. H. Lawrence).
Pinorman, 1954.
Lawrence of Arabia, 1954.

POETRY:

Images, Old and New, 1915.
Exile and other Poems, 1923.
A Fool i' the Forest, 1925.
Collected Poems, 1928.
A Dream in the Luxembourg, 1930.
Eaten Heart, 1931,
and others.

TRANSLATIONS:

The Poems of Anyte of Tegea, 1915.
Latin Poems of the Renaissance, 1915.
Greek Songs in the Manner of Anacreon, 1919.
The Good Humoured Ladies, 1922.
Voyages to the Moon and the Sun, 1923.
French Comedies of the XVIIIth Century:
    The Residuary Legatee, 1923.
    The Game of Love and Chance, 1923.
    The Conceited Count, 1923.
Dangerous Acquaintances (Les liaisons dangéreuses), 1924.
The Mystery of the Nativity, 1924.
The Fifteen Joys of Marriage, 1926
Candide and other romances, 1927.
Letters of Voltaire and Frederick the Great, 1927.

As a poet, Aldington began as an Imagist, and went on to write satirical and critical poetry in which the thought and feeling were not always fully integrated in the poetic texture. His novel *Death of a Hero* is a bitter satirical work which presents with extraordinary force the mood of disillusion which followed the First World War. The note of personal bitterness in Aldington's writing has often interfered with its artistic effectiveness.

WEST, Rebecca, b. 1892

NOVELS:

The Return of the Soldier, 1918.
The Judge, 1922.
Harriet Hume, 1929.
Ending in Earnest, 1931.
The Harsh Voice, 1935.
The Thinking Reed, 1936.
The Fountain Overflows, 1956.

CRITICAL AND MISCELLANEOUS WRITINGS:

Henry James, 1916.
St Augustine, 1933.
The modern 'Rake's Progress', 1934.
The Strange Necessity, 1938.
Black Lamb and Grey Falcon, 1942.
The Meaning of Treason, 1949.
A Train of Powder, 1955.

Black Lamb and Grey Falcon is a brilliant study of certain phases of Balkan history and politics. Rebecca's West's witty and incisive mind illuminates all she touches. Her novels are full of vitality. Her studies of modern treason have already become classics of their kind.

BUTTS, Mary (1892-1935)

Speed the Plough and Other Stories, 1923.
Armed with Madness, 1928.
Death of Felicity Taverner, 1932.
Ashes of Rings, 1933.
The Macedonian, 1933.
Last Stories, 1938.

Her stories are largely concerned with 'mystical' evil.

COMPTON-BURNETT, Ivy, b. 1892

Dolores, 1911.
Pastors and Masters, 1924.
Brothers and Sisters, 1929.

Men and Wives, 1931.
More Women than Men, 1933.
A House and its Head, 1933.
Daughters and Sons, 1937.
A Family and a Fortune, 1939.
Parents and Children, 1941.
Elders and Betters, 1944.
Manservant and Maidservant, 1947.
Two Worlds and their Ways, 1949.
Darkness and Day, 1951.
The Present and the Past, 1953.
Mother and Son, 1955.

———

BIOGRAPHY AND CRITICISM:

Pamela Hansford Johnson. I. Compton-Burnett (W.W.), 1953.
Robert Liddell, The Novels of I. Compton-Burnett, 1955.

GARNETT, David, b. 1892

NOVELS:

Lady into Fox, 1922.
A Man in the Zoo, 1924.
The Sailor's Return, 1925.
Go She Must!, 1927.
No Love, 1929.
The Grasshoppers Come, 1931.
Pocahontas, 1933.
Beany-Eye, 1935.
Aspects of Love, 1955.

SHORT STORIES:

The Old Dovecote, 1928.
A Terrible Day, 1932.

MISCELLANEOUS WRITINGS:

A Rabbit in the Air, 1932.
War in the Air, 1941.

AUTOBIOGRAPHY:

The Golden Echo, 1953.
Flowers of the Forest, 1955.

EDITED:

The Letters of T. E. Lawrence, 1938.
The Novels of Thomas Love Peacock, 1948.
The Essential T. E. Lawrence, 1951.

A novelist of sprightly imagination. *Lady into Fox* remains his most engaging work.

SAYERS, Dorothy Leigh (1893-1957)

DETECTIVE STORIES:

Whose Body? 1923.
Clouds of Witness, 1926.
Unnatural Death, 1927.
The Unpleasantness at the Bellona Club, 1928.
Lord Peter Views the Body, 1928.
The Documents in the Case (with Peter Eustace), 1930.
Strong Poison, 1930.
The Five Red Herrings, 1931.
Have His Carcase, 1932.
Hangman's Holiday, 1933.
Murder Must Advertise, 1933.
The Nine Tailors, 1934.
Gaudy Night, 1935.
Busman's Honeymoon, 1937.
In the Teeth of the Evidence, 1939.

PLAYS:

Busman's Honeymoon (with M. St Clare Byrne), 1936.
The Zeal of thy House, 1937.
The Devil to Pay, 1939.
Love All, 1940.
The Man Born to be King (radio play), 1942.
The Just Vengeance, 1946.
Where Do We Go from Here (radio play), 1948.
The Emperor Constantine, 1951.

CRITICAL AND MISCELLANEOUS WRITINGS:

Begin Here, 1940.
The Mind of the Maker, 1941.
Even the Parrot, 1944.
Unpopular Opinions, 1946.

Creed or Chaos? 1947.
The Lost Tools of Learning, 1948.
Introductory Papers on Dante, 1954.

TRANSLATIONS:
Dante's Inferno, 1949.
Dante's Purgatorio, 1955.

A writer of highly sophisticated detective stories who later turned to amateur theology and Christian apologetics both directly in prose argument and indirectly in religious drama and in work on Dante.

BLAKE, George, b. 1893

NOVELS:
The Shipbuilders, 1935.
Rest and be Thankful, 1934.
Late Harvest, 1938.
The Valiant Heart, 1940.
The Constant Star, 1945.
The Westering Sun, 1946.
The Voyage Home, 1952.
The Innocence Within, 1955.

PLAY:
Clyde-Built, 1922.

CRITICAL AND MISCELLANEOUS WRITINGS:
Vagabond Papers, 1922.
Wild Men, 1925.
Paper Money, 1928.
The Paying Guest, 1929.
The Seas Between, 1930.
David and Joanna, 1936.
The Five Arches, 1947.
The Piper's Tune, 1950.
Barrie and the Kailyard School, 1951.

An informed and sympathetic observer of the Scottish scene. *The Shipbuilders* gives an impressive picture of Glasgow and Clydeside during the depression.

WARNER, Sylvia Townsend, b. 1893

NOVELS:

Lolly Willowes, 1926.
Mr Fortune's Maggot, 1927.
The True Heart, 1929.

SHORT STORIES:

The Salutation, 1932.
More Joy in Heaven and other stories, 1935.
A Garland of Straw, 1943.
The Museum of Cheats, 1947.
Winter in the Air and other stories, 1955.

POETRY:

The Espalier, 1925.
Time Importuned, 1928.
Opus, 7, 1931.

MISCELLANEOUS WRITINGS:

Some World Far From Our and Stay Croydon, Thou Swain, 1929.
Summer will Show, 1936.
After the Death of Don Juan, 1938.
The Corner that Held Them, 1948.
The Flint Anchor, 1954.

HUXLEY, Aldous Leonard, b. 1894

NOVELS:

Crome Yellow, 1921.
Antic Hay, 1923.
Those Barren Leaves, 1925.
Point Counter Point, 1928.
Brave New World, 1932.
Eyeless in Gaza, 1936.
After Many a Summer, 1939.
Time Must Have a Stop, 1944.
The Genius and the Goddess, 1955.

SHORT STORIES:

Limbo, 1920.
Mortal Coils, 1922.

Little Mexican and other Stories, 1924 (Am. ed., Young Archimedes).
Two or Three Graces and other Stories, 1926.
Brief Candles, 1930.

CRITICAL AND MISCELLANEOUS WRITINGS:

On the Margin, 1923.
Along the Road, 1925.
Jesting Pilate, 1926.
Proper Studies, 1927.
Essays New and Old, 1926.
Do What You Will, 1929.
The Future of the Past, 1930.
Vulgarity in Literature, 1930.
Music at Night, 1931.
T. H. Huxley, 1932.
Texts and Pretexts, an anthology with commentaries, 1932.
Beyond the Mexique Bay, 1934.
The Olive Tree and other Essays, 1936.
Ends and Means, 1937.
Grey Eminence, 1941.
The Art of Seeing, 1942.
The Perennial Philosophy, 1946.
Science, Liberty and Peace, 1947.
Ape and Essence, 1948.
Themes and Variations, 1950.
The Devils of Loudon, 1952.
The Doors of Perception, 1954.
Heaven and Hell, 1956.

EDITED:

The Letters of D. H. Lawrence, 1932.

POETRY:

The Burning Wheel, 1916.
The Defeat of Youth, 1918.
Leda, 1920.
The Cicadas, 1931.

———

BIOGRAPHY AND CRITICISM:

J. Brooke, Aldous Huxley (W.W.), 1954.

PRIESTLEY, John Boynton, b. 1894

NOVELS:

Adam in Moonshine, 1927.
The Good Companions, 1929.
Angel Pavement, 1930.
Faraway, 1932.
Wonder Hero, 1933.
Doomsday Men, 1938.
Daylight on Saturday, 1943.
Three Men in New Suits, 1945.
Bright Day, 1946.
Jenny Villiers, 1947.
Festival at Farbridge, 1951.
The Magicians, 1954.

SHORT STORIES:

The Other Place, 1953.

PLAYS:

Dangerous Corner, 1932.
Laburnum Grove, 1933.
I Have Been Here Before, 1937.
Johnson Over Jordan, 1939.
They Came to a City, 1943.
An Inspector Calls, 1946.
Summer Day's Dream, 1949.

CRITICAL AND MISCELLANEOUS WRITINGS:

Figures in Modern Literature, 1924.
The English Comic Characters, 1925.
George Meredith, 1926.
Talking, 1926.
Peacock, 1927.
The English Novel, 1927.
English Humour, 1928.
Rain Upon Gadshill, 1939.
Low Notes on a High Level, 1954.
Journey Down a Rainbow, 1955 (with Jacquetta Hawkes).
All About Ourselves, 1956.

BIOGRAPHY AND CRITICISM:
Ivor Brown, J. B. Priestley (W.W.), 1957.

DOBRÉE, Valentine, b. 1894

Your Cuckoo Sings by Kind, 1927.
Emperor's Tigers, 1929.
To Blush Unseen, 1935.

Your Cuckoo Sings by Kind is a delicately rendered account of childhood and adolescence.

ARLEN, Michael (1895-1956)

NOVELS:

The Green Hat, 1924.
Young Men in Love, 1927.
Lily Christine, 1930.
Hell, said the Duchess, 1934.
Flying Dutchman, 1939.

SHORT STORIES:

The Romantic Lady, 1933.
These Charming People, 1923.
May Fair, 1925.
The Crooked Coronet, 1937.

The Green Hat is a period piece which beautifully epitomizes the spirit of the sophisticated 1920s.

GERHARDI, William Alexander, b. 1895

NOVELS:

Futility, 1922.
The Polyglots, 1925.
Jazz and Jasper, the story of Adams and Eva, 1928 (Eva's Apples, Am. Ed.).
My Sinful Earth, 1928.
Pending Heaven, 1930.

The Memoirs of Satan, 1932 (with Brian Lunn).
Resurrection, 1934.
Of Mortal Love, 1936.
My Wife's the Least of It, 1938.

SHORT STORIES:

A Bad End, 1926.
The Vanity Bag, 1927.
Pretty Creatures, 1927.

PLAYS:

The Immorality Lady 1927.
Rasputin 1956.

CRITICAL AND MISCELLANEOUS WRITINGS:

Anton Chehov, 1923.
Memoirs of a Polyglot, 1931.
The Casanova Fable, 1934 (with Hugh Kingsmill).
The Romanoffs, 1940.
My Literary Credo, 1947.
Highlights of Russian History, 1949.
The Life and Times of Lord Beaverbrook, 1956.

GOLDING, Louis, b. 1895

NOVELS:

Forward from Babylon, 1920.
Day of Atonement, 1925.
The Miracle Boy, 1927.
Magnolia Street, 1932.
Five Silver Daughters, 1934.
Mr Emmanuel, 1939.
The Glory of Elsie Silver, 1945.
Honey for the Ghost, 1949.
The Dangerous Places, 1951.
The Loving Brothers, 1952.
To the Quayside, 1954.
Mr Hurricane, 1957.
The Little Old Admiral, 1958.

SHORT STORIES:

The Doomington Wanderer, 1934.
Pale Blue Nightgown, 1944
Mario on the Beach, 1956.

TRAVEL:

Sunward, 1924.
Sicilian Noon, 1925.
In the Steps of Moses the Lawgiver, 1938.
Goodbye to Ithaca, 1955.

MISCELLANEOUS WRITINGS:

James Joyce, 1933.
The Jewish Problem, 1938.
Bare-knuckle Breed, 1952.

An accomplished and versatile writer, whose novels of Man-
chester Jewish life are particularly interesting. His travel books
are fine examples of their kind.

HARTLEY, Leslie Poles, b. 1895

NOVELS:

Simonetta Perkins, 1925.
The Shrimp and the Anemone, 1944.
The Sixth Heaven, 1946.
Eustace and Hilda, 1947.
The Boat, 1949.
My Fellow Devils, 1951.
The Go-Between, 1953.
A Perfect Woman, 1955.

SHORT STORIES:

Night Fears, 1924.
The Killing Bottle, 1932.
The Travelling Grave and other stories, 1951.
The White Wand, 1954.

CRONIN, Archibald Joseph, b. 1896

NOVELS:

Hatter's Castle, 1931.
Three Loves, 1932.

Grand Canary, 1933.
The Stars Look Down, 1935.
The Citadel, 1937.
The Keys of the Kingdom, 1942.
The Green Years, 1944.
Shannon's Way, 1948.
The Spanish Gardener, 1950.
Adventures in Two Worlds, 1952.

Hatter's Castle is a powerful novel of Scottish provincial life, obviously influenced by George Douglas Brown's *House with the Green Shutters*. Cronin's other early novels are strongly told stories illustrating economic, social or moral problems of modern industrial life. Later, he turned to more meditative religious themes. He now lives in America.

STRONG, Leonard Alfred George, b. 1896

NOVELS:

Dewer Rides, 1929.
The Jealous Ghost, 1930.
The Garden, 1931.
The Big Man, 1931.
The Brothers, 1932 (Brothers, Am. Ed.).
Sea Wall, 1933.
Corporal Tune, 1934.
Travellers, 1945.
Light Through the Cloud, 1946.

POETRY:

Dublin Days, 1921.
Lowery Road, 1923.
Difficult Love, 1927.
Northern Light, 1930.
Selected Poems, 1931.
Call to the Swan, 1936.

CRITICAL WRITINGS:

Common Sense about Poetry, 1931.
Defence of Ignorance, 1932.
A Letter to W. B. Yeats, 1932.

Life in English Literature, 1932 (with M. Redlich).
English for Pleasure, 1941.
John McCormack, 1941.
The Sacred River, 1949 (on James Joyce).
Dr Quicksilver, 1955.

A novelist and short-story writer of considerable narrative vigour. Some of his best short stories are set on the fishing-coasts of Ireland; the elemental situations provided by such settings are most congenial to his talent. His best novels are *The Garden* and *Sea Wall*.

MORGAN, Charles Langbridge, b. 1896

NOVELS:

The Gunroom, 1919.
My Name is Legion, 1925.
Portrait in a Mirror, 1929.
The Fountain, 1932.
Sparkenbroke, 1936.
The Voyage, 1940.
The Empty Room, 1941.
A Breeze of Morning, 1951.

PLAYS:

The Flashing Stream, 1938.
The River Line, 1952.
The Burning Glass, 1953.

COMMENTARY:

Liberties of the Mind, 1951.

A novelist of high seriousness, who works problems of art and morality into his novels with a relaxed dexterity that is not always convincing. Edwin Muir's sardonic observation is not wholly unfair: '*The Fountain* became a best-seller by demonstrating that mysticism was compatible with good form.'

KENNEDY, Margaret, b. 1896

NOVELS:

The Ladies of Lyndon, 1923.
The Constant Nymph, 1924.
The Fool of the Family, 1930.
Return I Dare Not, 1931.
The Midas Touch, 1938.
Troy Chimneys, 1953.
The Oracles, 1955.

PLAYS:

The Constant Nymph, from the novel of Margaret Kennedy, 1926
(with Basil Dean).
Escape Me Never, 1934.

O'BRIEN, Kate, b. 1897

NOVELS:

Without My Cloak, 1931.
The Ante-Room, 1934.
Mary Lavelle, 1936.
Pray for the Wanderer, 1938.
The Land of Spices, 1941.
The Last of Summer, 1943.
That Lady, 1946.
The Flower of May, 1953.

PLAYS:

Distinguished Villa, 1926.
The Bridge, 1927.
The Schoolroom Window, 1937,
and others.

O'FLAHERTY, Liam, b. 1897

NOVELS:

Thy Neighbour's Wife, 1923.
The Black Soul, 1924.
The Informer, 1925.
Mr Gilhooley, 1926.

The Assassin, 1928.
The Return of the Brute, 1929.
The House of Gold, 1929.
The Puritan, 1932.
Skerrett, 1932.
The Martyr, 1933.

SHORT STORIES:

Spring Sowing, 1924.
The Tent and other stories, 1926.
The Mountain Tavern and other stories, 1929.
The Wild Swan, 1932.
Short Stories of Liam Flaherty, 1937.
Land, 1946.
Two Lovely Beasts, 1948.

MISCELLANEOUS WRITINGS:

The Life of Tim Healy, 1927.
A Tourist's Guide to Ireland, 1929.
Two Years, 1930.
I Went to Russia, 1931.
Shame the Devil, 1934.

O'Flaherty is at his best when dealing vividly with strong real
life situations. He has the photographer's eye for the arresting
scene or movement, and his art needs solid objects to work on.

JAMESON, Margaret Storm, b. 1897

NOVELS:

The Pitiful Wife, 1923.
The Lovely Ship, 1927.
Farewell to Youth, 1928.
The Voyage Home, 1930.
A Richer Dust, 1931.
That was Yesterday, 1933.
A Day Off, 1933.
Company Parade, 1934.
Love in Winter, 1935.
In the Second Year, 1936.
None Turn Back, 1936.
Delicate Monster, 1937.

Civil Journey, 1939.
Europe To Let: memoirs of an obscure man, 1940.
Cousin Honoré, 1940.
The Fort, 1941.
Cloudless May, 1943.
The Other Side, 1945.
Before the Crossing, 1947.
The Black Laurel, 1948.
The Moment of Truth, 1949.
The Green Man, 1952.
The Hidden River, 1955.

CRITICAL AND MISCELLANEOUS WRITINGS:

Modern Drama in Europe, 1920.
No Time Like the Present, 1933.
The Writer's Situation, 1950.

MITCHISON, Naomi Margaret, b. 1897

NOVELS:

The Conquered, 1923.
Cloud Cuckoo Land, 1925.
The Corn King and the Spring Queen, 1931.

SHORT STORIES:

When the Bough Breaks and other stories, 1924.
Black Sparta: Greek Stories, 1928.
Barbarian Stories, 1929.
The Hostages, 1930.
The Delicate Fire: short stories and poems, 1933.

PLAYS:

Nix-Nought-Nothing (Four plays for Children), 1928.
Lobsters on the Agenda, 1952.
Graeme and the Dragon, 1954.
The Land the Ravens Found, 1955.
To the Chapel Perilous, 1955.

POETRY:

The Laburnum Branch, 1926.
The Delicate Fire, 1933,
and other works.

Classical scholar, political and educational reformer, and farmer in Scotland, Naomi Mitchison has one of the most interesting and versatile minds of our time. Her historical novels of ancient Greece and Rome shows a most effective union of scholarship and imagination.

WAUGH, Alexander (Alec) Raban, b. 1898

NOVELS:

The Loom of Youth, 1917.
The Lonely Unicorn, 1922. (Am. Ed., Roland Whately.)
Card Castle, 1924.
Kept, 1925.
Love in These Days, 1926.
Nor Many Waters, 1928. (Am. Ed., Portrait of a Celibate.)
Three Score and Ten, 1929.
So Lovers Dream, 1931.
The Balliols, 1934.
Eight Short Stories, 1937.
No Truce with Time, 1941.
His Second War, 1944.
Unclouded Summer, 1948.
Guy Renton, 1953.
Island in the Sun, 1956.

TRAVEL:

Sunlit Caribbean, 1948.

GREEN, Henry *pseud.* (Henry Yorke), b. 1905

NOVELS:

Blindness, 1926.
Living, 1929.
Party Going, 1939.
Caught, 1943.
Loving, 1945.
Back, 1946.
Concluding, 1948.
Nothing, 1950.
Doting, 1952.

(C) THE 1930s AND AFTER

BATES, Ralph, b. 1899

NOVELS:

Sierra, 1933.
Lean Men, 1934.
The Olive Field, 1936.
The Fields of Paradise, 1941.
The Undiscoverables, 1942.
The Journey to the Sandalwood Forest, 1947.
The Dolphin in the Wood, 1949.

BOWEN, Elizabeth Dorothea Cole, b. 1899

NOVELS:

The Hotel, 1927.
The Last September, 1929.
Friends and Relations, 1931.
To the North, 1932.
The House in Paris, 1935.
The Death of the Heart, 1938.
The Heat of the Day, 1949.
A World of Love, 1955.

SHORT STORIES:

Encounters, 1923.
Ann Lee's, 1926.
Joining Charles, 1929.
The Cat Jumps, 1934.
Look at all those Roses, 1941.
The Demon Lover, 1945.
Selected Stories, 1946.

CRITICAL AND MISCELLANEOUS WRITINGS:

Bowen's Court, 1942.
English Novelists, 1942.
Seven Winters, 1942.
Why do I Write? (with Graham Greene and V. S. Pritchett), 1948.

Collected Impressions, 1950.
The Shelbourne, 1951.

BIOGRAPHY AND CRITICISM:
Jocelyn Brooke, Elizabeth Bowen, 1952.

LINKLATER, Eric, b. 1899

NOVELS:

White Maa's Saga, 1929.
Poet's Pub, 1929.
A Dragon Laughed, 1930.
Juan in America, 1931.
The Men of Ness, 1932.
The Crusader's Key, 1933.
Magnus Merriman, 1934.
Ripeness is All, 1935.
God Likes Them Plain, 1935.
The Sailors Holiday, 1937.
Juan in China, 1937.
The Impregnable Women, 1938.
Private Angelo, 1946.
Laxdale Hall, 1951.
The House of Gair, 1953.
The Faithful Ally, 1954.

SHORT STORIES:

Sealskin Trousers, 1947.

CHILDREN'S BOOKS:

The Wind on the Moon, 1944.
Pirates in the Deep Green Sea, 1949.
Mr Byculla, 1950.

PLAYS:

The Devil's in the News, 1934.
Love in Albania, 1949.
The Mortimer Touch, 1952.

CRITICAL AND MISCELLANEOUS WRITINGS:

Ben Jonson and King James, 1931.
Mary Queen of Scots, 1933.
Robert the Bruce, 1934.
Lion and Unicorn, 1935.
The Cornerstones, 1941.
The Raft and Socrates Asks Why, 1942.
The Great Ship and Rabelais Replies, 1944.

A novelist of enormous talent, who has remained content to be one of the best comic novelists of his day, but whose wit, imagination and sense of life have always seemed to promise more than that.

WHITE, ANTONIA, b. 1899

NOVELS:

Frost in May, 1933.
The Lost Traveller, 1950.
The Sugar House, 1952.
Beyond the Glass, 1954.

SHORT STORIES:

Strangers, 1954.

A skilful and sensitive writer, who renders border-line psychological states with delicate precision (notably in *Beyond the Glass* and in some of her short stories). She has also translated a good deal from the French (including some of Colette's novels).

HUGHES, Richard Arthur Warren, b. 1900

NOVELS:

A Moment of Time, 1926.
A High Wind in Jamaica, 1929. (Am. Ed., The Innocent Voyage.)
In Hazard, 1938.

CHILDREN'S STORIES:

The Spider's Palace, 1938.
Don't Blame Me, 1940.

POETRY:

Gipsy Night, and other Poems, 1922.
Confessio Juvenis, 1926 (Collected Poems).

PLAYS:

The Sisters' Tragedy, 1922.
The Sisters' Tragedy and three other plays, 1924.
  (A Rabbit and a Leg, collected plays, Am. Ed.)

A High Wind in Jamaica is a remarkable study of children involved in a situation of not fully recognized moral horror, a classic of its kind. *In Hazard* is an account of storm at sea comparable in some ways to Conrad's *Typhoon*.

PRITCHETT, Victor Sawdon, b. 1900

NOVELS:

Clare Drummer, 1929.
Shirley Sanz, 1932.
Nothing Like Leather, 1935.
Dead Man Leading, 1937.
Mr Beluncle, 1951.

SHORT STORIES:

The Spanish Virgin, 1930.
You Make Your Own Life, 1938.
It May Never Happen, 1945.
Collected Short Stories, 1956.

CRITICAL WRITINGS:

The Living Novel, 1947.
Why do I Write? (with Graham Greene and Elizabeth Bowen), 1948.
Books in General, 1953.

A gifted short-story writer, Pritchett has a half-ironical, half-affectionate relish for the absurdities of human character and a sharp eye for the revealing detail. G. W. Stonier has aptly used the phrase 'wiry realism' about his writing. As a critic, Pritchett is lively, independent and undoctrinaire.

O'FAOLÁIN, Sean, b. 1900

NOVELS:
A Nest of Simple Folk, 1933.
Bird Alone, 1936.

SHORT STORIES:
Midsummer Night Madness, 1932.
A Purse of Coppers, 1937.
Teresa and other stories, 1946.

MISCELLANEOUS WRITINGS:
The Life Story of Eamon De Valera, 1933.
The Great O'Neill, 1942.
King of the Beggars, 1946.

PLAY:
She had to do Something, 1938.

One of the most gifted of the modern Irish novelists, whose sense of the Irish scene and the Irish imagination is an organic part of his response to life.

HANLEY, James, b. 1901

NOVELS:
The Furys, 1934.
The Maelstrom, 1935.
The Wall, 1936.
Hollow Sea, 1938.
Our Time is Gone, 1940.
No Directions, 1943.
Winter Song, 1950.
The Closed Harbour, 1952.
The Welsh Sonata, 1954.
Levine, 1955.

SHORT STORIES:
Men in Darkness, 1931.
Half-An-Eye, 1937.
At Bay, 1943.
Crilley, 1945.

A writer with a keen eye for the realistic detail and at the same time a powerful imagination; the combination can yield fiction of unusual force.

GIBBON, Lewis Grassic *pseud.* (James Leslie Mitchell) (1901-1935)

NOVELS:

Sunset Song, 1932.
Cloud Howe, 1933.
Grey Granite, 1934.
The above three novels constitute a trilogy, entitled *A Scots Quair*, published in one volume with a foreword by Ivor Brown in 1946.

BIOGRAPHY:

Niger: The Life of Mungo Park, 1934.

HISTORICAL AND ANTHROPOLOGICAL WORKS
(pub. under his own name):

Hanno, 1928.
Nine Against the Unknown, 1934.
The Conquest of the Maya, 1935.

In addition to these books, Gibbon wrote (under his own name) a large number of popular romances in order (as he put it to a journalist in 1933) 'to make some money out of books, so that I can devote lots of time and money to archaeological research'. His Scots trilogy is his only important work of fiction. It is an extremely interesting attempt to create a new kind of Scottish fiction, with an original use of Scots prose in dialogue and an attempt to anchor the novels solidly in the harsh realities of Scottish life in the north-east. In some respects, it represented the same kind of blow against the 'kailyard' school of sentimental rural Scottish fiction as George Douglas Brown's *House with the Green Shutters* had struck in 1901, but it was more ambitious and more original. The work has many flaws, both of style and of structure, as well as a disturbing arbitrariness in the patterning and interpretation of human affairs, but it remains a lonely attempt to achieve something really new in the modern Scottish novel.

SACKVILLE-WEST, Hon. Edward Charles, b. 1901

NOVELS:

Piano Quintet, 1925.
The Ruin, 1926.
Mandrake Over the Water Carrier, 1928.
Simpson, 1931.
Sun in Capricorn, 1934.

CRITICAL WRITINGS:

The Apology of Arthur Rimbaud, 1927.
A Flame in Sunlight, 1936 (a biography of De Quincey).
And So To Bed, 1947.
Inclinations, 1949.

A novelist with an unusually powerful and strange imagination.
An exceptionally intelligent and sensitive critic.

MORRISON, Nancy Brysson

NOVELS:

Breakers, 1930.
Solitaire, 1932.
The Gowk Storm, 1933.
The Strangers, 1935.
These are My Friends, 1946.
The Winnowing Years, 1949.
The Following Wind, 1954.

A Scottish novelist with a highly individual imaginative quality.
The Gowk Storm remains her best work.

GIBBONS, Stella Dorothea, b. 1902

NOVELS:

Cold Comfort Farm, 1932.
Bassett, 1934.
Enbury Heath, 1935.
The Untidy Gnome, 1935.
Miss Linsey and Pa, 1936.

Nightingale Wood, 1938.
My American, 1939.
The Rich House, 1941.
Ticky, 1943.
The Bachelor, 1944.
Westwood, 1946.
The Matchmaker, 1949.
The Swiss Summer, 1951.
Fort of the Bear, 1953.
The Shadow of a Sorcerer, 1955.
Here be Dragons, 1956.

SHORT STORIES:

Roaring Tower, 1937.
Christmas at Cold Comfort Farm, 1949.
Beside the Pearly Water, 1954.

POETRY:

The Mountain Beast, 1930.
The Priestess, 1934.
The Lowland Venus, 1938.
Collected Poems, 1950.

Cold Comfort Farm is a brilliant parody of the novel of rustic pessimism.

BEACHCROFT, Thomas Owen, b. 1902

NOVELS:

The Man Who Started Clean, 1937.
Asking for Trouble, 1948.
A Thorn in the Heart, 1952.

SHORT STORIES:

A Young Man in a Hurry, 1934.
You Must Break Out Sometimes, 1936.
The Parents Left Alone, 1940.
Collected Stories, 1946.
Malice Bites Back, 1948.
Goodbye Aunt Hesther, 1955.

WAUGH, Evelyn Arthur St John, b. 1903

NOVELS:

Decline and Fall, 1928.
Vile Bodies, 1930.
Black Mischief, 1932.
A Handful of Dust, 1937.
Scoop, 1938.
Put Out More Flags, 1942.
Work Suspended, 1942.
Brideshead Revisited, 1945.
Scott-King's Modern Europe, 1947.
The Loved One, 1948.
Helena, 1950.
Men at Arms, 1952.
Love Among the Ruins, 1953.
Officers and Gentlemen, 1954.

MISCELLANEOUS WRITINGS:

Rossetti, 1928.
Remote People, 1931.
Ninety-Two Days, 1934.
Edward Campion, 1935.
Waugh in Abyssinia, 1936.
Robbery Under Law, 1939.
When the Going Was Good, 1946.
The Holy Places, 1953.

————

BIOGRAPHY AND CRITICISM:

Christopher Hollis, Evelyn Waugh (W.W.), 1954.

STONIER, George Walter, b. 1903

MISCELLANEOUS WRITINGS:

Gog Magog, 1933.
The Shadow Across the Page, 1937.
Shaving through the Blitz, 1943.
My Dear Bunny, 1946.
The Memoirs of a Ghost, 1947.
Round London with the Unicorn, 1951.

A literary journalist whose stories and sketches show humour, observation, and a keen relish of life.

ORWELL, George *pseud.* (Eric Hugh Blair) (1903-1950)

NOVELS:

Burmese Days, 1934.
A Clergyman's Daughter, 1935.
Keep the Aspidistra Flying, 1936.
Coming Up for Air, 1939.
Animal Farm, 1945.
Nineteen Eighty-Four, 1949.

CRITICAL AND MISCELLANEOUS WRITINGS:

Down and Out in Paris and London, 1933.
The Road to Wigan Pier, 1937.
Homage to Catalonia, 1938.
Inside the Whale, 1940.
The Lion and the Unicorn: Socialism and the English Genius, 1941.
Critical Essays, 1946.
The English People, 1947.
Shooting an Elephant, 1950.
Such, Such Were the Joys. New York, 1953.
England Your England, and Other Essays, 1953.

BIOGRAPHY AND CRITICISM:

Tom Hopkinson, George Orwell (W.W.), 1953.
Laurence Brander, George Orwell, 1954.
Christopher Hollis, A Study of George Orwell, 1956.

Orwell had a vigorous, independent mind, and he contemplated the social, political and literary scene with an ironically innocent eye. His accounts of the vulgar picture-postcard in England ('The Art of Donald McGill', in *Critical Essays*) and his essay on Boys' Weeklies (in both *Inside the Whale* and *Critical Essays*) are classics of sociological criticism, and his essays on *Gulliver's Travels* ('Politics v. Literature', in *Shooting an Elephant*), on Dickens (in both *Inside the Whale* and *Critical Essays*), on 'Lear, Tolstoy and the Fool' (in *Shooting an Elephant*) and on Kipling (in *Critical Essays*) are admirable examples of an approach which, ignoring the apparatus of professional literary criticism, looks at a work of literature with a deliberate naïveté and discusses it in the light of what can and ought to be said about man as a political and ethical creature. This method is, understandably, less successful in dealing with works where the meaning is achieved obliquely through the formal patterning of image and symbol (e.g. his essay on Yeats, in *Critical Essays*).

Animal Farm, which Orwell described as a 'fairy tale', is a witty satire on the movement from social revolution to totalitarian dictatorship. *Nineteen Eighty-Four*, written when Orwell was a dying man, is a nightmarish picture of the totalitarian state, presented with masochistic horror as a possible development of English Socialism. As a study of the final corruption of power, it has a certain savage cogency, but as a criticism of English socialism it is fantastically irrelevant and even as a picture of the ultimate evil of the totalitarian state it is too obsessed and self-lacerating to arouse serious political reflection.

PLOMER, William Charles Franklyn, b. 1903

NOVELS:

Turbott Wolfe, 1926.
Sado, 1931. (Am. Ed., They Never Come Back.)
The Case is Altered, 1932.
The Invaders, 1934.
Ali the Lion, 1936.
Museum Pieces, 1952.

SHORT STORIES:

I Speak of Africa, 1928.
Paper Houses, 1929.
The Child of Queen Victoria, 1933.
Four Countries, 1949.

POETRY:

Notes for Poems, 1928.
The Family Tree, 1929.
The Fivefold Screen, 1932.
Selected Poems, 1940.
The Dorking Thigh, 1945.
A Shot in the Park, 1955.

MISCELLANEOUS WRITINGS:

Cecil Rhodes, 1933.
Kilvert's Diary (ed.), 1938.
Double Lives (autobiography), 1950.

A lively and sensitive novelist and short-story writer. As a poet, he has a gift for ironic description.

ISHERWOOD, Christopher William, b. 1904

NOVELS:

All the Conspirators, 1928.
The Memorial, 1932.
Mr Norris Changes Trains, 1935.
Goodbye to Berlin, 1939.
Prater Violet, 1945.
The World in the Evening, 1954.

PLAYS (in collaboration with W. H. Auden):

The Dog Beneath the Skin, 1935.
Ascent of F.6, 1936.
On the Frontier, 1938.

TRANSLATIONS:

The Bhagavad-Gita, 1944 (with Swami Prabhavananda).
Shankara's Crest-Jewel of Discrimination, 1947 (with Swami Prabhavananda).
Baudelaire's Intimate Journals, 1947.
How to Know God: the Yogi aphorisms of Patanjah, 1953 (with Swami Prabhavananda).

Isherwood's stories of Berlin in the early 1930s are brilliant evocations of the atmosphere of the time and place.

LEHMANN, Rosamond Nina, b. 1904

NOVELS:

Dusty Answer, 1927.
A Note in Music, 1930.

Invitation to the Waltz, 1932.
The Weather in the Streets, 1936.
The Ballad and the Source, 1944.
The Gypsy's Baby, 1946.
The Echoing Grove, 1943.

PLAY:

No More Music, 1939.

GREENE, Graham, b. 1904

NOVELS:

The Man Within, 1929.
The Name of Action, 1930.
Rumour at Nightfall, 1931.
It's a Battlefield, 1934.
England Made Me, 1935.
Brighton Rock, 1938.
The Power and the Glory, 1940.
The Heart of the Matter, 1948.
The End of the Affair, 1951.
The Quiet American, 1955.

SHORT STORIES:

The Basement Room, 1935 (reprinted with additions as Nineteen Stories, 1947; Twenty-One Stories, 1954).
The Bear Fell Free, 1935.

ENTERTAINMENTS:

(Greene has given the name 'entertainment' to those of his novels which he wishes to distinguish from his more serious work. Many of these are thrillers, but they often show something of the concern with moral ambiguities in a confused and cruel world which characterizes his serious novels. *Brighton Rock* was classified as an entertainment in the American edition.)

Stamboul Train, 1932.
A Gun for Sale, 1936.
The Confidential Agent, 1939.
The Ministry of Fear, 1943.
The Third Man and the Fallen Idol (stories written for the scripts of the films of these titles), 1950.
Loser Take All, 1955.

PLAY:

The Living Room, 1953.

MISCELLANEOUS WRITINGS:

Journey Without Maps, 1936.
The Lawless Roads; 1939.
Why do I Write? 1948. (An exchange of letters between Elizabeth Bowen, Graham Greene and V. S. Pritchett.)
The Lost Childhood and Other Essays, 1951.

POETRY:

Babbling April, 1925.

Graham Greene has also written children's books, illustrated by Miss D. Craigie.

———

BIOGRAPHY AND CRITICISM:

J. Madaule, Graham Greene, Paris, 1949.
P. Rostenne, Graham Greene témoin des temps tragiques, Paris, 1949.
K. Allott and M. Farris, The Art of Graham Greene, 1951.
M.-B. Mesnet, Graham Greene and the heart of the matter, 1954.
F. Wyndham, Graham Greene (W.W.), 1955.

MITFORD, Hon. Nancy, b. 1904

NOVELS:

Highland Fling, 1931.
Christmas Pudding, 1932.
Wigs on the Green, 1935.
Pigeon Pie, 1940.
Pursuit of Love, 1945.
Love in a Cold Climate, 1949.
The Blessing, 1951.

BIOGRAPHY:

Madame de Pompadour, 1951.

A novelist who casts a coldly intelligent eye on the human emotions and what they produce. Her manner is cunningly frivolous, comic and ironical.

WARNER, Rex, b. 1905

NOVELS:

The Wild Goose Chase, 1937.
The Professor, 1938.
The Aerodrome, 1941.
Why Was I Killed?, 1943.

CRITICAL AND MISCELLANEOUS WRITINGS:

English Public Schools, 1945.
The Cult of Power, 1946.
Men of Stones, 1949.
John Milton, 1949.
Men and Gods (Greek myths), 1950.
E. M. Forster (W.W.), 1950.
Eternal Greece, 1953.

POETRY:

Poems, 1937.

TRANSLATIONS:

Euripides: Medea, 1944.
Aeschylus: Prometheus Bound, 1947.
Xenophon: Anabasis, 1949.
Euripides: Hippolytus, 1950.
Thucydides: The Peloponnesian War, 1954.

BATES, Herbert Ernest, b. 1905

NOVELS:

The Two Sisters, 1926.
Catherine Foster, 1929.
Charlotte's Row, 1931.
The Fallow Land, 1932.
The Poacher, 1935.
A House of Women, 1936.
Spella Ho, 1938.
Fair Stood the Wind for France, 1944.
The Purple Plain, 1947.
The Jacaranda Tree, 1949.
Dear Life, 1950.

The Scarlet Sword, 1950.
Love For Lydia, 1952.
The Feast of July, 1954.

SHORT STORIES:

Day's End, 1928.
Seven Tales and Alexander, 1929.
The Black Boxer, 1932.
A German Idyll, 1932.
The Women Who Had Imagination, 1934.
Cut and Come Again, 1935.
Country Tales, 1938.
The Flying Goat, 1939.
My Uncle Silas, 1939.
The Beauty of the Dead, 1940.
The Bride Comes to Evensford, 1943.
Colonel Julien, 1951.
The Nature of Love, 1953.
The Daffodil Sky, 1955.
The Sleepless Moon, 1956.

CRITICAL AND MISCELLANEOUS WRITINGS:

The Modern Short Story, 1941.
Through the Woods, 1936.
The Seasons and the Gardener, 1942.
How Sleep the Brave, 1945.

SNOW, Sir Charles Percy, b. 1905

NOVELS:

Death Under Sail, 1932.
New Lives for Old, 1933.
The Search, 1934.
Strangers and Brothers, 1940.
The Light and the Dark, 1947.
Time of Hope, 1949.
The Masters, 1951.
The New Men, 1954.
Homecoming, 1956.

PLAY:

View Over the Park, 1950.

The last six novels listed above are part of a projected sequence of ten or more volumes (with the general title *Strangers and Brothers*) dealing with personal and moral problems arising in an academic and scientific community.

POWELL, Anthony Dymoke, b. 1905

NOVELS:

Afternoon Men, 1931.
Venusberg, 1932.
From a View to a Death, 1933.
What's Become of Waring, 1939.
A Question of Upbringing, 1951.
Buyer's Market, 1952.
The Acceptance World, 1955.

HOPKINSON, Henry Thomas, b. 1905

FICTION:

A Wise Man Foolish, 1930.
A Strong Hand at the Helm, 1933.
The Man Below, 1939.
Mist in the Tagus, 1946.
The Transitory Venus, 1948 (collected short stories).
Down the Long Slide, 1949.

MISCELLANEOUS WRITINGS:

Love's Apprentice, 1953.

STEWART, John Innes Mackintosh, b. 1906

NOVELS:

Mark Lambert's Supper, 1954.
The Guardsman, 1955.

DETECTIVE NOVELS (under the pseudonym of Michael Innes):

Murder in the President's Lodging, 1936.
Hamlet, Revenge! 1937.

The Hawk and the Handsaw, 1948.
The Journeying Boy, 1949.
Christmas as Candleshow, 1953.

CRITICAL AND MISCELLANEOUS WRITINGS:

Character and Motive in Shakespeare, 1949.
James Joyce (W.W.), 1957.

An unusual combination of scholar, critic, and writer of detective stories. His detective stories are done with wit and cunning, superior examples of their kind.

HUTCHINSON, Ray Coryton, b. 1907

NOVELS:

Thou Hast a Devil, 1930.
The Answering Glory, 1932.
The Unforgotten Prisoner, 1933.
One Light Burning, 1935.
Shining Scabbard, 1936.
Testament, 1938.
The Fire and the Wood, 1940.
Interim, 1945.
Elephant and Castle, 1949.
Recollection of a Journey, 1952.
The Stepmother, 1955.

CALDER-MARSHALL, Arthur, b. 1908

NOVELS:

Two of a Kind, 1933.
About Levy, 1933.
At Sea, 1934.
Dead Centre, 1935.
Pie in the Sky, 1937.
A Date with a Duchess, 1937.
The Way to Santiago, 1940.
A Man Reprieved, 1949.
Occasion of Glory, 1955.

MANNING, Olivia

NOVELS:

The Wind Changes, 1938.
Artist among the Missing, 1949.
School for Love, 1951.
A Different Face, 1953.
The Doves of Venus, 1955.

SHORT STORIES:

The Remarkable Expedition, 1947.

TRAVEL:

The Dreaming Shore, 1950.

SANSOM, William, b. 1912

NOVELS:

The Body, 1949.
The Face of Innocence, 1951.
It Was Really Charlie's Castle, 1953.
A Bed of Roses, 1954.

SHORT STORIES:

Fireman Flower, 1944.
Three, 1946.
Something Terrible, Something Lovely, 1948.
The Passionate North, 1950.
A Touch of the Sun, 1952.
Pleasures Strange and Simple, 1953.
The Light that Went Out, 1953.
A Contest of Ladies, 1956.

MISCELLANEOUS WRITINGS:

Westminster in War, 1947.
South: Aspects and Images from Corsica, Italy and Southern France, 1948.

POETRY:

Lord Love Us, 1954.

A clever and versatile writer, who has a tendency to play tricks on the reader. His most characteristic device (which he employs in *South, The Passionate North, A Touch of the Sun* and elsewhere) is to incorporate stories or a novel into a travel book, as it were, where an account of human relationships is set against a carefully described topographical background. His carefully wrought prose is a considerable achievement. But his skill has still to come to terms with his imagination.

WILSON, Angus Frank Johnstone, b. 1913

NOVELS:
Hemlock and After, 1952.
Anglo-Saxon Attitudes, 1956.

SHORT STORIES:
The Wrong Set, 1949.
Such Darling Dodos, 1950.

CRITICAL AND MISCELLANEOUS WRITINGS:
Emile Zola, 1950.
For Whom the Cloche Tolls, 1953 (A Scrapbook of the Twenties).

PLAY:
The Mulberry Bush, 1956.

TOYNBEE, Philip, b. 1916

NOVELS:
School in Private, 1941.
The Barricades, 1943.
Tea with Mrs Goodman, 1947.
The Garden to the Sea, 1953.

AUTOBIOGRAPHY:
Friends Apart, 1954.

Friends Apart is a fascinating account of Toynbee and two friends during his undergraduate days at Oxford just before the War.

SCOTT, John Dick, b. 1917

NOVELS:

The Cellar, 1947.
The Margin, 1949.
The Way to Glory, 1952.
The End of an Old Song, 1954.

An interesting Scottish novelist whose *The End of an Old Song* promised to be a rendering of phases of modern Scottish life and character but which deviated into melodrama at the end.

NEWBY, Percy Howard, b. 1918

NOVELS:

A Journey to the Interior, 1945.
Agents and Witnesses, 1947.
The Spirit of Jem, 1947.
Mariner Dances, 1948.
The Snow Pasture, 1949.
The Loot Runners, 1949.
The Young May Moon, 1950.
A Season in England, 1951.
A Step to Silence, 1952.
The Retreat, 1953.
The Picnic at Sakkara, 1955.

CRITICAL WRITINGS:

Maria Edgeworth, 1950.
The Novel 1945-50, 1951.

The Picnic at Sakkara is a brilliant comic novel, combining criticism and compassion, irony and affection, in an unusual and most effective manner.

See also under POETRY: Masefield, De la Mare, Williams, Sassoon, Muir, E. Sitwell, Turner, O. Sitwell, V. Sackville-West, Shanks, Church, Read, Graves, Day-Lewis, Spender, Scarfe. Under DRAMA: Barrie, Ervine, Sherriff, Van Druten.

DRAMA

BARRIE, Sir James Matthew, Bt. (1860-1937)

PLAYS:

The Professor's Love Story, 1895.
Quality Street, 1901.
The Admirable Crichton, 1903.
Peter Pan, 1904.
Alice Sit-by-the-Fire, 1905.
What Every Woman Knows, 1908.
Der Tag, 1914.
The Old Lady Shows her Medals, 1917.
Dear Brutus, 1917.
Mary Rose, 1920.
Shall We Join the Ladies, 1922.

NOVELS, SHORT STORIES, ETC.:

Better Dead, 1888.
Auld Licht Idylls, 1888.
When a Man's Single, 1888.
A Window in Thrums, 1889.
My Lady Nicotine, 1890.
The Little Minister, 1891.
Sentimental Tommy, 1896.
Margaret Ogilvy (biography of his mother), 1896.
Tommy and Grizel, 1900.
The Little White Bird, 1902.
Peter Pan in Kensington Gardens, 1906.
Peter and Wendy, 1911.
Farewell, Miss Julie Logan, 1932.

A skilled literary craftsman, who knew all the tricks of the writing trade and of writing for the theatre. He was quite out of touch with any of the new literary movements of his time, but exploited with determination and virtuosity the emotions, whimsies and sentimentalities implicit in the Scottish 'kailyard' tradition and in Victorian and Edwardian middle-class literature generally. Edwin Muir diagnosed him shrewdly when he wrote that 'his softness was really a kind of toughness, and the most deplorable

324

fault of his work is not sensibility run to seed, but obduracy'. A man of very great gifts, who used them cunningly and often brilliantly but never fully creatively.

ERVINE, St John Greer, b. 1883

PLAYS:

The Magnanimous Lover, 1907.
Mixed Marriage, 1910.
Jane Clegg, 1911.
John Ferguson, 1914.
The First Mrs Fraser, 1928.
Boyd's Shop, 1935.
Robert's Wife, 1937.
Friends and Relations, 1940.
Private Enterprise, 1947.
My Brother Tom, 1952.

NOVELS:

Mrs Martin's Man, 1914.
Alice and a Family, 1915.
Changing Winds, 1917.
The Wayward Man, 1927.

CRITICAL AND MISCELLANEOUS WRITINGS:

Some Impressions of My Elders, 1922.
How to Write a Play, 1928.
The Theatre in My Time, 1933.

A versatile and talented writer, St John Ervine has written popular plays and intelligent middlebrow criticism. He has a clear and forceful style, and his miscellaneous prose writings reveal an independent mind and a strong personality.

O'CASEY, Sean, b. 1884

PLAYS:

The Shadow of a Gunman, 1925.
Juno and the Paycock, 1925.
The Plough and the Stars, 1926.

The Silver Tassie, 1929.
Within the Gates, 1933.
Windfalls, 1934.
The Star Turns Red, 1940.
Purple Dust, 1940.
Red Roses for Me, 1942.
Oak Leaves and Lavender, 1946.
Cockadoodle Dandy, 1949.
Collected Plays, 1949, 1951.
The Bishop's Bonfire, 1955.

AUTOBIOGRAPHY:

I Knock at the Door, 1939.
Pictures in the Hallway, 1942.
Drums under the Window, 1945.
Inishfallen, Fare Thee Well, 1949.
Rose and Crown, 1952.
Sunset and Evening Star, 1951.

BRIDIE, James *pseud.* (Dr O. H. Mavor) (1888-1951)

PLAYS:

The Anatomist and other Plays, 1931.
The Amazed Evangelist, 1932.
Jonah and the Whale, 1932.
The Black Eye, 1933.
A Sleeping Clergyman, 1933.
A Sleeping Clergyman and other Plays, 1934.
Marriage is No Joke, 1934.
Colonel Witherspoon and other Plays, 1938.
The Letter-Box Rattles, 1938.
The Christmas Card, 1949.
Daphne Laureola, 1949.
Dr Angelus, 1950.
Mr Gillie, 1950.
Plays, 1953.

A witty and inventive dramatist whose intellectual liveliness is sometimes reminiscent of Shaw. It looked at one time as though his work was going to help produce a new awakening in the Scottish theatre (he was a Glasgow man, who remained in Glasgow), but, in spite of his originality and success, he did not quite possess either the imagination or the grasp of dramatic structure to enable him to fulfil that promise.

MUNRO, Charles Kirkpatrick *pseud.* (Charles Walden Kirkpatrick Macmullan), b. 1889

PLAYS:

Wanderers, 1915.
At Mrs. Beam's, 1922.
The Rumour, 1923.
Storm, 1924.
The Mountain, 1926.
Cocks and Hens, 1927.
Mr Eno, 1928.
Veronica, 1930.
Bluestone Quarry, 1931.
Ding and Co., 1934.

ESSAYS:

The True Woman, 1931.
Watching a Play, 1933.
The Fountains in Trafalgar Square, 1952.

SHERRIFF, Robert Cedric, b. 1896

PLAYS:

Journey's End, 1929.
Badger's Green, 1930.
Windfall, 1933.
St Helena (with Jeanne de Casalis), 1934.
Miss Mabel, 1948.
Home at Seven, 1950.
The White Carnation, 1953.
The Long Sunset, 1955.

NOVELS:

The Fortnight in September, 1931.
Greengates, 1936.
The Hopkins Manuscript, 1939.
Chedworth, 1944.
Another Year, 1946.
King John's Treasure, 1954.

COWARD, Noel, b. 1899

PLAYS:

I'll Leave it to You, 1920.
The Young Idea, 1924.
The Vortex, 1924.
Fallen Angels, 1925.
Hay Fever, 1925.
Easy Virtue, 1926.
The Queen Was in the Parlour, 1926.
This Was a Man, 1926.
Home Chat, 1927.
The Marquise, 1927.
Siroco, 1927.
Bitter Sweet, 1929.
Private Lives, 1930.
Post-Mortem, 1931.
Cavalcade, 1932.
Design for Living, 1933.
Play Parade, 1933.
Conversation Piece, 1934.
Point Valaine, 1935.
Operette, 1938.
Blithe Spirit, 1941.
Present Laughter, 1943.
This Happy Breed, 1943.
Peace in Our Time, 1947.
Relative Values, 1951.
Quadrille, 1952.
Nude with Violin, 1956.

AUTOBIOGRAPHY:

Present Indicative, 1937.
Middle East Diary, 1945.
Future Indefinite, 1954.

Writer, actor, composer, sentimentalist and wit, satirist of England and emotional patriot, Noel Coward represents in a most illuminating way the trend of sophisticated thought and response from 1920 onwards.

LEVY, Benn Wolfe, b. 1900

This Woman Business, 1926.
Mud and Treacle, 1928.
Mrs Moonlight, 1930.
Art and Mrs Bottle, 1929.
The Devil, 1930.
Evergreen, 1930.
Springtime for Henry, 1931.
The Poet's Heart, 1936.
The Jealous God, 1938.
Clutterbuck, 1946.
Return to Tyassi, 1950.
Cupid and Psyche, 1952.

JOHNSTON, William Denis, b. 1901

PLAYS:

The Old Lady Says 'No!' 1929.
The Moon in the Yellow River, 1931.
A Bride for the Unicorn, 1933.
Storm Song, 1934.
Blind Man's Buff, 1936.
The Golden Cuckoo, 1939.
The Dreaming Dust, 1940.
A Fourth for Bridge, 1948.

AUTOBIOGRAPHY:

Nine Rivers from Jordan, 1953.

An Irish playwright who has experimented in expressionist and other new techniques with a remarkable combination of the grotesque and the ironical.

VAN DRUTEN, John William, b. 1901

PLAYS:

Young Woodley, 1928.
After all, 1929.
London Wall, 1931.

Behold We Live, 1932.
The Distaff Side, 1933.
Flowers of the Forest, 1934.
Gertie Maude, 1937.
Leave Her to Heaven, 1950.
The Voice of the Turtle, 1943.
The Druid Circle, 1947.
Bell, Book and Candle, 1950.
I am a Camera (from Christopher Isherwood's stories), 1951.
I've Got Sixpence, 1952.

NOVELS:

A Woman on Her Way, 1930.
And Then You Wish, 1936.
The Vicarious Years, 1955.

MISCELLANEOUS WRITINGS:

The Way to the Present, 1938.
Playwright at Work, 1953.

FRY, Christopher, b. 1907

PLAYS:

The Boy with a Cart. Cuthman, Saint of Sussex, 1939.
A Phoenix Too Frequent, 1946.
The First Born, 1946.
The Lady's Not for Burning, 1949.
Thor, with Angels, 1949.
Venus Observed, 1950.
Ring Round the Moon (an English version of Jean Anouilh's *L'Invitation au Château*), 1950.
A Sleep of Prisoners, 1951.
The Dark is Light Enough, 1954.
The Lark (a version of Anouilh's *L'Alouette*), 1955.
Tiger at the Gates (a version of J. Giraudoux's *La Guerre de Troie n'aura pas lieu*), 1955.

————

BIOGRAPHY AND CRITICISM:

Derek Stanford, Christopher Fry (W.W.), 1954.

RATTIGAN, Terence Marvyn, b. 1911

French without Tears, 1936.
After the Dance, 1939.
Flare Path, 1942.
While the Sun Shines, 1943.
Love in Idleness, 1944. (O Mistress Mine in U.S.A.)
The Winslow Boy, 1946.
The Browning Version, 1948.
Harlequinade, 1948.
Adventure Story, 1949.
Who is Sylvia, 1950.
The Deep Blue Sea, 1952.
The Sleeping Prince, 1953.
Separate Tables, 1954.

The dates are those of first production of the plays.

USTINOV, Peter Alexander, b. 1921

House of Regrets, 1943.
Beyond, 1944.
The Banbury Nose, 1945.
Plays about People, 1950.
The Love of Four Colonels, 1951.
The Moment of Truth, 1953.
Romanoff and Juliet, 1956.

An interesting and extremely witty playwright whose work is full of unusual promise.

See also: Under FICTION: Galsworthy, Maugham, Joyce, Compton Mackenzie, Jesse, Lawrence, Sayers, Blake, Priestley, Morgan, Kennedy, Mitchison, Linklater, Isherwood, Greene, Snow, Wilson. Under POETRY: Yeats, Sturge Moore, Masefield, Abercrombie, Drinkwater, Young, Eliot, Turner, Auden, Spender, Durrell, Ridler, Thomas, Nicholson, Kirkup.

GENERAL PROSE

(A) HISTORY AND BIOGRAPHY

OLIVER, F. S. (1864-1934)

Alexander Hamilton, 1906.
Ordeal by Battle, 1915.
The Endless Adventure Vol. I (1710-1727), 1930.
    Vol. II (1727-1735), 1931. Vol. III, 1935.
The Anvil of War, 1935.

Oliver's work is the comment of a man of affairs who is also a thinker about the way things are done in the world politically. *The Endless Adventure* follows the career of Walpole, and is illuminating reading. *The Anvil of War* contains his correspondence with his brother during the First World War, and was edited by Stephen Gwynn.

FISHER, Herbert Albert Laurens (1865-1940)

The Mediaeval Empire, 1898.
Bonapartism, 1908.
Napoleon Bonaparte, 1913.
Life of Lord Bryce, 1926.
A History of Europe, 3 vols., 1935.
England and Europe, 1936.
A Political History of England, 1940.

HAMMOND, John Lawrence Le Breton (1872-1949)

Charles James Fox, 1903.
The Life of C. P. Scott, 1934.

With his wife, Lucy Barbara Hammond, b. 1873
The Village Labourer 1760-1832, 1911.
The Town Labourer, 1760-1832, 1917.
The Skilled Labourer, 1760-1832, 1919.
Lord Shaftesbury, 1923.
The Rise of Modern Industry, 1925.

333

The Age of the Chartists, 1930.
James Stansfeld, 1932.
The Bleak Age, 1934.

The Hammonds were pioneers in English economic and industrial history: *The Village Labourer* and *The Town Labourer* are standard works.

CHURCHILL, Sir Winston Leonard Spencer, b. 1874

The Story of the Malakand Field Force, 1898.
The River War, 1899.
Savrola, 1900.
London to Ladysmith via Pretoria, 1900.
Ian Hamilton's March, 1900.
Lord Randolph Churchill, 1906.
My African Journey, 1908.
The World Crisis, 4 vols., 1923-29. (One-vol. abridged ed., 1931.)
My Early Life, 1930.
The Eastern Front, 1931.
Thoughts and Adventures, 1932.
Marlborough, 4 vols., 1933-38.
Great Contemporaries, 1937.
Arms and the Covenant (speeches), 1938.
Step by Step, 1939.
Into Battle (speeches), 1941. And other volumes of speeches, among them:
　The Unrelenting Struggle, 1942.
　The End of the Beginning, 1943.
　Onwards to Victory, 1944.
The Second World War:
　I. The Gathering Storm, 1948.
　II. Their Finest Hour, 1949.
　III. The Grand Alliance, 1950.
　IV. The Hinge of Fate, 1951.
　V. Closing the Ring, 1952.
　VI. Triumph and Tragedy, 1954.
A History of the English Speaking Peoples, Vol. I, The Birth of Britain, 1956. Vol. II, The New World, 1956.

———

BIOGRAPHY AND CRITICISM:

Philip Guedalla, Mr Churchill, 1942.
E. C. Wingfield-Stratford, Winston Churchill: The Making of a Hero, 1942.
R. E. G. George, Winston Churchill, 1943.

J. Coulter, Churchill, 1944.
G. Eden, Portrait of Churchill, 1945.
R. L. Taylor, Winston Churchill, 1953.
C. L. Broad, Winston Churchill, rev. and enlarged ed., 1953.
C. R. Coote (ed.), Churchill by his Contemporaries, 1953.
B Tucker, Winston Churchill, 2nd rev. ed., 1955.
V. S. Cowles, Winston Churchill: The Era and the Man, 1956.
John Connell, Winston Churchill (W.W.), 1956.

TREVELYAN, George Macaulay, b. 1876

England in the Age of Wycliffe, 1899.
England Under the Stuarts, 1904.
Garibaldi's Defence of the Roman Republic, 1907.
Garibaldi and the Thousand, 1909.
Garibaldi and the Making of Italy, 1911.
The Poetry and Philosophy of George Meredith, 1912.
Clio: a Muse, and other Essays, 1913.
The Life of John Bright, 1913.
Recreations of an Historian, 1919.
Scenes from Italy's War, 1919.
Lord Grey of the Reform Bill, 1920.
British History in the Nineteenth Century, 1922.
Manin and the Venetian Revolution of 1848, 1923.
History of England, 1926.
England Under Queen Anne: I. Blenheim, 1930.
    II. Ramillies and the Union with Scotland, 1932.
    III. The Peace and the Protestant Succession, 1934.
Sir George Otto Trevelyan, a Memoir, 1932.
Grey of Fallodon, 1937.
The English Revolution, 1688, 1938.
English Social History, 1944.
An Autobiography and other Essays, 1949.
The Seven Years of William IV, 1952.
A Layman's Love of Letters, 1954.

STRACHEY, Giles Lytton (1880-1932)

Landmarks in French Literature, 1912.
Eminent Victorians, 1918.
Queen Victoria, 1921.
Books and Characters, 1922.
Elizabeth and Essex, 1928.
Portraits in Miniature, 1931.
Pope, 1925.
Characters and Commentaries, 1933.

The mocking wit of Strachey's biographical studies has not found as much favour with a later generation as it did in his own time. *Books and Characters* contains some acute and helpful criticism, especially of French writers.

———

BIOGRAPHY AND CRITICISM:
R. A. Scott-James, Lytton Strachey (W.W.), 1955.

TAWNEY, Richard Henry, b. 1880

The Agrarian Problem in the Sixteenth Century, 1912.
English Economic History, Select Documents (with Bland and Brown), 1914.
The Acquisitive Society, 1921.
Tudor Economic Documents (with Prof. E. Power), 1924.
Religion and the Rise of Capitalism, 1926.
Equality, 1931.
Land and Labour in China, 1932.
The Attack and other Papers, 1953.

Religion and the Rise of Capitalism is a classic study of the relation between Protestant thought and economic behaviour in the sixteenth and seventeenth centuries.

YOUNG, George Malcolm, b. 1882

Gibbon, 1932.
Origin of the West-Saxon Kingdom, 1934.
Early Victorian England (ed.), 1934.
Charles I and Cromwell, 1932.
Portrait of an Age, 1936.
Daylight and Champaign, 1937.
Mr Gladstone, 1944.
Today and Yesterday, 1948.
Last Essays, 1950.
Stanley Baldwin, 1952.

An admirable prose writer. *Portrait of an Age*, expanded from a chapter in *Early Victorian England*, is a standard work, and a model of how such things should be done.

MACKENZIE, Agnes Mure (-1955)

An Historical Survey of Scottish Literature to 1714, 1933.
Robert Bruce, King of Scots, 1934.
The Rise of the Stewarts, 1935.
The Scotland of Mary and the Religious Wars, 1936.
The Passing of the Stewarts, 1937.
The Foundations of Scotland, 1938.

NICOLSON, Hon. Sir Harold George, b. 1886

Paul Verlaine, 1921.
Sweet Waters, 1921. (A novel)
Tennyson, 1923.
Byron, the Last Journey, 1924.
Swinburne, 1926.
The Development of English Biography, 1928.
Lord Carnock, 1930.
People and Things, 1931.
Public Faces, 1932.
Peacemaking, 1919, 1933.
Curzon, the Last Phase 1919-1925, 1934.
Dwight Morrow, 1935.
Small Talk, 1937.
Diplomacy, 1939.
Marginal Comment, 1939.
Why Britain is at War, 1939.
The Desire to Please, 1943.
Friday Mornings, 1944.
The Congress of Vienna, 1946.
The English Sense of Humour, 1947.
Comments, 1948.
Benjamin Constant, 1949.
King George V, 1952.
Evolution of Diplomatic Method, 1954.
Good Behaviour, 1955.

An accomplished biographer and historian whose experience in the Diplomatic Service helped to give him his approach to modern history. An urbane curiosity about men and civilization provides the motive power for much of his work, which is in the best English tradition of cultured amateurism.

337

SCOTT, Geoffrey (1886-1928)

The Architecture of Humanism, 1914, revised 1924.
Portrait of Zélide, 1925.

Scott was an extremely graceful writer. The first book had a considerable influence in reviving interest in the Baroque. The second is a sympathetic and beautifully ordered biography.

SADLEIR, Michael, b. 1888

Political Career of Richard Brinsley Sheridan, 1912.
Excursions in Victorian Bibliography, 1922.
Desolate Splendour, 1923. (A novel)
Daumier, 1924.
The Noblest Frailty, 1925. (A novel)
Trollope: a Commentary, 1927, 1945.
Trollope: a Bibliography, 1928.
Bulwer and his Wife, 1803-1836, 1931.
Blessington-D'Orsay: a Masquerade, 1933, 1947.
Fanny by Gaslight, 1947. (A novel)
Forlorn Sunset, 1947. (A novel)
Michael Ernest Sadler: a Memoir by his Son, 1949.
Nineteenth-Century Fiction: a Bibliographical Record, 2 Vols., 1951.

Biographer, bibliographer, and novelist. *Fanny by Gaslight*, the most successful of his novels, is an interesting period piece. His biographies of Trollope and of Blessington-D'Orsay are his best work.

NAMIER, Sir Lewis Bernstein, b. 1888

Germany and Eastern Europe, 1915.
The Structure of Politics at the Accession of George III, 1929.
England in the Age of the American Revolution, Vol. I, 1930.
Skyscrapers, 1931.
In the Margin of History, 1939.
Conflicts, 1942.
1848: The Revolution of the Intellectuals, 1946.
Facing East, 1947.
Diplomatic Prelude, 1938-39, 1948.
Europe in Decay, 1936-1940, 1950.
Avenues of History, 1952.
In the Nazi Era, 1952.
Personalities and Powers, 1955.

Sir Lewis Namier's detailed studies of political and diplomatic history have set new standards of scholarship, accuracy and interpretation for a whole generation of historians.

TOYNBEE, Arnold Joseph, b. 1889

Nationality and the War, 1915.
The New Europe, 1915.
The Western Question in Greece and Turkey, 1922.
Greek Historical Thought, 1924.
Greek Civilization and Character, 1924.
A Survey of International Affairs for 1920-23, and annually from 1924 until 1938.
Turkey (with K. P. Kirkwood), 1926.
A Journey to China, 1931.
British Commonwealth Relations (ed.), 1934.
A Study of History, Vols. I-X, 1934-1954.
Civilization on Trial, 1947.
War and Civilization, 1951.
The World and the West, 1953.

A Study of History is an ambitious attempt to survey the whole history of civilization and to deduce from it some general laws governing the rise and fall of individual civilizations.

GUEDALLA, Philip (1889-1944)

Palmerston, 1926.
The Duke, 1931. (Biography of Wellington.)
Conquistador, 1927.
The Partition of Europe 1715-1815, 1914.
Supers and Supermen, 1920.
The Second Empire, 1922.
Masters and Men, 1923.
Napoleon and Palestine, 1925.
Gladstone and Palmerston, 1928.
The Queen and Mr Gladstone, 1933.
The Hundred Days, 1934.
The Hundred Years, 1936.
Mr Churchill, 1941.

An historian and biographer with a witty ironical style, superficially in the Strachey manner though Guedalla's writing is rather more lush than Strachey's.

CLARK, Sir George Norman, b. 1890

The Seventeenth Century, 1929.
The Later Stuarts, 1934.
Science and Social Welfare in the Age of Newton, 1937.
The Wealth of England, 1946.

NEALE, Sir John Ernest, b. 1890

Queen Elizabeth, 1934.
The Age of Catherine de Medici, 1943.
The Elizabethan Political Scene, 1948.
The Elizabethan House of Commons, 1949.
Elizabeth I and her Parliaments 1559-1581, 1953.

BRYANT, Sir Arthur, b. 1899

King Charles II, 1931.
Macaulay, 1932.
Samuel Pepys, the Man in the Making, 1933.
The National Character, 1934.
The England of Charles II, 1934.
The Letters and Speeches of Charles II, 1935.
Samuel Pepys, the Years of Peril, 1935.
George V, 1936.
The American Ideal, 1936.
Postman's Horn, 1936.
Stanley Baldwin, 1937.
Humanity in Politics, 1938.
Samuel Pepys, the Saviour of the Navy, 1938.
Unfinished Victory, 1940.
English Saga, 1940.
The Years of Endurance, 1942.
Dunkirk, 1943.
Years of Victory, 1944.
Historian's Holiday, 1947.
The Age of Elegance, 1950.
The Story of England: Makers of the Realm, 1953.
The Turn of the Tide, 1957.

BUTTERFIELD, Herbert, b. 1900

The Historical Novel, 1924.
The Peace Tactics of Napoleon 1806-8, 1929.
The Whig Interpretation of History, 1931.
Napoleon, 1939.
The Statecraft of Machiavelli, 1940.
The Englishman and his History, 1944.
The Study of Modern History (inaugural lecture as prof. of modern history at Cambridge), 1944.
George III, Lord North and the People, 1949.
The Origins of Modern Science, 1949.
Christianity and History, 1949.
History and Human Relations, 1951.
Christianity in European History, 1951.
Christianity, Diplomacy and War, 1953.
Man on his Past, 1955.

ROWSE, Arthur Leslie, b. 1903

Sir Richard Grenville of the *Revenge*, 1937.
Tudor Cornwall, 1941.
Poems of a Decade, 1931-41.
A Cornish Childhood, 1942. (Autobiography)
The Spirit of English History, 1943.
The English Spirit, 1944.
Poems Chiefly Cornish, 1944.
The Use of History, 1946.
Poems of Deliverance, 1946.
The End of an Epoch, 1947.
The England of Elizabeth, 1950.
The English Past, 1951.
History of France (by Lucien Romier, translated and completed), 1953.
An Elizabethan Garland, 1953.
The Expansion of England, 1955.
The Early Churchills, 1956.

TAYLOR, Alan John Percival, b. 1906

The Italian Problem in European Diplomacy 1847-49, 1934.
Germany's First Bid for Colonies 1847-49, 1938.
The Habsburg Monarchy 1815-1918, 1941 (rewritten 1946).
The Course of Germany History, 1945.

From Napoleon to Stalin, 1950.
Rumours of Wars, 1952.
The Struggle for Mastery in Europe, 1848-1918, 1954.
Bismarck, 1955.
Englishmen and Others, 1956.

WEDGWOOD, Cicely Veronica, b. 1910

Strafford, 1935.
The Thirty Years' War, 1938.
Oliver Cromwell, 1939.
William the Silent, 1944.
Velvet Studies, 1946.
Richelieu and the French Monarchy, 1949.
Seventeenth-Century Literature, 1950.
The Last of the Radicals, 1951.
Montrose, 1952.
The King's Peace, 1955.

TREVOR-ROPER, Hugh Redwald, b. 1914

Archbishop Laud, 1941.
The Last Days of Hitler, 1947.
The Gentry 1540-1640, 1953.
Hitler's Table Talk (ed.), 1953.
Historical Essays, 1957.

(B) CRITICISM AND SCHOLARSHIP

BOAS, Frederick Samuel (1862-1957)

Shakespeare and his Predecessors, 1896, 1940.
University Drama in the Tudor Age, 1914.
Shakespeare and the Universities, 1922.
An Introduction to Tudor Drama, 1933.
Christopher Marlowe, 1940.
An Introduction to Stuart Drama, 1946.
Thomas Heywood, 1950.
Introduction to Eighteenth-Century Drama, 1952.
Sir Philip Sidney, 1955.

SIMPSON, Percy, b. 1865

Shakespeare's Punctuation, 1911.
The Plays of Ben Jonson (with C. J. Herford), vols. I-V, 1925-27.
                    (with E. M. Simpson), vols. VI-XI, 1938-52.
Studies in Elizabethan Drama, 1955.

CHAMBERS, Sir Edmund Kerchever (1866-1954)

The Mediaeval Stage, 3 vols., 1903.
The Elizabethan Stage, 3 vols., 1923.
Shakespeare: a Survey, 1925.
Arthur of Britain, 1927.
William Shakespeare (2 vols.), 1930.
The English Folk Play, 1933.
Sir Henry Lee, 1936.
Samuel Taylor Coleridge, 1938.
English Literature at the Close of the Middle Ages, 1945.

Scholar, bibliographer, biographer, stage historian, critic and editor, Sir Edmund Chambers contributed particularly to Elizabethan and Shakespearean studies. His two-volume life of Shakespeare is now the standard work.

FRY, Roger Eliot (1866-1934)

Giovanni Bellini, 1899.
Sir Joshua Reynolds' Discourses (ed.), 1905.
Vision and Design, 1920.
A Sampler of Castille, 1923.
Transformations, 1926.
Cézanne, 1927.
Flemish Art, 1927.
Henri Matisse, 1930.
Characteristics of French Art, 1932.
Reflections on British Painting, 1934.

An important art critic who was a pioneer in introducing in England modern French painting. His biography was written by Virginia Woolf, 1940.

GRIERSON, Sir Herbert John Clifford, b. 1866

The First Half of the Seventeenth Century, 1905.
The Poems of John Donne, ed. with introduction and commentary, 2 vols., 1912.
Metaphysical Poets, Donne to Butler, 1921. (Anthology)
The Background of English Literature, 1925.
Lyrical Poetry from Blake to Hardy, 1928.
Cross-Currents in English Literature of the Seventeenth Century, 1929.
Milton and Wordsworth, 1937.
The Letters of Sir Walter Scott (ed. with Davidson Cook, W. M. Parker and others), 12 vols., 1932-1937.
Rhetoric and English Composition, 1945.

Grierson's work on Donne and the other seventeenth-century metaphysical poets contributed significantly to the revival of interest in those poets and to the change in poetic taste which resulted.

SPURGEON, Caroline F. E. (1869-1942)

Mysticism in English Literature, 1913.
Five Hundred Years of Chaucer Criticism and Allusion, 1925.
Keats's Shakespeare, 1928.
Shakespeare's Imagery and What it Tells Us, 1935.

Miss Spurgeon's study of Shakespeare's imagery has proved to be one of the most germinal works of Shakespeare criticism of the century.

CHAMBERS, Raymond Wilson (1874-1942)

Widsith, a Study in Old English Heroic Legend, 1912.
England Before the Norman Conquest, 1926.
The Continuity of English Prose from Alfred to More (in Harpsfield's Life of Sir Thomas Moore, ed. E. V. Hitchcock), 1932.
Thomas More, 1935.

The Continuity of English Prose is an important attempt to establish a continuous tradition in English prose (mostly through religious and devotional prose) from Anglo-Saxon times to the sixteenth century. *Thomas More* is now the standard biography of its subject.

MACCARTHY, Sir Desmond (1878-1952)

The Court Theatre 1904-1907, 1907.
Lady John Russell, a memoir, with selections from her diaries and correspondence (with Agatha Russell), 1910.
Remnants, 1918.
Portraits, 1931, ff.
Criticism, 1932.
Letters of the Earl of Oxford and Asquith, 1933.
Experience, 1935.
Leslie Stephen, 1937.
Drama, 1940.

One of the finest of modern non-academic literary and dramatic critics. His criticism was vigorous, perceptive, independent, wholly undoctrinaire and if he lacked the analytic rigour of some of his younger academic contemporaries, he more than made up for it by his honesty, sensitivity and liveliness, which did so much to raise the standard of literary journalism.

LUBBOCK, Percy, b. 1879

The Craft of Fiction, 1921.
Earlham, 1922.

Roman Pictures, 1923.
The Region Cloud, 1925. (Novel)
Shades of Eton, 1929.
Mary Cholmondeley, 1937.
Portrait of Edith Wharton, 1947.

The Craft of Fiction is an important critical work in the Henry James tradition, and has proved germinal in the development of a closer technical treatment of the novel. *Earlham* is an attractive reminiscent account of childhood in an East Anglian country house.

BELL, Clive, b. 1881

Art, 1914.
Since Cézanne, 1922.
Landmarks in Nineteenth-Century Painting, 1927.
Civilization, 1928.
Proust, 1929.
An Account of French Painting, 1931.
Enjoying Pictures, 1934.
Old Friends, 1956.

WILSON, John Dover, b. 1881

Life in Shakespeare's England, 1911.
New Cambridge Edition of Shakespeare's Plays (with Sir A. T. Quiller-Couch and others), 1921 ff.
The Schools of England (ed.), 1928.
The Essential Shakespeare, 1932.
Matthew Arnold's Culture and Anarchy (ed.), 1932.
The Manuscript of Shakespeare's Hamlet, 1934.
What Happens in Hamlet, 1935.
The Fortunes of Falstaff, 1943.

SISSON, Charles Jasper, b. 1885

Thomas Lodge and other Elizabethans, 1933.
Lost Plays of Shakespeare's Age, 1936.
The Judicious Marriage of Mr Hooker, 1940.
Shakespeare: Complete Works (ed.), 1954.
Shakespeare, 1954.
New Readings in Shakespeare, 1955.

TILLYARD, Eustace Mandeville Wetenhall, b. 1889

The Poetry of Sir Thomas Wyatt, 1929.
Milton, 1930.
Poetry Direct and Oblique, 1934.
Shakespeare's Last Plays, 1938.
The Elizabethan World Picture, 1943.
Shakespeare's History Plays, 1944.
Five Poems, 1948.
The English Epic and its Background, 1954.

Milton, an interpretation of Milton's poetry with reference to the development of his thought and emotion throughout his life, has had considerable influence on Milton criticism.

MURRY, John Middleton (1889-1957)

Fyodor Dostoevsky, 1916.
Still Life, 1917. (Novel)
The Evolution of an Intellectual, 1919.
Aspects of Literature, 1920.
Countries of the Mind, 1922.
The Problem of Style, 1922.
The Things We Are, 1922. (Novel)
Pencillings, 1923.
Discoveries, 1924.
To the Unknown God, 1924.
Between Two Worlds, 1924. (Autobiography)
The Voyage, 1924. (Novel)
Keats and Shakespeare, 1925.
The Life of Jesus, 1926.
Things to Come, 1928.
God, 1929.
D. H. Lawrence, Two Essays, 1930.
Studies in Keats, 1930.
Countries of the Mind, 2nd Series, 1931.
Son of Woman, the Story of D. H. Lawrence, 1931.
The Necessity of Communism, 1932.
The Life of Katherine Mansfield (with Ruth E. Mantz), 1933.
Reminiscences of D. H. Lawrence, 1933.
William Blake, 1933.
Shakespeare, 1936.
The Necessity of Pacifism, 1937.
The Pledge of Peace, 1938.

347

The Price of Leadership, 1939.
Adam and Eve, 1944.
The Challenge of Schweitzer, 1948.
The Free Society, 1948.
Katherine Mansfield and other Literary Portraits, 1949.
The Mystery of Keats, 1949.
The Conquest of Death, 1951.
Community Farm, 1951.
Jonathan Swift, 1954, and in (W.W.), 1955.
The Journal of Katherine Mansfield (ed.), 1954.
Unprofessional Essays, 1955.
Love, Freedom and Society, 1957.

WADDELL, Helen, b. 1889

Lyrics from the Chinese, 1913. (Trans.)
The Wandering Scholars, 1927.
Mediaeval Latin Lyrics, 1929. (Trans.)
Manon Lescaut, 1931. (Trans.)
Peter Abelard, 1933. (Novel)
The Abbé Prévost, 1933.
Beasts and Saints, 1934.
The Desert Fathers, 1936.

The Wandering Scholars is a classic study of the *vagantes* of the
Middle Ages, showing a deep understanding of mediaeval Latin
poetry. The translations in *Mediaeval Latin Lyrics* reflect the same
kind of sympathetic scholarship. Helen Waddell possesses a true
historical imagination.

CHARLTON, Henry Buckley, b. 1890

The Senecan Tradition in Renaissance Tragedy, 1921.
The Art of Literary Study, 1924.
Shakespearean Comedy, 1938.
Shakespearean Tragedy, 1948.

DOBRÉE, Bonamy, b. 1891

Histriophone, 1921.
Restoration Comedy, 1924.
Essays in Biography, 1925.

Timotheus, or the Future of the Theatre, 1925.
Vanbrugh (ed., Nonesuch), 1927.
Sarah Churchill, 1927.
The Lamp and the Lute, 1929.
The Sofa, by Crébillon Fils, 1929. (Trans.)
Restoration Tragedy, 1930.
Letters of Lord Chesterfield (ed.) with Life, 1930.
St Martin's Summer, 1931. (Novel)
The London Book of English Prose (with Herbert Read), 1931.
   (Anthology)
Variety of Ways, 1932.
William Penn, 1932.
John Wesley, 1933.
As Their Friends Saw Them, 1933.
Giacomo Casanova, 1933.
Modern Prose Style, 1934.
Open Letter to a Professional Man, 1935.
The Floating Republic (with G. E. Mainwaring), 1935.
English Revolts, 1937.
The Victorians and After (with Edith Batho), 1938.
The Unacknowledged Legislator, 1942.
English Essayists, 1947.
The Amateur and the Theatre, 1947.
The London Book of English Verse (with Herbert Read), 1949.
   (Anthology)
Alexander Pope, 1951.
Rudyard Kipling (W.W.), 1951.
The Broken Cistern, 1954.
John Dryden (W.W.), 1956.

A critic, scholar and stylist who combines a deep interest in the life and letters of the past with a lively concern with the literature of his own day, Bonamy Dobrée exhibits in his writing an unusual blend of the academic and the creative. His critical studies are done with liveliness and elegance. His books on Restoration drama and his edition of Lord Chesterfield's Letters are standard works.

RICHARDS, Ivor Armstrong, b. 1893

Foundations of Aesthetics (with C. K. Ogden and Jas. Wood), 1921.
The Meaning of Meaning (with C. K. Ogden), 1923.
Principles of Literary Criticism, 1924.
Science and Poetry, 1925.

Practical Criticism, 1929.
Mencius on the Mind, 1931.
Coleridge On Imagination, 1934.
Interpretation in Teaching, 1938.
How to Read a Page, 1942.
The Republic of Plato (a simplified version), 1942.
Basic English and its Uses, 1943.
Speculative Instruments, 1955.

LUCAS, Frank Laurence, b. 1894

Seneca and Elizabethan Tragedy, 1922.
Euripides and his Influence, 1923.
Authors Dead and Living, 1926.
Tragedy, 1927.
The Complete Works of John Webster (ed.), 1928.
Eight Victorian Poets, 1930.
The Criticism of Poetry, 1933.
Studies French and English, 1934.
The Decline and Fall of the Romantic Ideal, 1935.
Style, 1955.
Tennyson (W.W.), 1956.

A distinguished classical scholar, who holds to the classical
ideals of clarity and moderation. His criticism is scholarly and balanced, but he is completely out of sympathy with most modern
movements in literature. His edition of Webster is a model of its
kind.

ELLIS-FERMOR, Una Mary, b. 1894

Christopher Marlowe, 1926.
Jacobean Drama, 1936.
Some Recent Research in Shakespeare's Imagery, 1937.
The Irish Dramatic Movement, 1939 (2nd ed., 1954).
Masters of Reality, 1942.
The Frontiers of Drama, 1945.

KNIGHT, George Wilson, b. 1897

Myth and Miracle, 1929.
The Wheel of Fire, 1930.

The Imperial Theme, 1931.
The Shakespearian Tempest, 1932.
The Christian Renaissance, 1933.
Principles of Shakespearian Production, 1936.
Atlantic Crossing, 1936.
The Burning Oracle, 1939.
This Sceptred Isle, 1940.
The Starlit Dome, 1941.
Chariot of Wrath, 1942.
The Olive and the Sword, 1944.
The Dynasty of Stowe, 1945.
The Crown of Life, 1947.
Christ and Nietzsche, 1948.
Lord Byron: Christian Virtues, 1952.
Byron's Dramatic Prose, 1954.
The Mutual Flame, 1955.
The Laureate of Peace (Pope), 1954.
Lord Byron's Marriage, 1957.

PINTO, Vivian de Sola, b. 1895

Sir Charles Sedley, a Study in the Life and Literature of the Restoration,
    1927.
The Poetical and Dramatic Works of Sir Charles Sedley (ed.), 1928.
Peter Sterry, Platonist and Puritan, 1934.
Rochester: Portrait of a Restoration Poet, 1935.
Lord Berners, a Selection from his Works, 1937.
The English Renaissance, 1938.
Crisis in English Poetry 1880-1940, 1951.
English Biography in the Seventeenth Century, 1951.
Poems of John Wilmot, Earl of Rochester (ed.), 1953.

BATHO, Edith, b. 1895

The Ettrick Shepherd, 1927.
The Later Wordsworth, 1934.
The Poet and the Past, 1937.
The Victorians and After (with Bonamy Dobrée), 1938.
Chronicles of Scotland by Hector Boece, trans. by Bellenden (ed.)
    Vol. I, with R. W. Chambers, 1936.
    Vol. II, with H. W. Husbands, 1941.

LEAVIS, Frank Raymond, b. 1895

Mass Civilization and Minority Culture, 1930.
New Bearings in English Poetry, 1932.
For Continuity, 1933.
Culture and Environment (with Denys Thompson), 1933.
Revaluations, 1936.
Education and the University, 1943.
The Great Tradition, 1948.
The Common Pursuit, 1952.
D. H. Lawrence: Novelist, 1955.

Dr Leavis edited *Scrutiny* from its foundation in 1932 until its demise in 1953.

WILLEY, Basil, b. 1897

The Seventeenth-Century Background, 1934.
The Eighteenth-Century Background, 1940.
Nineteenth-Century Studies, 1949.
More Nineteenth-Century Studies, 1956.

BOWRA, Sir Maurice, b. 1898

Tradition and Design in the Iliad, 1930.
Greek Lyric Poetry, 1936.
Early Greek Elegists, 1938.
The Heritage of Symbolism, 1943.
Sophoclean Tragedy, 1944.
From Virgil to Milton, 1945.
The Creative Experiment, 1949.
The Romantic Imagination, 1950.
Heroic Poetry, 1952.

A classical scholar and a gifted modern linguist, Bowra is an unusually wide-ranging critic of ancient and modern European literature.

LEWIS, Clive Staples, b. 1898

The Pilgrim's Regress, 1933.
The Allegory of Love, 1936.
Rehabilitations, 1938.

The Personal Heresy (with E. M. W. Tillyard), 1939.
The Problem of Pain, 1940.
The Screwtape Letters, 1942.
A Preface to Paradise Lost, 1942.
Perelandra, 1943.
Christian Behaviour, 1943.
Abolition of Man, 1944.
Miracles, 1947.
Mere Christianity, 1952.
English Literature in the Sixteenth Century, 1954.
Surprised by Joy, 1955. (Autobiography)

The Allegory of Love is the standard work on the development of the Courtly Love ideal in English and European literature, a brilliant example of a particularly difficult kind of literary and intellectual history.

COGHILL, Nevill Henry Kendal Aylmer, b. 1899

Visions from Piers Plowman, 1949.
The Poet Chaucer, 1949.
The Canterbury Tales (in mod. English), 1951.
Chaucer (W.W.), 1956.

SUTHERLAND, James, b. 1900

The Medium of Poetry, 1934.
Defoe, 1937.
Background for Queen Anne, 1939.
A Preface to Eighteenth-Century Poetry, 1948.
The Oxford Book of English Talk (ed.), 1953.

POTTER, Stephen, b. 1900

D. H. Lawrence, a First Study, 1930.
Coleridge and S.T.C., 1935.
The Muse in Chains, 1937.
Gamesmanship, 1947.
Lifemanship, 1950.
One-Upmanship, 1952.
Humour Anthology, (ed.), 1954.
Potter on America, 1956.

Potter began his writing career as a serious critic (he also edited the Nonesuch *Coleridge* and edited the letters of Mrs Coleridge under the title *A Minnow Among the Tritons*, 1934). But he revealed his true métier when he embarked on the series of books beginning with *Gamesmanship*. These mock-serious studies of how to establish superiority on all kinds of social occasions created a new kind of English humour.

BULLOUGH, Geoffrey, b. 1901

Philosophical Poems of Henry More (ed.), 1931.
The Oxford Book of Seventeenth-Century Verse (with H. J. C. Grierson), 1934.
The Trend of Modern Poetry, 1934 (revised ed. 1949).
Poems and Dramas of Fulke Greville (ed.), 1939.

CECIL, Lord David, b. 1902

The Stricken Deer: Life of William Cowper, 1929.
Sir Walter Scott, 1933.
Early Victorian Novelists, 1934.
Jane Austen, 1935.
The Young Melbourne, 1939.
Hardy the Novelist, 1943.
Two Quiet Lives, 1948.
Poets and Storytellers, 1949.
Lord M. (second part of biography of Melbourne), 1954.
Walter Pater, 1956.

STOKES, Adrian Durham, b. 1902

The Thread of Ariadne, 1925.
Sunrise in the West, 1926.
The Quattro Cento, 1932.
Stones of Rimini, 1934.
Tonight the Ballet, 1934.
Russian Ballets, 1935.
Colour and Form, 1937.
Venice, an Aspect of Art, 1945.
Inside Out, 1947.
Cézanne, 1947.

Art and Science, 1949.
Smooth and Rough, 1951.
Michelangelo: A Study in the Nature of Art, 1955.
Raphael, 1956.

CLARK, Sir Kenneth McKenzie, b. 1903

The Gothic Revival, 1929.
Leonardo da Vinci, 1939.
L. B. Alberti on Painting, 1944.
Constable's Hay Wain, 1944.
Florentine Painting: Fifteenth Century, 1945.
Landscape into Art, 1949.
Piero della Francesca, 1951.
Moments of Vision, 1954.
The Nude, 1956.

CONNOLLY, Cyril Vernon, b. 1903

Enemies of Promise, 1938.
The Unquiet Grave, 1944.
The Condemned Playground, 1944.
Ideas and Places, 1953.

Cyril Connolly edited *Horizon* from 1939 until its demise in 1950. Witty, ironical, not optimistic about the prospects for the writer in the present stage of civilization, he writes of his time with a combination of sadness and frolic. He is an able parodist, and some of his best criticism is in that form. *Enemies of Promise* contains both autobiography and criticism of contemporary life and letters; *The Condemned Playground* is a book of critical essays which show his characteristic mixture of pessimism and mischief. *The Unquiet Grave* is a miscellany of personal pieces which reveal the author's tastes, habits and temperament.

QUENNELL, Peter, b. 1905

Baudelaire and the Symbolists, 1929.
A Superficial Journey through Tokyo and Peking, 1932.
Byron, the Years of Fame, 1935.
Caroline of England, 1940.

Byron in Italy, 1941.
Four Portraits, 1945.
Byron (Nonesuch, ed.) 1949.
John Ruskin, 1949.
Byron: A Self-Portrait (ed. Letters and Diaries, 1798-1824), 2 vols., 1950.
Mayhew's London Labour and the London Poor (ed. selections), 3 vols., 1949-51.
Spring in Sicily, 1952.
Selections: Writings of John Ruskin ed., 1952.
The Singular Preference, 1953.
Hogarth's Progress, 1955.
Ruskin (W.W.), 1956.

A skilled biographer, with a feeling for oddity of character and a fine prose style.

JAMES, David Gwilym, b. 1905

Scepticism and Poetry, 1937.
The Romantic Comedy, 1938.
The Life of Reason, 1949 (The Augustans).
The Dream of Learning, 1951 (The Elizabethans).
The Universities and the Theatre (ed.), 1952.

A notable exponent of philosophic criticism.

TILLOTSON, Geoffrey, b. 1905

On the Poetry of Pope, 1938.
Twickenham Edition of Pope's Poems, vol II, 1940.
Essays in Criticism and Research, 1942.
The Moral Poetry of Pope, 1946.
Thackeray the Novelist, 1954.

KNIGHTS, Lionel Charles, b. 1906

Drama and Society in the Age of Jonson, 1937.
Explorations: Essays in Literary Criticism, 1946.

EMPSON, William, b. 1906

Seven Types of Ambiguity, 1930 (rev. ed. 1954).
Poems, 1935.

Some Versions of Pastoral, 1935.
The Gathering Storm, 1940.
The Structure of Complex Words, 1951.
Collected Poems, 1955.

LEHMANN, John Frederick, b. 1907

Prometheus and the Bolsheviks, 1937.
The Age of the Dragon, 1951. (Coll. Poems)
The Open Night, 1952.
Edith Sitwell (W.W.), 1952.
The Whispering Gallery, 1955. (Autobiography)

Lehmann's importance in modern literature has been less for his own creative work than for his encouragement of new writers, as editor and anthologist. He edited *New Writing* (in its various manifestations), *The Chatto Book of Modern Verse* (with C. Day Lewis), and other collections of modern literature, and edits the *London Magazine*.

MUIR, Kenneth, b. 1907

The Voyage to Illyria (with Sean O'Loughlin), 1937.
English Poetry, 1938.
Collected Poems of Sir Thomas Wyatt (ed.), 1949.
Macbeth (new Arden ed.), 1951.
King Lear (new Arden ed.), 1952.
Elizabethan Lyrics, 1953.
John Milton, 1955.
Shakespeare's Sources, 1957.

DAICHES, David, b. 1912

New Literary Values, 1936.
The Novel and the Modern World, 1939.
Poetry and the Modern World, 1940.
The King James Version of the Bible, 1941.
Virginia Woolf, 1942.
R. L. Stevenson, a Revaluation, 1947.
A Study of Literature, 1948.
Robert Burns, 1951 and in (W.W.), 1957.
Willa Cather, 1951.
Critical Approaches to Literature, 1956.
Literary Essays, 1956.
Two Worlds, 1956. (Autobiography)

(C) PHILOSOPHY AND SCIENCE

The grand manner in philosophy is gone; the typical philosophical work of our time is the short technical monograph rather than the large work covering the whole field of ethics or metaphysics. As a result, there are few philosophers listed here. Two of the most influential of the older generation of philosophers in our time have been G. E. Moore (*Principia Ethica*, 1903) and Bertrand Russell; the former is not listed here as his important work belongs to an earlier period, and is dealt with in the previous volume in this series. The great influence on the younger philosophers of the 1930s was Wittgenstein, whose *Tractatus Logico-Philosophicus* (1922) was an important influence on the work of the logical analysts. In science, the tradition of trying to give a picture of the universe as seen by the modern physicist and astronomer persists, though intermittently, in spite of the increasing difficulty of the task.

WHITEHEAD, Alfred North (1861-1947)

A Treatise on Universal Algebra, 1989.
Principia Mathematica (with Bertrand Russell), 3 vols., 1910-13.
Science and the Modern World, 1925.
Religion in the Making, 1926.
Process and Reality, 1929.
The Aims of Education, 1929.
Adventures of Ideas, 1933.
Nature and Life, 1934.

Whitehead derives an idealist philosophy, aiming at knowledge of the absolute in God, from a mathematical base. *Science and the Modern World* and *Adventures of Ideas* have been his most influential works.

BRAGG, Sir William Henry (1862-1942)

Studies in Radioactivity, 1912.
X-Rays and Crystal Structure, 1915.
The World of Sound, 1920.
Concerning the Nature of Things, 1925.
The Universe of Light, 1933.

His prose is in the best tradition of scientific writing.

RUSSELL, Bertrand Arthur William (Earl Russell), b. 1872

PHILOSOPHY:

A Critical Exposition of the Philosophy of Leibnitz, 1900.
The Principles of Mathematics, 1903.
Principia Mathematica (with A. N. Whitehead), 3 vols., 1910-13.
Philosophical Essays, 1910.
The Problems of Philosophy, 1912.
Scientific Method in Philosophy, 1914.
Our Knowledge of the External World, 1914.
The Philosophy of Bergson, 1914.
Principles of Social Reconstruction, 1916.
Roads to Freedom, 1918.
Mysticism and Logic, and other Essays, 1918.
An Introduction to Mathematical Philosophy, 1919.
The Practice and Theory of Bolshevism, 1920.
The Analysis of Mind, 1921.
Free Thought and Official Propaganda, 1922.
ABC of Atoms, 1923.
Icarus: or the Future of Science, 1924.
ABC of Relativity, 1925.
What I Believe, 1925.
The Analysis of Matter, 1927.
An Outline of Philosophy, 1927.
Sceptical Essays, 1928.
Marriage and Morals, 1929.
The Conquest of Happiness, 1930.
The Scientific Outlook, 1931.
Freedom and Organization, 1814-1914, 1934.
Religion and Science, 1935.
In Praise of Idleness and other Essays, 1935.
Which Way to Peace? 1936.
Power, 1938.
An Inquiry into Meaning and Truth, 1940.
Let the People Think, 1941.

A History of Western Philosophy, 1945.
Physics and Experience, 1946.
The Faith of a Rationalist, 1947.
Human Knowledge, its Scope and its Limits, 1948.
Towards World Government, 1948.
Unpopular Essays, 1950.
Portraits from Memory, 1956.

JEANS, Sir James Hopwood (1877-1946)

The Dynamical Theory of Gases, 1904.
Theoretical Mechanics, 1906.
The Mathematical Theory of Electricity and Magnetism, 1908.
Radiation and the Quantum-Theory, 1914.
Problems of Cosmogony and Stellar Dynamics, 1919.
Atomicity and Quanta, 1926.
Astronomy and Cosmogony, 1928.
The Universe Around Us, 1929.
The Mysterious Universe, 1930.
The Stars in Their Courses, 1931.
The New Background of Science, 1933.
Through Space and Time, 1934.
Science and Music, 1937.

The Mysterious Universe and *The Universe Around Us* have proved to be Jeans's most popular works of exposition; they are intended for the layman.

EDDINGTON, Sir Arthur Stanley (1882-1944)

Stellar Movements and the Structure of the Universe, 1914.
Report on the Relativity Theory of Gravitation, 1918.
Space, Time and Gravitation, 1920.
The Mathematical Theory of Relativity, 1923.
Internal Constitution of the Stars, 1926.
Stars and Atoms, 1927.
The Nature of the Physical World, 1928.
Science and the Unseen World, 1929.
The Expanding Universe, 1933.
New Pathways in Science, 1935.
Relativity Theory of Protons and Electrons, 1936.
The Philosophy of Physical Science, 1939.
The Combination of Relativity Theory and Quantum Theory, 1943.

The Nature of the Physical World is a masterpiece of exposition.

HUXLEY, Julian Sorell, b. 1887

The Individual in the Animal Kingdom, 1911.
Essays of a Biologist, 1923.
The Stream of Life, 1926.
Religion without Revelation, 1927.
Animal Biology (with J. B. S. Haldane), 1927.
The Science of Life (with H. G. and H. P. Wells), 1929.
Ants, 1929.
Bird-Watching and Bird Behaviour, 1930.
Africa View, 1931.
What Dare I Think? 1931.
An Introduction to Science (with E. N. De C. Andrade), Vols. 1-4, 1931-
    35.
Problems of Relative Growth, 1932.
The Captive Shrew and other Poems, 1932.
The Elements of Experimental Embryology (with G. R. de Beer), 1934.
Scientific Research and Social Needs, 1934.
If I Were Dictator, 1934.
We Europeans (with C. H. Haddon), 1935.
At the Zoo, 1936.
The Living Thoughts of Darwin, 1939.
The Uniqueness of Man, 1941.
Democracy Marches, 1941.
Evolution, the Modern Synthesis, 1942.
TVA: Adventure in Planning, 1943.
Evolutionary Ethics, 1943.
On Living in a Revolution, 1944.
Man in the Modern World, 1947.
Soviet Genetics and World Science, 1949.
Evolution in Action, 1952.
From An Antique Land, 1954.

Biologist, general scientist, essayist, humanist, Julian Huxley writes with clarity and authority on a great variety of subjects.

COLLINGWOOD, Robin George (1889-1943)

Religion and Philosophy, 1916.
Roman Britain, 1923.
Specculum Mentis, 1924.
Outlines of a Philosophy of Art, 1925.
Faith and Reason, 1928.
The Philosophy of History, 1930.
An Essay on Philosophical Method, 1933.

Roman Britain and the English Settlements (with J. N. L. Myres), 1936.
Principles of Art, 1937.
Autobiography, 1939.
An Essay on Metaphysics, 1940.
The New Leviathan, 1942.
The Idea of History (ed. T. M. Knox), 1945.
The Idea of Nature (ed. T. M. Knox), 1946.

An original and versatile thinker, who discussed art, religion, science and history as related parts of the complex map of human intellectual and spiritual activity; also, an authority on Roman Britain. His *Autobiography* is a work of great interest.

***

BIOGRAPHY AND CRITICISM

E. W. F. Tomlin, R. G. Collingwood (W.W.), 1953.

BRONOWSKI, Jacob, b. 1908

The Poet's Defence, 1939.
William Blake, a Man without a Mask, 1944.
The Face of Violence (radio play), 1950.
The Common Sense of Science, 1951.

An unusual combination of scientist, literary critic and playwright.

AYER, Alfred Jules, b. 1910

Language, Truth and Logic, 1936.
The Foundations of Empirical Knowledge, 1940.
Thinking and Meaning, 1947.
Philosophical Essays, 1954.
The Problem of Knowledge, 1956.

Illustrates the modern philosopher's approach to truth and logic through a study of the nature of language. His *Language, Truth and Logic* has been a widely-read exposition of logical positivism.

(D) TRAVEL

BELL, Gertrude Margaret Lowthian (1868-1926)

The Desert and the Sown, 1907.
Amurath to Amurath, 1911.
The Palace and the Mosque of Ukhaidir, 1914.
Letters, 1927.

TOMLINSON, H. M., b. 1873

The Sea and the Jungle, 1912.
Old Junk, 1918.
London River, 1921, 1951.
Waiting for Daylight, 1922.
Tidemarks, 1924.
Gifts of Fortune, 1926.
Under the Red Ensign, 1926.
Gallions Reach, 1927. (Novel)
Between the Lines, 1928.
All Our Yesterdays, 1930. (Novel)
The Snows of Helicon, 1933. (Novel)
Below London Bridge, 1934.
South to Cadiz, 1934.
The Wind is Rising, 1941.
Morning Light, 1946.
The Face of the Earth, 1950.
Malay Waters, 1950.

A highly individual imagination is at work both in the travel books and in the novels.

LAWRENCE, Thomas Edward (1888-1935)

Seven Pillars of Wisdom, a Triumph, 1926 and 1935.
Revolt in the Desert (abridgement of the above), 1927.
The Odyssey of Homer (prose trans.), 1932.
Crusader's Castles, 1936.

Letters, ed. David Garnett, 1938.
Secret Despatches from Arabia, 1939.
The Essential T. E. Lawrence, selected with Pref. by D. Garnett, 1951.
Selected Letters, ed. D. Garnett, 1952.
The Home Letters of T. E. Lawrence and his Brothers, 1954.
The Mint, 1955.

Controversy about this remarkable personality (a man of action who achieved a special kind of relationship with the Arabs and produced in his *Seven Pillars of Wisdom* a brilliant and personal account of the Arab campaign in the First World War) continues. Among the books about Lawrence are:

B. H. Liddell-Hart, T. E. Lawrence, 1934.
T. E. Lawrence by his Friends, ed. A. W. Lawrence, 1937.
T. E. Lawrence to his Biographer Liddell-Hart, 1938.
T. E. Lawrence to his Biographer Robert Graves, 1938.
Richard Aldington, T. E. Lawrence, 1955.

STARK, Freya

Bagdad Sketches, 1933.
The Valleys of the Assassins, 1934.
The Southern Gates of Arabia, 1936.
Seen in the Hadramaut, 1938.
A Winter in Arabia, 1940.
Letters from Syria, 1942.
East is West, 1945.
Perseus in the Wind, 1948.
Traveller's Prelude, 1950.
Beyond the Euphrates, 1951.
The Coast of Incense, 1953.
Ionia, a Quest, 1954.
The Lycian Shore, 1956.

An intrepid traveller, shrewd observer, and original thinker, Freya Stark has produced some of the finest travel literature in English.

See also: Under POETRY: S. Sitwell, V. Sackville West, Auden, MacNeice, Durrell. Under FICTION: N. Douglas, Maugham, Lawrence, Huxley, Gunn, Benson, E. Waugh, A. Waugh, Golding, R. Macaulay, O'Flaherty, Manning. Under CRITICISM AND SCHOLARSHIP: Quennell.

(E) POLITICS AND ECONOMICS

BARKER, Sir Ernest, b. 1874

The Political Thought of Plato and Aristotle, 1906.
Political Thought in England from Herbert Spencer to Today, 1915,
    1947.
National Character, 1927, 1948.
Reflections on Government, 1942.
Britain and the British People, 1942, 1955.
Aristotle's Politics (translated), 1946.
The Character of England (ed.), 1947.
Traditions of Civility, 1948.
Principles of Social and Political Theory, 1951.
Age and Youth (Autobiography), 1953.
The European Inheritance (joint ed.), 1954.
From Alexander to Constantine, 1955.

One of the last of British historians and political thinkers to be
trained on the classics and to have the broad humanistic approach
to men and affairs produced by such a training.

ANGELL, Sir Norman, b. 1874

Patriotism under Three Flags, 1903.
Europe's Optical Illusion, 1909.
The Great Illusion, 1910.
Peace Theories and the Balkan War, 1912.
The Foundations of International Polity, 1914.
The Economic Chaos and the Peace Treaty, 1919.
Must Britain Travel the Moscow Road? 1926.
The Public Mind, 1926.
The Unseen Assassins, 1932.
The Press and the Organisation of Society, 1933.
Preface to Peace, 1936.
Let the People Know, 1943.
After All, 1951.

A skilful and passionate publicist whose exposition of the fatuity
of war in *The Great Illusion* had a world-wide influence.

WOOLF, Leonard Sidney, b. 1880

International Government, 1916.
The Future of Constantinople, 1917.
Co-operation and the Future of Industry, 1918.
Empire and Commerce in Africa, 1920.
Socialism and Co-operation, 1921.
Hunting the Highbrow, 1927.
Imperialism and Civilization, 1928.
After the Deluge, Vol. I, 1931, Vol. II, 1939.
The Intelligent Man's Way to Prevent War (ed.), 1933.
Quack, Quack (anti-Nazi satire), 1935.
Barbarians at the Gate, 1939.
The War for Peace, 1940.
Principia Politica, 1953.

A humane and liberal commentator on the contemporary political and economic scene. His novel *The Village in the Jungle* exposes some of the evils of colonialism, and *Empire and Commerce in Africa* attacks directly Britain's exploitation of the black races.

KEYNES, John Maynard, Lord (1883-1946)

The Economic Consequences of the Peace, 1919.
A Treatise on Probability, 1921.
A Revision of the Treaty, 1922.
A Tract on Monetary Reform, 1923.
A Short View of Russia, 1925.
The End of Laissez-Faire, 1926.
A Treatise on Money, 2 Vols., 1930.
Essays in Persuasion, 1931.
Essays in Biography, 1933.
The General Theory of Employment, Interest and Money, 1936.
How to Pay for the War, 1940.

A brilliant and versatile mind, responsible in large measure for the economics of both the American 'New Deal' and of modern Britain. The *General Theory* has had an enormous influence on modern politics and economics. Keynes was a man of wide cultural and artistic interests as well as the leading economist of his day.

COLE, George Douglas Howard, b. 1889

The World of Labour, 1913.
Self-Government in Industry, 1917.
Labour in the Commonwealth, 1918.
Social Theory, 1920
Chaos and Order in Industry, 1920.
A Short History of the British Working-Class Movement, 1789-1947, revised ed., 1948.
Literature and Politics, 1929.
The Intelligent Man's Guide through World Chaos, 1932.
Principles of Economic Planning, 1935.
Chartist Portraits, 1941.
The Means of Full Employment, 1943.
Samuel Butler, 1947.
Socialist Thought, 3 vols., 1953-55.

A prolific Left-wing economist with an effective expository style who has poured out books commenting on the modern economic and political scene, over the last forty years. He has also written over thirty detective stories, in co-operation with his wife, Margaret I. Cole.

LASKI, Harold Joseph (1893-1950)

The Problem of Sovereignty, 1917.
Authority in the Modern State, 1919.
Political Thought from Locke to Bentham, 1920.
Foundations of Sovereignty, 1921.
A Grammar of Politics, 1925.
Communism, 1927.
Liberty in the Modern State, 1930.
The Dangers of Obedience, 1930.
An Introduction to Politics, 1931.
The Crisis and the Constitution, 1932.
Democracy in Crisis, 1933.
The State in Theory and Practice, 1935.
The Rise of European Liberalism, 1936.
Parliamentary Government in England, 1938.
The American Presidency, 1938.
Faith, Reason and Civilization, 1944.
The American Democracy, 1948.
The Holmes-Laski Correspondence, 1954.

A lively and influential Left-wing political thinker, who played an important part in shaping the political thought of the younger generation in the 1930s. His fascinating correspondence with the great American jurist Oliver Wendell Holmes (who was his senior by more than fifty years) reflects vividly the personalities of both men.

CROSSMAN, Richard Howard Stafford, b. 1907

Plato Today, 1937.
Socrates, 1938.
Government and the Governed, 1939.
How we are Governed, 1939.
Palestine Mission, 1947.
The God that Failed (ed.), 1950.

A Left-wing intellectual of the 1930s who went into practical politics thus shifting his interests from political theory to political practice. *The God that Failed* is a collection of essays by writers who had been attracted to Communism in the 1930s and were later disillusioned: it is a very important document for anyone who wishes to understand the 'red thirties' and their aftermath in British thought.

INDEX

Numbers in roman type refer to the Introductory Chapters, in *italics* to the
Bibliography.

A selected list of MIDLAND BOOKS

(continued on next page)

MIDLAND BOOKS